BIBLE
Encouragement
for Every Day

Daily Devotions for a
Woman's Heart

© 2014 by Barbour Publishing, Inc.

Print ISBN 978-1-63609-612-4

Adobe Digital Edition (.epub) 978-1-63609-764-0

Published by Barbour Publishing, Inc., 1810 Barbour Drive, Uhrichsville, Ohio 44683, www.barbourbooks.com

Our mission is to inspire the world with the life-changing message of the Bible.

ecpa Member of the Evangelical Christian Publishers Association

Printed in China.

BIBLE
Encouragement
for Every Day

Daily Devotions for a
Woman's Heart

BARBOUR
PUBLISHING

Bible Encouragement for Your Heart. . .

The Bible is filled with thousands of fascinating verses that describe God, people (including ourselves), and the world we live in. Some of them make us confident in our faith, while others puzzle us.

The Old and New Testament scriptures in these pages may be favorite verses you learned as a child or those you've wondered about for a long time. Some you may have never noticed before. Whatever the case, *Bible Encouragement for Every Day* is designed to help you appreciate the Word and walk more deeply in it. Here you can daily share the authors' delight in well-known scriptures, come to know some elusive verses better and feel encouraged to make each one part of your own life, and meditate on the soul-stirring devotions and prayers.

The Bible is the most wonderful book on earth. As these scriptures and daily devotions challenge your faith, encourage your soul, and help you understand more about the God who loves you, His words will touch your heart and soul—and you'll be encouraged to make them an everyday part of your vibrant spiritual life.

—*The Publishers*

~ Day 1 ~

In the beginning God created the heaven and the earth.
GENESIS 1:1 KJV

Sometimes the simplest things are the most profound.

The Bible begins with a clear, direct statement of where our universe came from: God. What the Bible doesn't try to explain is where God Himself comes from. At the very start, scripture simply assumes His existence.

But read a few pages into the Bible, and you'll find God's explanation of His own being. . .kind of. Though it's tough for the time-bound human mind to understand, God called Himself "I AM" in response to Moses' question, "What is [Your] name?" (Exodus 3:13–14 KJV). Those two little words clearly imply existence, and interestingly, always in the present tense. There was never a time that God wasn't, and there will never be a time when He won't be. God simply is.

Scientists and philosophers have debated the origins of the universe and everything in it—including people—for about as long as people have existed in the universe. But the Bible states clearly and simply that everything originated with God.

It takes faith to accept that. But it takes a lot more faith to disbelieve!

Father, many things about You are beyond my comprehension. When I don't understand, please help me just to trust You, have faith in You, and believe. Amen.

～ Day 2 ～

This is how God showed his love among us: He sent his one and only Son into the world that we might live through him.
1 JOHN 4:9 NIV

This short verse packs an enormous amount of significance. God has always been there to guide us, even when we didn't know He was doing it. He continues to assist us in ways we may never realize, all because of His love for us. And as we know, He sent His only Son to this world to offer us salvation.

Many things about God are quite a mystery. We could never begin to understand the way in which He works and thinks. If there is anything at all that we can understand for sure, though, we can know He loves us. For that, we love Him. There is nothing we could ever do to make God stop loving us, because certainly we did nothing to make Him start.

God is concerned about everything we do. He celebrates our victories and cries with us during our difficult times. As we see in 1 John 4:9, God proved His love for us long before we were ever born! How could we not love such a God who first loved us so much?

You have always loved me, God, and You will love me forever. I am so grateful! Compared to Yours, my love is small, but I love You with all of my heart. Amen.

*Now unto him that is able to do exceeding abundantly above all
that we ask or think, according to the power that worketh in us. . .*
EPHESIANS 3:20 KJV

This scripture concludes Paul's prayer for the Ephesian church for spiritual growth, inner strength, and knowledge of God's love (vv. 14–19). The passage is a doxology giving praise to God and assurance to every believer of the omnipotence of our loving Lord.

The apostle declares that God is able to do "exceeding abundantly." The Greek word *huperekperissou* is a rare double compound meaning that God not only is able to accomplish all things, but does so "super-abundantly above the greatest abundance"—or "beyond measure."

"Above all that we ask or think" is just that. Imagine every good thing that God has promised in His Word—or things you've only dreamed about. Think of wonderful things that exceed the limits of human comprehension or description; then imagine that God is able and willing to do even more!

The last part of this verse indicates that the Holy Spirit works within the Christian's life to accomplish the seemingly impossible. Our highest aspirations are within God's power—but like Paul, we must pray. When we do, God does far more for us than we could ever guess.

*O Lord, You accomplish things I perceive as impossible.
You know my hopes and dreams, and I believe that You
are able to exceed my greatest expectations. Amen.*

Do you not know that you are God's temple
and that God's Spirit dwells in you?
1 Corinthians 3:16 rsv

The Samaritan woman asked Jesus where people ought to worship God—on Mount Gerizim (where a Samaritan temple once stood) or at the Jewish temple in Jerusalem. Jesus surprised her by saying that the time was soon coming when men would not worship God at *either* spot but "the true worshipers will worship the Father in spirit and truth" (John 4:19–24 rsv). Indeed, as Stephen later said, "The Most High does not dwell in temples made with hands" (Acts 7:48 nkjv).

If God doesn't dwell in temples built by men, where does He dwell? Jesus promised His disciples that although, up to that time, the Holy Spirit dwelled *with* them, He would soon dwell *in* them (John 14:17).

Paul stated it clearly when he asked Christians, "Do you not know that you are God's temple and that God's Spirit dwells in you?" (1 Corinthians 3:16 rsv). He further stated, "Your body is a temple of the Holy Spirit within you," and emphasized that that was why we ought to live holy lives (1 Corinthians 6:19 rsv; 2 Corinthians 6:16–17).

What an awesome privilege—to be a temple of the Spirit of God!

Heavenly Father, how wonderful it is that You have
chosen my body as a dwelling place for Your Holy Spirit.
Keep me always aware of Your presence. Amen.

∽ Day 5 ∽

"But they did not listen or pay attention; instead,
they followed the stubborn inclinations of their evil
hearts. They went backward and not forward."
JEREMIAH 7:24 NIV

Jews of Jeremiah's time excelled at following the external trappings of the law; as long as they offered the appropriate sacrifices in abundance, they thought they would please God.

In Jeremiah 7:22–23, the Lord told them otherwise. "I did not just give them commands about burnt offerings. . .but. . .this command: . . . Walk in obedience to *all* I command you" (NIV, italics added). Instead, they did as they wanted, resulting in a backward religion.

The literal wording of the last sentence reads: "They *were* backward and not forward." They had their religion the wrong way around; they had focused on external actions and not internal obedience.

Earlier, the prophet Isaiah said that the people would fall backward, into captivity, because they had a "little" religion: "The word of the LORD to them will become: Do this, do that, a rule for this, a rule for that; a little here, a little there—so that as they go they will fall backward; they will be injured and snared and captured" (28:13 NIV).

The goal for Christians today remains the same: "This is love for God: to keep his commands" (1 John 5:3 NIV). True devotion will express itself in every area of our lives.

Sometimes, Lord, I am guilty of focusing on the
world instead of on You. Help me to obey Your
commands and to keep moving forward. Amen.

Grace to you and peace from God
our Father and the Lord Jesus Christ.
1 CORINTHIANS 1:3 NKJV

The Romans had a particular format for beginning a letter. A typical opening line might read: "Hermas, to my dear brother Aristarchus, greetings."

Paul followed this format in his epistles. He began by identifying himself: "Paul," and often "Paul, an apostle of Jesus Christ." He would then identify the recipient of his letter by saying, "to Timothy," or "to the saints who are in Ephesus."

Instead of simply saying, "greetings," however, Paul invariably invoked blessings upon his readers. "Grace to you and peace from God our Father and the Lord Jesus Christ." The wording is almost identical throughout his epistles. Before anything else, Paul wished believers to have God's grace and peace filling their lives.

In his last letters of Titus and 1 and 2 Timothy—as an aging man looking back over a lifetime of hardships and persecution—Paul added one more blessing. Now he wrote, "Grace, *mercy*, and peace from God our Father and Jesus Christ our Lord" (1 Timothy 1:2 NKJV, italics added).

God's grace and peace are gifts of His Holy Spirit, helping us make it through difficult times. But sometimes we do fall—and it's good to know God's mercy is there to lift us up.

Father God, I thank You for blessing me daily and for filling
my life with Your gifts of grace, mercy, and peace. Amen.

In the multitude of my anxieties within me,
Your comforts delight my soul.
PSALM 94:19 NKJV

Do you worry when evil people seem to prosper and when life gets in your way? You are not alone.

We don't know for sure who wrote Psalm 94, but we can be certain that the psalmist was annoyed and anxious when he wrote it. He cries out to God, asking Him to "pay back to the proud what they deserve" (v. 2 TNIV). Then he goes on with a list of accusations about the evil ones. The psalmist's anxiety builds until finally, in verses 8–11, he warns his enemies to shape up and start following God. Verse 19 is the turning point—the place in the psalm where the writer is at a loss for words. Completely and utterly exasperated, he turns from his rant and starts praising God. "In the multitude of my anxieties within me," he says, "Your comforts delight my soul" (NKJV).

"In the multitude of my anxieties within me." Does that phrase describe you? When anxiety overwhelms us, we find relief in the words of Psalm 94:19. When we turn our anxious thoughts over to God, He brings contentment to our souls.

Dear God, on those days when frustration and
anxiety overwhelm me, please come to me, comfort
my soul, and remind me to praise You. Amen.

Day 8

*They chose Stephen, a man full of faith and of
the Holy Spirit. . .grace and power.*
ACTS 6:5, 8 NIV

From reading Acts 6, one has a suspicion that committees were the
brainchild of the early church. The good news is that the group
described here was assembled to bring help to the hurting—Greek
widows who were not receiving their fair share. The committee
included Stephen, a young man full of faith, grace, power, and
God's Holy Spirit.

What makes this passage so important is its emphasis on spiritual
armor's role in performing good deeds. For Stephen, that armor
included "faith," a conviction that his life was totally directed by God;
"grace," a lifestyle that spoke of Christ, even when he was silent;
and "power," the result of allowing the Holy Spirit to have His way.

Ultimately, Stephen's uncompromising life so antagonized his
enemies that after a no-holds-barred discourse, he was dragged
outside and stoned to death—making him Christianity's first martyr.

Standing by that day was Saul, a slayer of Christians. Undoubtedly,
the influence of a young man filled with faith, grace, and power followed Saul until the day he encountered God on a road to Damascus.
That's when Saul became the apostle Paul.

*I want to set a good example, Lord. Bless me with
strong faith, Your grace, and the power of Your Holy
Spirit. Teach me to be a blessing to others. Amen.*

"The city and everything in it are to be
destroyed as an offering to the LORD."
JOSHUA 6:17 NCV

Fortified with massive walls, Jericho appeared undefeatable. But God miraculously gave the Israelites victory over the city by collapsing that barrier.

In those days, conquering armies would confiscate everything of value from their victims. God, however, instructed Joshua not to take anything from Jericho except articles of gold, silver, bronze, and iron.

The banned spoils included the city's supply of harvested grain, an extremely valuable trading commodity. No doubt some Israelites wondered why God wanted the grain destroyed—especially since their daily manna had ceased only a short time before. Nevertheless, soldiers burned the grain along with everything else in the city.

In recent years, archaeologists have excavated the ancient ruins of Jericho. Their findings match the biblical account right down to clay jars filled with charred grain. Though some consider this battle a myth, the burned jars sit as silent witnesses to the accuracy of the Bible.

Millennia ago, a command to burn grain may have seemed wasteful to some. But God had His purposes. Today, when God assigns us jobs that appear odd or unimportant, believe that He still has His reasons.

Lord, sometimes Your ways are mysterious to me.
Still, I believe that You know the way, and I will
keep moving forward with faith. Amen.

But if anyone is deficient in wisdom, he should ask God, who gives to all generously and without reprimand, and it will be given to him. But he must ask in faith without doubting, for the one who doubts is like a wave of the sea, blown and tossed around by the wind. For that person must not suppose that he will receive anything from the Lord, since he is a double-minded individual, unstable in all his ways.
JAMES 1:5–8 NET

James, the half brother of Jesus, was not an early believer. It must have been difficult growing up in a household with perfection personified. But after Jesus' death, burial, and resurrection, James became a strong leader of the church. The book of James reads like a practical-Christian-living Frequently Asked Questions list.

At the beginning of this passage, James tells us that if we lack wisdom, we should ask God for it—and He'll grant that request. The three prior verses (James 1:2–4) tell that God gives us wisdom by trials and testing, which produce endurance and finally maturity.

So if you ask, be ready for the storm. When it comes, believe—don't doubt. If we weather that storm, we'll become wise.

Father, when I face tests and trials, help me to endure the storm by holding tightly to You. Open my eyes, Lord. Teach me. Make me wise. Amen.

~ Day 11 ~

"Study this Book of Instruction continually. Meditate on it day and night so you will be sure to obey everything written in it. Only then will you prosper and succeed in all you do."
JOSHUA 1:8 NLT

It is so easy for sin to creep into our lives, particularly in this age of technology in which we live. With a single click of the mouse, we can view anything we wish. We can study any subject and instantly have a library of resources on hand.

Unfortunately, this technology has a dark side as well. A phrase that has been used often throughout recent years is "garbage in, garbage out." With another click of the mouse, we can allow images and ideas to enter our minds that we know better than to allow.

Joshua 1:8 speaks clearly to the solution to any temptation we may encounter. Just as the Bible is as relevant today as it was when it was written, we can use its instruction to be successful in our Christian walk. When we fill our minds with God's Word, there will be neither room nor desire to fill our minds with the garbage of this world. As Joshua 1:8 points out, only then will we prosper and succeed in everything we do!

Let us thank the Lord for His Holy Word!

"Lead me not into temptation, but deliver me from evil." Lord, plant those words in my heart, and let Your Holy Word, the Bible, always be my guide. Amen.

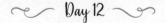

For God so loved the world, that he gave his only begotten Son, that whosoever believeth in him should not perish, but have everlasting life.
JOHN 3:16 KJV

Every once in a while we find a succinct statement that sums up a series of themes in a neat sentence. No, we're not talking about "Lather, rinse, repeat." John 3:16 is fascinating because in one verse we find the fullness of God's message in a nutshell.

We learn that God so loved. God's love was not a pitying love of pure emotion, but a practical love. God saw our sinfulness, and He loved. He expressed His love by the greatness of the gift of His Son. When sin would drag us down to perish in the awful pit, Christ died and went there as our substitute.

Sin separated us from God. Jesus' resurrection connects us again to a life-giving God, to an eternal life where we know that God is love. By faith we enter into this relationship. In our sin, deserving of death, we could do no good works to dig ourselves out of our hole. By God's grace, He extends salvation as a gift, obtained by believing in His Son. What a message! What a gift!

God, how can I ever thank You for the gift of salvation through Your Son, Jesus? Let my life be a testimony to His sacrifice and Your eternal love. Amen.

Trust in the LORD with all your heart and lean not on
your own understanding; in all your ways submit to
him, and he will make your paths straight.
PROVERBS 3:5–6 NIV

Have you ever had to make a decision but didn't know what to do? As Christians, we have a reliable resource for counsel. When decision-making poses a threat to our serenity and peace, Proverbs 3:5–6 provides sound advice.

First, trust in the Lord. Trusting God is fundamental to our relationship with God. And not just trusting, but doing so with everything within us.

The second bit of advice tells us to avoid the temptation to handle problems or decisions apart from God. Our thoughts and opinions are loaded with misleading personal biases. So King Solomon, author of this proverb, points us to full dependence on the wisdom of God's Word rather than human reasoning. Finally, God provides the solution to decision-making with a promise—namely, if we take all our concerns to God, He will direct our paths.

When we're tempted to act on our own wisdom, the Lord tells us to stop, reflect, and prayerfully consider each matter. He gives us uncomplicated advice for our major and not-so-major decisions. The question is, will we listen? That's the most important decision of all.

Often, Lord, I run on ahead of You and make decisions
on my own. Help me to remember that even with
small decisions I need to seek Your will. Amen.

Day 14

We must pay the most careful attention, therefore, to
what we have heard, so that we do not drift away.
HEBREWS 2:1 NIV

The fishing industry flourished in the Sea of Galilee, since no other freshwater lake existed nearby. This body of water lay nearly seven hundred feet below the level of the Mediterranean Sea, which was about thirty miles to the west.

The nearby hills reached as high as fifteen hundred feet. To the east, mountains with peaks of more than thirty-three hundred feet surrounded the sea, whose name means "circle." The geography created a beautiful but dangerous setting, subject to sudden and violent storms.

The fishing boats commonly used held four men, and a boat's typical small size at that time made it quite vulnerable to vicious weather. If fishermen were careless as to what was happening around them—where they were and whether the clouds showed signs of changing—they could find themselves in trouble quickly. Their boat would be carried off by the wind and waves.

A similar drifting can easily happen to us as we navigate the sea of life. Keeping an eye open for the early warning signs of danger helps us stay on the course God has given us. We need to pay careful attention to all we have learned in order to arrive safely at the end of our journey.

Heavenly Father, I know that Satan can find countless
ways to send me off course. Help me to keep my eyes
open and my destination set on You. Amen.

Then King David went in and sat before the Lord, and he said: "Who am I, Sovereign Lord, and what is my family, that you have brought me this far?"
2 SAMUEL 7:18 NIV

It's a very humbling experience when we stop and consider all God has done for us and all He has promised to do.

This is how David felt after Nathan the prophet visited him. Nathan informed David of what God had said concerning him. After reminding David of some of the things He had already brought him out of, God spoke of all that He still intended to do in David's life. God made promises so majestic and full that they must have been overwhelming to this man who had once been a simple shepherd boy.

David wasn't the only one who received promises of God's blessings. Abram (Genesis 15:1–17), Moses (Exodus 3:1–22), and Joshua (Joshua 1:1–9) are just a few of the others who were given promises—promises they were astonished God would offer.

God's willingness to shower His people with such blessings speaks of His wonderful grace, a grace that is generously and daily extended to us. Let us express our appreciation as David did, with a humble attitude and a grateful prayer of praise.

Father, I praise You! Your blessings are endless and so beyond what I deserve. I accept them with sincere gratefulness and absolute joy. Amen.

And this is love: that we walk in obedience to his commands. As you have heard from the beginning, his command is that you walk in love.
2 JOHN 1:6 NIV

"Walk in love." It sounds so easy, so attractive. So why don't more people do it?

Because it goes against our worst instincts. Let's not forget we were rebels from the start. Eve, encouraged by the serpent, feared God was keeping something from her. So she went her own way—and took Adam with her. They ran from God. You might think we would be wiser, but we're all still doing our own thing—and still getting it wrong.

It's human nature to rebel when someone is keeping you down, taking advantage of you, or playing you for a fool. But this is *God* we're talking about, not some con artist, dodgy politician, or tin-pot dictator. He doesn't have anything to prove, and He doesn't have anything to gain. He made everything, so it's already His. To put it bluntly, we can trust Him.

So put aside those fears. If you must rebel, rebel against rebellion. God's "commands" are simply instructions for how to walk beside Him. Stop going your own way and start going His—and you will know what it's like to truly "walk in love."

God, You love me. You desire to go with me and lead me. Why then would I go my own way? Take my hand. I want us to walk together. Amen.

~ Day 17 ~

*"What is truth?" retorted Pilate. With this he went
out again to the Jews gathered there and said,
"I find no basis for a charge against him."*
JOHN 18:38 NIV

Most of us are familiar with the trumped-up charges and the kanga-
roo court that convened to set in motion Jesus' journey to the cross.
As Jesus is shuffled from one jurisdiction to another, an interesting
conversation begins with Pontius Pilate, the Roman authority figure
for the region.

In an attempt to make sense of this latest crisis, which no doubt
has interrupted his breakfast, Pilate begins to question Jesus. As
Pilate tries to sort out the mayhem the Jewish priests have brought
to his door, he finds himself engaging in a philosophical discussion
about truth with the prisoner.

Jesus asserts that His purpose is to testify to truth, and for this
reason He was born (18:37). The Way, the Truth, and the Life is
testifying in a legal proceeding about who He is.

Pilate asks the right question: "What is truth?" He's on the
right track, looking for a semblance of justice in the midst of pro-
cedural mockery. But his failing lies in the fact that he doesn't wait
for Jesus' answer. Instead, he returns to the bloodthirsty mob who
aren't interested in truth—they're only interested in having their
position justified.

Jesus approaches all of us with the answer of truth. Will we listen?

*Jesus, You are the way and the truth and the life—the
only way to the Father. Help me always to walk in
Your truth and to listen to Your words. Amen.*

Day 18

Hezekiah dammed up the source of the waters of the Upper
Gihon and directed them down to the west side of the City
of David. Hezekiah succeeded in all that he did.
2 Chronicles 32:30 net

Jerusalem sits atop a mountain and has long been a formidable fortress, but it has always had one perennial vulnerability: it must draw its water from the spring of Gihon, which lies outside the walls.

Early in the city's history, a twenty-foot-deep trench was dug and then covered with rock slabs to provide a covered aqueduct draining into the Pool of Siloam, inside the walls. Later it was replaced by the steep Warren's Shaft, which allowed people to get to the spring directly. These weren't very effective, because King David's men first captured the city through one of them.

King Hezekiah solved the problem by covering the exterior access to the Gihon spring entirely and cutting a 533-meter tunnel and aqueduct back to the pool, where water could be safely gathered. Jerusalem has been besieged at least twenty-three times and captured forty-four times, but this solved the water problem.

Tourists in Jerusalem can visit Hezekiah's tunnel today, 2,700 years after it was built!

Wherever the way is blocked, You know a detour.
Whenever there is a problem, You know its solution.
So lead me, Lord. I want to follow You. Amen.

He that dwelleth in the secret place of the most High
shall abide under the shadow of the Almighty.
PSALM 91:1 KJV

What a wonderful promise! God will cover—in a cloud of glory and protection—anyone who enters into His presence and stays in continual communion with Him. Under the old covenant, this applied only to the high priest entering into the Holy of Holies. But under the new covenant, all Christians can enter into God's presence through the blood of Jesus Christ.

As we daily abide in the scriptures and come into God's presence, He assures us safety and security no matter the circumstances. The word *shadow* indicates a shelter, covering, or protection from the heat and storms of life. Just as a tree's looming branches shield us from the hot sun, God provides refuge and protection wherever we are and whatever challenges we encounter.

The names given to God in this verse define the various aspects of His loving protection and care. *Most High* means that He is greater than any threat or problem we face, and *Almighty* emphasizes His power and majesty.

In another verse, the psalmist wrote, "God is our refuge and strength, a very present help in trouble" (Psalm 46:1 KJV). The Lord is present at all times to help and protect us. He *is* our dwelling place.

Most high and almighty God, nothing can harm
me and no evil will come to me because You are my
eternal protection and my strength. Amen.

∽ Day 20 ∽

Let the message about Christ, in all its richness, fill your lives. Teach and counsel each other with all the wisdom he gives. Sing psalms and hymns and spiritual songs to God with thankful hearts.
COLOSSIANS 3:16 NLT

As we think about what real wisdom is, we realize that the only wisdom worth having comes from God.

No matter how smart we think we have become, nothing compares to God's wisdom. He shares His wisdom with us and instructs us to share it with others.

Colossians 3:16 indicates that we become wise when our lives are filled with God's Word. We need to study and learn and meditate on God's Word. We then will feel moved to sing praises to Him for what He gives us. We need to live the Word of God every day. It will shine through us! The old song says, "They will know we are Christians by our love." This means reflecting the love of God in everything we do.

When we spend time in God's Word, we find peace, wisdom, and contentment that we get from no other place. This is a peace we love to have. This is happiness! Imagine being anything but thankful to God for filling us with His love, peace, and wisdom!

O Lord, my Rock and my Redeemer, may my words and my actions be a reflection of Your Word and pleasing in Your sight. Amen.

Jesus reached out his hand and touched the man. "I am willing,"
he said. "Be clean!" And immediately the leprosy left him.
LUKE 5:13 NIV

This touching verse sums up Jesus' mission. The leper asked for
healing—if Jesus was willing. Of course, Jesus was willing. He
willingly took human form; He willingly suffered ridicule. Willingly
He cured many—and willingly He died.

He didn't have to do any of it, but He did.

In return, God asks the same from us. He can do great works
through us—if we are willing. But that's difficult, isn't it? After all,
who are we? We can't perform miracles. And there lies the stumbling
block—for God to work in the world, we have to get past thinking of
ourselves as His *partners*. The apostles didn't cure anyone. God used
them to perform many cures, but none of the power came from them.
They simply allowed themselves to be instruments in His hands.

Great things are yet to be done in this world—and we can be
a part of them when we stop worrying about our capabilities and
put more faith in *His*.

In the quest to be more like Christ, the simplest and most
effective thing we can do is be willing. Then hand that willingness
over to God and see what He does with it.

God, I am willing. Use me. Work through me to
accomplish whatever You desire. Whether it is something
great or something small, I am ready. Amen.

"The LORD bless you and keep you."
NUMBERS 6:24 NKJV

"God bless you." How many times have you said it? How often has it been said to you?

In church you hear this familiar blessing found in Numbers 6:24–26 (NKJV):

> *"The LORD bless you and keep you; the LORD make His face*
> *shine upon you, and be gracious to you; the LORD lift*
> *up His countenance upon you, and give you peace."*

God gave the words for this blessing, sometimes called "the priestly blessing," to Moses. It is the oldest blessing in the Bible.

What does it mean for the Lord to bless you? Webster's defines the word *bless* as "to hallow or consecrate by religious rite or word." To be blessed by God is to be granted His favor and protection. In Matthew 5, Jesus offers illustrations of those who are blessed. He tells the blessed ones, "Rejoice and be exceedingly glad" (v. 12 NKJV). The result of God's blessing is happiness. We find joy knowing that God loves and protects us.

Paul says in Ephesians 1:3 that we should react to God's blessings with praise: "Give praise to the God and Father of our Lord Jesus Christ. He has blessed us with every spiritual blessing" (NIrV).

How has the Lord blessed you today? Praise Him!

I praise You, Lord, for the abundance of blessings You give me each day. Morning and night You bless me, and I am so grateful! Amen.

∽ Day 23 ∽

When he had received the drink, Jesus said, "It is finished."
With that, he bowed his head and gave up his spirit.
JOHN 19:30 NIV

"It is finished"—Jesus' words on the cross have inspired music and thrilled the hearts of Christians ever since His death.

John wrote his Gospel in Greek, a language rich with possibilities. The original word is *tetelestai*. This verb in the perfect tense implies an action completed in the past with continuing results in the present. When Jesus died, God's plan for our salvation had come to fruition—and we are still saved today by that onetime sacrifice.

More meaning comes through when we consider the actual Hebrew words Jesus spoke on the cross. "*Tam ve'nishlam*" is taken from the prayer offered at the conclusion of a book of the Torah: "*Tam ve'nishlam Shevach La'el Boreh Olam.*" Translated into English, it means "It is completed and fulfilled, blessed be God, the Creator of the world." The high priest spoke the "*Tam ve'nishlam*" at the end of Passover.

In saying, "It is finished," Jesus not only said He had completed the work of our salvation; He also said His death fulfilled the law and identified Himself with the Passover lamb. Once again, He staked His claim as the Jewish Messiah.

Let us give thanks for Jesus, our Passover Lamb.

Thank You, Jesus, for completing God's plan of salvation.
Thank You for standing in my place that I might be
saved to enjoy His gift of eternal life. Amen.

"There is no one righteous, not even one."
ROMANS 3:10 NIV

Those who have prayed for a father's or mother's salvation will relate to the following conversation:

"Dad, what is keeping you from accepting the Lord into your life?"

"I'm not worthy."

"No one is, but He wants you to come to Him in spite of that."

"I can't do that, son, until I can give up my bad habits."

Today's scripture verse highlights Paul's conviction that everyone is under the influence of sin. Since Adam's fall, all humankind is in the same boat—all have the need of being made righteous by accepting Christ's gift of salvation and allowing the Holy Spirit to take over in their day-by-day walk.

According to Paul, righteousness is both being and doing. It is a right relationship with God and conduct that's in accord with His will. In the original Greek, "not even one" is like shutting the door on the subject. That's it! No exceptions!

All who feel they must get their spiritual houses in order before approaching God should recall an old gospel song:

> *Come just as you are. O come just as you are. Turn from your*
> *sin, let the Savior come in, but come just as you are.*
> HALDOR LILLENAS

Father, on days when I feel not good enough for
You, myself, or others, I come to You believing that
You will accept me just as I am. Amen.

⟿ Day 25 ⟿

"But God raised him from the dead, freeing him from the agony of death, because it was impossible for death to keep its hold on him."
ACTS 2:24 NIV

According to science and the natural order, which statement is true?

It is impossible for the dead to return to life.

It is impossible for the dead to stay dead.

Even movies like *The Night of the Living Dead* play on our rock-solid assumption that dead people are meant to remain in the grave.

In his sermon on the day of Pentecost, Peter told his audience that Jesus of Nazareth had indeed died, put to death at their hands only weeks before. For the members of that audience, that should have been the end. If even the great King David's body lay entombed in Jerusalem, how much more this troublesome prophet from Galilee (Acts 2:29)?

But in Jesus, God turned the normal course of nature on its head. He reversed the poles; He turned the impossibility of coming back to life to the impossibility of staying dead. He raised Jesus to life and exalted Him to His right hand (Acts 2:32–33).

May we bow in worship to the one who turned His funeral upside down and opened a new world of (im)possibilities.

Lord, I worship You because You are the only one who brings eternal life to all believers. Thanks to You, I look forward to a new life in heaven someday. Amen.

But when Peter came to Antioch, I had to oppose
him to his face, for what he did was very wrong.
GALATIANS 2:11 NLT

When Peter first arrived in Antioch, Jewish and Gentile believers
fellowshipped together during mealtime. Although the food prepa-
ration didn't follow Jewish dietary laws and Jewish law considered
Gentiles unclean, Peter didn't hesitate to participate in these meals.
After all, God had declared Gentiles and all food to be clean in
Peter's vision at Joppa.

However, when James and other Jewish Christian leaders came to
Antioch, Peter stopped eating and fellowshipping with the Gentile
believers. Then the other Jewish Christians followed Peter's hypocrisy,
and even Barnabas was influenced to join them in their hypocrisy
(see Galatians 2:13).

Alarmed by Peter's behavior and its influence on others, Paul
confronted him face-to-face. If left unchecked, Peter's actions could
have resulted in a heretical teaching that claimed there were two
bodies of Christ, one for Jews and the other for Gentiles.

Out of fear of what others would think, Peter, a pillar of the early
church, shrank back from doing the right thing without considering
the ramifications of his actions.

We all want to fit in. However, compromising God-given convictions isn't the answer. To combat compromise, pray for guidance,
memorize appropriate scripture, and stand firm. Anything less is
hypocrisy.

God, make my armor strong. Help me not to compromise
my convictions. Guide me in Your ways and arm me with
Your Word that I might always stand firm. Amen.

Uzziel son of Harhaiah, one of the goldsmiths, repaired the next section; and Hananiah, one of the perfume-makers, made repairs next to that. They restored Jerusalem as far as the Broad Wall.
NEHEMIAH 3:8 NIV

When Nehemiah started rebuilding the walls of Jerusalem, he used all sorts of people. The perfume makers and goldsmiths may have supplied the means, or they may actually have put stone upon stone. Beside these artisans were merchants and rulers of districts. Men of different tribes worked side by side. Some repaired areas they had a personal interest in. Shallum repaired a section "with the help of his daughters" (v. 12). Priests and temple servants labored. Some were less than diligent; others were zealous.

Nehemiah called *all* believers to do the Lord's work. And, working together, they rebuilt the city walls in an amazing fifty-two days! The fact that they were surrounded on all sides by enemies may have been a further incentive.

Faith is in a similar position today. We only have one enemy, but we make him stronger when we treat our brothers and sisters as Satan's reinforcements. By allowing politics and differing interpretations to divide church from church, we only weaken the city of God.

Make the common denominator belief in Him, and we will build a wall with all His people on the inside and only Satan left on the outside.

Heavenly Father, lead me to unite with my fellow believers, because when we band together, nothing can destroy our love and devotion toward You and Your work. Amen.

But Mary treasured up all these things and
pondered them in her heart.
LUKE 2:19 NIV

The Bible records two different accounts of Mary pondering events surrounding her son, Jesus. The first was at the Savior's birth—following the angels' appearance to the shepherds—when she carefully weighed every circumstance she'd experienced and seen.

The second time was when the twelve-year-old Jesus separated from His parents to sit at the feet of teachers in the temple. When Jesus' anxious parents found Him in Jerusalem, they scolded their son. His response? "Why were you searching for me? . . . Didn't you know I had to be in my Father's house?" (Luke 2:49 NIV). Then He obeyed and went with them.

The Bible portrays Jesus' mother as a tender, loving, patient, and humble woman. Yet she was still very human. On one hand, she knew Jesus was the Messiah; on the other, Jesus was her son—the boy she nurtured, taught, and cared for. So Mary stored in her memory the things that had already taken place, to try to understand the divine nature and mission of her beloved son.

We have no record of Mary verbalizing questions, thoughts, and perhaps—at times—concerns. But we know she pondered (and undoubtedly prayed) as all good Christian parents do.

Too often I jump to conclusions, Lord, without taking time
to ponder Your example and Your Word. Remind me to slow
down, even stop, and turn my thoughts toward You. Amen.

And the Lord *said unto him,*
What is that in thine hand?
Exodus 4:2 kjv

God astonished Moses by miraculously appearing as a flame in a desert bush. He told Moses that He was sending him to Egypt to liberate the Israelites and lead them to the Promised Land. When Moses objected that he was nobody, God assured him, "I will certainly be with you." Again Moses protested: "But suppose they will not believe me" (Exodus 3:11–12; 4:1 nkjv).

God did not need to "suppose" any such thing. He had just said, "I will *certainly* be with you." Nevertheless, God was willing to throw in an extra sign to strengthen Moses' faith and asked, "What is that in your hand?" (Exodus 4:2 nkjv).

Well, what *was* it? It was a shepherd's staff, a rod made of an almond sapling. God told Moses to cast it down, and when he did, it transformed into a serpent. When Moses seized its tail, it morphed back into a wooden rod.

This verse is often used to teach the principle "Help yourself with what you have on hand," but that's missing the point. The real point is that even after we have a showstopping "burning bush" encounter with God, even after God assures us He's with us to help us—we *still* doubt. And God often then does another miracle to *re*assure us.

Sometimes I feel conflicted in my faith just like the
boy's father in Mark 9:17–26. So I say to You, Lord,
"I do believe; help me overcome my unbelief!" Amen.

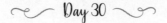

~ Day 30 ~

*In your hearts revere Christ as Lord. Always be prepared to give
an answer to everyone who asks you to give the reason for the
hope that you have. But do this with gentleness and respect.*
1 PETER 3:15 NIV

Isn't the relevance of God's Word amazing? This verse is part of a letter, written by the apostle Peter, for Christians living in a non-Christian society. His letter is filled with encouragement and advice. Peter gives three parts of advice with several key words.

First, Peter advises, set God apart from everything else in your heart; in other words, "sanctify" God, or recognize God's holiness and treat Him with deserved awe.

Second, be prepared to explain your hope in Christ and eternal life, having a full grasp of what and in whom you believe.

Finally, remember that *how* you say something is equally as important as *what* you say. Peter instructs believers to explain Christ with "gentleness and respect."

In other words, we must walk the walk before we can reveal the hope we have in Jesus Christ. And when God is ready for us to speak on His behalf, we will know whom we represent, and we will do so with utmost respect and gentleness.

*Dear God, please prepare me to explain my hope in Christ
and eternal life. Teach me to explain it in a way that
honors You with gentleness and respect. Amen.*

～ Day 31 ～

*Wisdom makes one's face shine, and the hardness
of one's countenance is changed.*
ECCLESIASTES 8:1 NRSV

Do you remember this sunny Sunday school chorus?

> *You can smile when you can't say a word.*
> *You can smile when you cannot be heard.*
> *You can smile when it's cloudy or fair.*
> *You can smile anytime, anywhere.*
> A. H. Ackley

From today's fascinating verse, it's obvious that Solomon's insight on wisdom isn't necessarily aimed at PhDs or brainiacs. Obviously, he is taking aim at those of us who need to understand the correlation between wisdom and our outlook on life.

Not even the beautician class in your community college can provide the know-how to change one's point of view or disposition. Such a permanent adjustment doesn't come from hair tint or lipstick color; it springs from something much more permanent—it's an interior makeover.

The poet who supplied today's ditty understands this. In many ways, a smile is the direct reaction to what's being felt within. As a vacation Bible school kid observed, "When I smile, I feel all bubbly inside." Short of bubbles, a hard countenance greatly changes with a smile.

A positive, happy point of view is the result of a major mind and heart change.

*Father, put a smile on my face today. Even if it rains
and frustration comes my way, bless me with a positive
outlook that I can share with others. Amen.*

Jesus answered them, "You are deceived, because
you don't know the scriptures or the power of God."
MATTHEW 22:29 NET

The Sadducees were trying to trap Jesus.

They asked Him question after question to try to make Him contradict Himself. They wanted to show the crowd the importance of their religious ways and their superiority over Jesus. It irritated them that Jesus drew a big crowd everywhere He went with His teaching. They wanted to be the authority, but instead it seemed that the crowds preferred to listen to every word that came from Jesus. Imagine being alive during the time Jesus was teaching and being able to hear the voice of the Son of God as He spoke!

On this occasion, as recorded in Matthew 22, Jesus again could see the motivation behind the Sadducees' questions. His answer to them amazes us even today. These religious, self-righteous Sadducees must have thought very highly of themselves to try to trip up Jesus the way they did. What better answer could there be for such a person than to be told, "You are deceived, because you don't know the scriptures or the power of God"?

The scriptural illiteracy these men displayed was certainly not impressive to Jesus. This is just another affirmation of why we only put our faith in the Word of God.

God, as I read Your Word, enlighten me. Teach me Your
ways. Help me to apply them to my everyday life so
that I may walk in the footsteps of Jesus. Amen.

Jesus said to him, "Love the Lord your God with all your heart, with all your soul, and with all your mind."
MATTHEW 22:37 NET

The Sadducees couldn't trap Jesus, so the Pharisees tried to do it. They asked Him which of the commandments was the most important.

Everything Jesus did, He did with love. Even when He was angry with people, it was because He knew their actions were contrary to God's will. There was never a time when Jesus spoke to another person, went anywhere, or did anything without being filled with love for people. We can almost imagine that as Jesus went about His daily routine, He must have been absolutely glowing with love!

When asked about the most important commandment, Jesus cited Deuteronomy 6:5, which says that we should be completely full of love for God. He then mentioned that the second most important commandment was just like it, to love others as we love ourselves. Everything Jesus ever taught and lived revolved around love.

This is how we should live. Our Lord is the God of love, and nothing is more important. We should focus on what is right with the world and with other people and not be so concerned about what is wrong with them. Long before John Lennon and Paul McCartney wrote their song, Jesus was saying it. "All you need is love."

In these chaotic times, I sometimes find it hard to focus on the goodness in people. Change that, Lord. Lead me to love others just as You love them. Amen.

I say to myself, "The LORD is my portion;
therefore I will wait for him."
LAMENTATIONS 3:24 NIV

For the Israelites, the word portion held multiple meanings. It could refer to a piece of land or an inheritance. Portions could also imply the necessities of life like daily food, water, and clothing. Old Testament writings often designate the kind of life one was born into and the family one was raised in as our portion in life.

In this verse, the writer declares that the Lord is his portion. He states clearly that he inherited the right to worship God, and that God provides the essentials to support his life. He is also welcomed to be a part of the family of God.

The Lord is our portion too. But when will we fully receive this inheritance and celebrate with Him? We know it is coming, but it's difficult to wait.

Hope gives us strength as we anticipate our return to God. We belong to God and know someday we will worship Him face-to-face in His presence. Knowing God will keep His promise, we can say with confidence, "'The LORD is my portion; therefore I will wait.'"

What an amazing promise You have made to me,
Father, that one day I will be with You in heaven.
My hope is in You as I wait for that day. Amen.

∾ Day 35 ∾

Let the morning bring me word of your unfailing
love, for I have put my trust in you.
PSALM 143:8 NIV

How did your day begin today? Did you arise early and enjoy the peaceful quiet of the morning after a good night's sleep? Or maybe you spent a sleepless night tending to the needs of a sick child, and you faced the day running on empty.

We don't know if David was a morning person or a night owl, but he chose to start his day looking for visible reminders of God's unfailing love. It might have been easy to remember God's love for him if he had witnessed a glorious morning sunrise, but if the night had been stormy and he was dealing with spooked sheep in the midst of a downpour, God's unfailing love may have felt a little distant.

Regardless of the circumstances, David decided to trust in God first thing in the morning. Whether or not conditions were favorable for faith, David believed in God's unfailing love—even if he couldn't see it in the world around him.

I awake in the morning, and You are there. You are with
me all day long and throughout the night. Thank You,
heavenly Father, for Your ever-present love. Amen.

*"The one is who is victorious I will make a pillar in the temple
of my God. Never again will they leave it. I will write on them
the name of my God and the name of the city of my God, the
new Jerusalem, which is coming down out of heaven from
my God; and I will also write on them my new name."*
REVELATION 3:12 NIV

An old hymn by C. Austin Miles states, "There's a new name written
down in glory, and it's mine." In Revelation 2:17 (NIV), Jesus promised to give the one who overcomes "a white stone with a new name
written on it, known only to the one who receives it." In the Old
Testament, God promised a new name to Zion when "the nations
will see your vindication" (Isaiah 62:2 NIV).

But God's people weren't the only ones to receive a new name.
In the letter to the church at Philadelphia, the One "who is holy
and true, who holds the key of David" (Revelation 3:7 NIV) spoke of
His *new* name (v. 12). Both God the Father and God the Son will
mark their own with their names: their names will be inscribed on
the 144,000 (Revelation 14:1) and those who are allowed into the
New Jerusalem (Revelation 22:4).

Our Savior has adopted us (Ephesians 1:5) and bestowed His
name on us.

That's a name change we can all welcome.

*Dear God, I am special! You made me Your child and
marked me with Your name. Already, my name is
inscribed in Your book. Thank You, Father! Amen.*

∾ Day 37 ∾

"But will God really live on earth? Why, even the highest heavens
cannot contain you. How much less this Temple I have built!"
1 Kings 8:27 nlt

A masterpiece of quarried stone, wood paneling, and carvings with
gold overlay, Solomon's temple required the efforts of over thirty
thousand men, working seven years, for its completion.

During the temple's dedication service, the priests carried the ark
of the covenant into the Most Holy Place, and "the glorious presence
of the LORD filled the Temple" (1 Kings 8:11 nlt).

Offering a prayer of dedication, Solomon recognized that God
isn't confined to one place. Perhaps he had memorized his father's
words, written years before: "I can never get away from your presence!
If I go up to heaven, you are there. . . . If I dwell by the farthest
oceans, even there your hand will guide me, and your strength will
support me" (Psalm 139:7–10 nlt).

God Himself says, "Am I not everywhere in all the heavens and
earth?" (Jeremiah 23:24 nlt).

Out of love for the Israelites, God displayed His presence in
their temple through a brilliant cloud.

Our God is not some impersonal force that considers us mere
specks of humanity existing on the earth. He sees and cares for us
as individuals. And more comforting, He knows our whereabouts
at all times and is at hand to guide us through good and bad times.

When I am lost in this journey called "life," You
know exactly where I am. I call and You lead me.
I am grateful, Lord! I love You, Lord! Amen.

"For my yoke is easy and my burden is light."
MATTHEW 11:30 NIV

Ever felt like a beast of burden? With all the pressures and expectations of this life, it would be hard not to sometimes. If you had to be such a creature, what kind of master would you choose?

Horses and oxen still plow fields all around the world. They wear yokes across their shoulders, and their burdens are not light. We who feel wearied by the world might sympathize with them as they drag plows through hard, stony ground. They don't get to choose their masters. They can only walk where the reins or the whip make them go. And when their working life is over. . .

So why would anyone choose to wear a yoke?

Because the one Christ offers really is light. So light in fact that He actually carries our burdens! There is no harness; there is no whip. We get to choose our Master!

All He asks for a lifetime of companionship followed by an eternity of bliss is that we wear the "yoke" of the love of God. With Jesus guiding our steps, plowing a straight furrow will be our pleasure. And when our working life is over, we'll find the furrow led all the way to heaven.

*Father, I am proud to call You Master. You are good
and kind to me. You allow me freedom, and when
I obey You, You fill my heart with joy. Amen.*

He performs wonders that cannot be fathomed,
miracles that cannot be counted.
JOB 5:9 NIV

In Job 5, Job's friend Eliphaz tries to put in plain words the reason for Job's suffering. In his opinion, Job must have done something sinful to be in such a dreadful state. Eliphaz tells Job what he would do if he were suffering because of his sins. He would appeal to God. He would confess his sins and hope for God's mercy. After all, God "performs wonders that cannot be fathomed, miracles that cannot be counted."

In other words, Eliphaz says Job should seek God's justice, because God is greater than anyone can imagine. He alone is the one who forgives our sinfulness and heals our suffering.

Job's afflictions were not due to anything that he had done, but Eliphaz's instructions to him would have been good, if he had sinned. We see them again in 1 John 1:9 (NIV), "If we confess our sins, he is faithful and just and will forgive us our sins and purify us from all unrighteousness."

Are you feeling guilty about some sin in your life? Remember the greatness of God. Romans 10:13 (NIV) says: "Everyone who calls on the name of the Lord will be saved."

Sometimes I feel so ashamed of my sins that I avoid
confessing them to You. Help me to remember that You
will forgive me if I just come to You and ask. Amen.

～ Day 40 ～

For our conversation is in heaven; from whence also
we look for the Saviour, the Lord Jesus Christ.
PHILIPPIANS 3:20 KJV

In this passage, the Greek translation of the word *conversation* is *politeum*, meaning "citizenship." The word is broad in its translation, indicating our citizenship, thoughts, and affections are already in heaven.

For every Christian, heaven is home. From the moment we accept Christ, we are adopted into God's family with the promise of spending eternity with Him and all the saints who have gone before us. We are no longer citizens of this earth; we are born from above, and our names are written in God's celestial register.

Because our citizenship is in heaven, so are our hopes, thoughts, and affections. We are *in* the world, but not *of* it any longer. In his letter to the Hebrews, Paul expounded on how Abraham and his descendants were "looking forward to the city with foundations, whose architect and builder is God" (Hebrews 11:10 NIV). They considered themselves strangers on this earth because "they were longing for a better country—a heavenly one" (Hebrews 11:16 NIV).

As heaven's citizens, we will enjoy all the rights and privileges of our heavenly Father. Meanwhile, we look to Jesus and stay steadfast to His Word until He ushers us home.

Heavenly Father, I know that my forever home is there
with You. I cannot imagine how wonderful it is! Thank
You for my road home—Your gift of salvation. Amen.

Day 41

For the eyes of the LORD range throughout the earth to strengthen those whose hearts are fully committed to him.
2 CHRONICLES 16:9 NIV

God is on a quest. He explores throughout the world and searches in every corner. He is relentless in His pursuit for something.

What is the object of His exploration? He wants people with a particular type of heart condition—hearts fully devoted to Him.

God seeks a relationship with those who have open and receiving hearts. He is not looking to condemn or judge, but to find hearts committed to knowing Him and learning His way. He desires people who want to talk and listen to Him and who have a deep thirst to serve and please Him.

God gives loyal hearts a gift—His strength. He eagerly pours His Spirit into these open hearts in order to draw them closer and build an intimate relationship with them.

God looks for us, and the only requirement is for each of us to have a fully devoted heart. As we open our hearts and hands to receive Him, He will find us.

Find me, Lord; draw me near to You. Open up my heart so that I may fully receive all You want to pour into it. Amen.

Day 42

*When Jesus heard what had happened, he withdrew
by boat privately to a solitary place. Hearing of this,
the crowds followed him on foot from the towns.*
MATTHEW 14:13 NIV

Jesus went out onto the sea in search of privacy in which to mourn John the Baptist. He must have been distraught. But might He also have spared a thought for Himself? After all, both He and John had been gifts from God and heralded by angels. They were both part of the same plan.

John had prepared the way—and now he was gone. Jesus must have felt alone in a way He never had before. Perhaps there was a sense of "Now it's My turn." The prospect of the long walk to the cross must have seemed, somehow, more real at that moment.

Did He gather His strength on that boat?

Then He came back to the shore. The crowd swept away any possibility of self-pity. Seeing them and their needs, He "had compassion on them" (Matthew 14:14 NIV). Then, in one of His best-remembered miracles, He went on to feed five thousand of them.

When He stepped onto the shore, Jesus encapsulated one of the most important tenets of Christianity: it isn't about you; it's about the wonderful things you can achieve for God when you put your own fears behind you and have compassion on others.

*I don't want my life to be all about me, God. Teach me to
step outside of myself and into a life of service. Amen.*

*Jesus Christ our Lord, who was. . .declared to be
the Son of God with power according to the Spirit of
holiness, by the resurrection from the dead.*
ROMANS 1:3–4 NKJV

When Jesus was baptized and the Holy Spirit descended upon Him, God the Father declared out loud, "This is My beloved Son, in whom I am well pleased" (Matthew 3:16–17 NKJV).

Jesus also declared to the Jewish people, "I am the Son of God," and said that if they didn't believe it when He *said* so, to at least believe because of the miracles (John 10:36–38 NKJV). Jesus' miracles also declared that He was the Son of God.

But when the Holy Spirit of God raised Jesus back to life after He had lain dead in the grave for three days, this was the final and greatest proof that Jesus was the long-awaited Messiah, the Son of God. Jesus Christ was "declared to be the Son of God with *power*" (Romans 1:4 NKJV, italics added).

This final declaration has great personal relevance to us who believe on Jesus, for if the Spirit of God had the power to raise Jesus from the dead, and that same Spirit dwells in our hearts, He will raise us to endless life as well (Romans 8:11).

*Jesus, I believe You are the Son of God. I know that
God's powerful Holy Spirit raised You from death, and
someday He will do the same for me. Amen.*

∾ Day 44 ∾

If you fulfill the royal law as expressed in this scripture, "You shall love your neighbor as yourself," you are doing well.
JAMES 2:8 NET

Sometimes we wonder if we are doing enough for God. We think about the commandments and the teachings of Jesus and wonder if we are living "Christlike" lives.

A rich young ruler came to Jesus one time and asked him what he must do to be saved. But the answer Jesus gave reflected the idea that He always taught: there is nothing we can do to earn our way into heaven. It is not a matter of earning our salvation, and certainly God is not impressed by our work. Our walk with Jesus is about a real relationship. It is about loving Him and loving others as ourselves. Isn't it wonderful that we have a God of love?

As we see in James 2:8, we are living as we should if we obey God's law to love one another. We know that this is not always easy to do. It seems that the way we love the person we like the least is how we love God the most. Sometimes it is quite challenging to look upon others as Jesus does. If we see people through the eyes of Jesus, though, in His words we are "doing well."

Give me Your eyes, Lord. Allow me to see others as You see them. Then, with Your help, I can love those who to me seem unlovable. Amen.

～ *Day 45* ～

And the LORD God planted a garden eastward in Eden;
and there he put the man whom he had formed.
GENESIS 2:8 KJV

Adam wasn't created in the Garden of Eden. He was formed from the dust somewhere to the west of the garden. The first thing God did, after giving him life, was to lead the father of mankind to paradise.

Then Adam and Eve blew it and were thrown out. God could have let it go and left mankind scrabbling in the dust, but He didn't. He sacrificed His Son to give us another way to paradise. That's how much He wants us there! Because that's where we were meant to be!

But mankind has been fallible from the start, and as a result, we often don't think we deserve the kind of love God offers. The dust of this world is all many ever aspire to. Heaven is for better folk, special folk, saints perhaps, not weak, inconsistent, scared people like us. And when we think like that, we break God's heart. He's not waiting for us to prove ourselves worthy. He made the invitation, and it's still valid. We just have to accept.

The garden was planted for *you* to walk in. Not some "better" person. You have another chance. Take it. Head eastward or upward. God wants you to come home!

I accept Your invitation, O Mighty God! I accept that
Jesus died for my sins because You believe that I am
good enough for eternal life in heaven. Amen.

*For they are the spirits of the demons performing signs who
go out to the kings of the earth to bring them together for
the battle that will take place on the great day of God, the
All-Powerful. Now the spirits gathered the kings and their
armies to the place that is called Armageddon in Hebrew.*
REVELATION 16:14, 16 NET

The Valley of Armageddon is the coastal plain and associated plateau
called Megiddo, about halfway between the southern tip of the Sea
of Galilee and the Mediterranean coast. It is broad and flat, ideal
for armies, and dominates the coastal trade route between Egypt
and Mesopotamia.

People have been fighting ever since Cain killed Abel, but the
first recorded battle of which we have real details was fought at
Megiddo between Egyptian pharaoh Thutmose III and a coalition of
Canaanite kings led by Durusha, king of Kadesh, on or about April
16, 1457 BC. The Egyptians surprised and defeated the Canaanites,
who retreated to the nearby city of Megiddo, where they were starved
out. The Egyptians killed 83 and captured 340.

Aren't you glad that when we read the book of Revelation we
know the outcome of the last battle that will be fought at Megiddo
as well?

*God, we hear about Armageddon, and we fear that day when
the last battle comes. Help me to remember that the outcome
is good and it leads the righteous to heaven. Amen.*

I appeal to you to show kindness to my child, Onesimus.
I became his father in the faith while here in prison.
PHILEMON 1:10 NLT

During Paul's imprisonment in Rome, he encountered Onesimus, a runaway slave from the city of Colossae. Curiously, Onesimus belonged to Philemon, an acquaintance of Paul and host of the house church in Colossae. Perhaps in times past, Paul had seen the slave while visiting Philemon.

Onesimus had apparently stolen from his master before running away—perhaps to cover traveling expenses to Rome. Such actions usually meant a death sentence for the slave, if caught.

While in Rome, through Paul's influence, Onesimus became a follower of Christ. Now he realized his need to return to Philemon and also to make restitution. However, doing so could mean his death.

Determined to do the right thing, whatever the cost, Onesimus made plans to travel back to his master. To soften the slave's return, Paul wrote a personal letter to Philemon, asking his friend to forgive Onesimus and regard him as a brother in Christ.

Even with Paul's letter, Onesimus displayed great courage along with his commitment to Christ by returning to Philemon.

How courageous are you in your walk with Christ? Are you willing to lay everything on the line for Him?

Father, strengthen my walk with Christ. Take away the
barriers that prevent me from being a brave soldier, one
willing to lay everything on the line for You. Amen.

"Neither," he replied, "but as commander of the army of the Lord I have now come." Then Joshua fell facedown to the ground in reverence, and asked him, "What message does my Lord have for his servant?"

Joshua 5:14 niv

Oh, Joshua really did the right thing here! He'd wanted to know if this strange man with the drawn sword was on his side or the enemy's side. But the "man" was above and beyond such concepts.

Even though the Israelites were God's chosen people, He wasn't on their side. Their enemies were being destroyed—and the man with the sword would tell Joshua how to do that—because they worshipped false gods. It was up to the Israelites to be on God's side!

We sometimes fool ourselves into thinking that because God loves us, He must hate our enemies. Armies have often marched to war under the same mistaken premise. But if we neglect our duties to the Lord and our enemies are diligent in theirs, then we become the enemy, no matter how much He has blessed us in the past.

There *are* two sides we should be interested in, but they aren't ours and our enemy's—they are God's and His enemy's.

Joshua wasn't so proud as to think it was all about him and his victories. Neither should we be.

Lord, teach me to be watchful and aware of Your enemies. Then help me to stand against them, not for my own sake, but for Yours. Amen.

So He said, "Come." And when Peter had come down out
of the boat, he walked on the water to go to Jesus.
MATTHEW 14:29 NKJV

Maybe you've seen the bumper sticker: IF YOU THINK YOU'RE SO
PERFECT, TRY WALKING ON WATER. It refers to those times in the
Bible when Jesus, the perfect Son of God, broke the rules of physics
by hiking over the waves. But there was someone far from perfect
who also walked on water.

Earlier, Jesus had told His disciples to get into a boat and go
on without Him to the other side of the lake. He stayed behind to
send the crowds away—and then to pray. Later that evening, the
disciples, wrestling their boat against a contrary wind, saw a ghostly
figure approaching. Jesus assured them it was He, and Peter asked
the Lord to command him to come. Jesus did—and Peter, briefly,
walked on water.

What does it take for an ordinary person to walk on water? A
command of God. By the power of God, ordinary men and women,
responding to God's call, have successfully accomplished difficult,
even impossible, tasks.

Don't give up when things seem the worst. That's the time to
find the strength of God.

You are my strength, O Lord. Whenever I feel like
giving up, I will turn to You believing that You
will give me the power to carry on. Amen.

But just as he who called you is holy, so be holy in all you do; for it is written: "Be holy, because I am holy."
1 PETER 1:15–16 NIV

Peter reiterates one of God's seemingly impossible commands in his epistle: be holy.

God had first given the command to the nation of Israel. He emphasized it by repeating "be holy" three times in the book of Leviticus alone (11:44; 19:2; 20:7).

The word *be* can also be translated "become." We are in the process of becoming holy. "Perfecting" holiness involves purifying ourselves from contaminants of body and spirit (2 Corinthians 7:11)—empowered by the refining fire of the Holy Spirit. When Christ returns, we will be like Him. That hope encourages us to purify ourselves in the here and now (1 John 3:3).

Perhaps the meaning of the word *holy* becomes clearer when we examine the companion command to "consecrate yourselves" (Leviticus 11:44 NIV). We dedicate ourselves to God—one hundred percent pure. No impurities (1 Thessalonians 4:7). No distractions. Just one hundred percent commitment to God.

One hundred percent? We're not there yet. But we will be. "For he chose us in him before the creation of the world to be holy and blameless in his sight" (Ephesians 1:4 NIV).

I give myself to You, Father, as a work in progress. Come into my heart. Shape me and direct me toward holiness so that I might please You. Amen.

Peter said, "I don't have any silver or gold for you.
But I'll give you what I have. In the name of Jesus
Christ the Nazarene, get up and walk!"
ACTS 3:6 NLT

Financially, Peter and John might have felt right at home in our slumping economy. But unlike many in today's world, they had other wealth to spend—the riches found in Jesus Christ.

Setting: the temple gate. Beneficiary of the disciples' generosity: a crippled beggar. Results: a lame man healed, the opportunity to share Jesus with the crowd that gathered—and a jail sentence.

It's Peter's confidence that fascinates most readers. Temple leaders demanded that Peter keep quiet about Jesus, but the disciple had experienced too much with Jesus to keep quiet. When the leaders tried to minimize the miracle, Peter pointed out irrefutable evidence—the man was walking! Finally, Peter was asked his secret, which enabled the disciple to speak of the inexhaustible power found in Jesus Christ (Acts 4:7–12)!

What a contrast: a circle of sophisticated temple leaders attempting to silence two country fishermen who could not help speaking about what they had seen and heard (Acts 4:20).

Christian friend, don't let a checkbook dictate your generosity; share what you have with the spiritually crippled and those who hunger and thirst after righteousness.

You can do it through the power of Jesus Christ.

Dear God, especially when those who don't believe
outnumber me, make me willing and eager to speak
out about You and the power of Your love. Amen.

Deborah, a prophet, the wife of Lappidoth,
was leading Israel at that time.
JUDGES 4:4 NIV

How did a woman end up ruling Israel, a culture steeped in patriarchy? Who is this prophet, Deborah?

A leader of Israel around 1200 BC, Deborah is described as a prophet, a judge, and a military leader who delivered God's word to Barak and inspired him to follow God. She must have been a remarkable woman, to be accepted by men and given power at a time in history when women were rarely seen in leadership roles.

A prophet is one called by God to speak on His behalf. Deborah inspired people to turn their hearts toward God. She joins only a few other biblical women described as prophets—Miriam, Huldah, the wife of Isaiah, and Anna.

Deborah serves as a role model for men and women today in our witness for God. Our simple daily acts of kind service inspire others. We can speak God's Word, sharing hope and encouragement with others in letters, emails, and even simple conversations in the grocery line. Simply being present with a grieving friend often shows Christ to others when words seem inadequate.

We may not see ourselves as prophets or leaders, but we all can draw others closer to God through our prayers and service.

Heavenly Father, sometimes I miss seeing opportunities to
help and to share You with others. Open my eyes and my
heart! Show me new ways to pray and to serve. Amen.

This gospel of the kingdom shall be preached in all the world
for a witness unto all nations; and then shall the end come.
MATTHEW 24:14 KJV

If you ask many people if we're already living in the end-times, they'll answer, "Yes, we are, and Jesus could come any day now." However, Jesus tells us that the gospel must first "be preached in all the world for a witness unto all nations"—and only then shall the end come.

We tend to think that in this modern era the gospel has surely already been preached in all nations—thanks to radios, television, and the internet—even in nations closed to the gospel. But the Greek word translated as "nations" is *ethnos* and literally means "ethnic groups" or "people groups." Many closed nations are made up of dozens of people groups and tribes in remote mountain valleys and hinterlands who don't have access to modern media—yet they too need to hear the gospel.

We desire Jesus to return, and when He declares, "Surely I come quickly," we pray, "Amen. Even so, come, Lord Jesus" (Revelation 22:20 KJV). But we must do our part to hasten that day: we must help see to it that the gospel goes to the ends of the earth (Acts 1:8).

Lord, in this age when the whole world seems connected,
there are still some who haven't heard Your name. Lead
us, Your people, to the ones who need to hear. Amen.

Whether you turn to the right or to the left, your ears will hear
a voice behind you, saying, "This is the way; walk in it."
Isaiah 30:21 niv

Many times in life we find ourselves at a crossroads, faced with a pivotal choice about the direction of the future. Israel was at such a juncture, challenged by the prophet Isaiah to return to a lifestyle that embraced their compassionate and gracious God. Rejection of the challenge would result in desolation; repentance would bring the blessings of a restored relationship.

Monumental decisions are not unique to people of faith, but Isaiah's verse offers encouragement and hope to those who call upon the name of the Lord while making crucial choices. This verse speaks directly to the God Positioning System eternally available to each of us. In contrast to the satellite-based Global Positioning System popular today, users of the God Positioning System enjoy the voice of God speaking directly into their lives.

When we walk with God and use His navigational system, we can rest assured that His map for our lives is trustworthy. He will never lead us down dead-end roads or route us onto nonexistent streets. Instead, He promises to hear us when we cry for help (Isaiah 30:19). And from that request, He gives direction that is unequaled by any earthly GPS.

I'm grateful, Father, for Your God Positioning System.
Each morning, remind me to turn it on so that Your
voice can direct me in the way I should go. Amen.

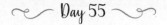

Whoever claims to love God yet hates a brother or sister is a
liar. For whoever does not love their brother and sister, whom
they have seen, cannot love God, whom they have not seen.
1 John 4:20 niv

This is the verse that risks making hypocrites of us all. Who among us does not know someone we'd cross the road to avoid? That person might be obnoxious, a liar, might have caused all sorts of grief—but is still beloved by God, and He wants that soul brought home.

What about the guys begging on the street? There are so many these days, and lots of them are con artists, so we preserve our dignity by walking on by. Well, some of them are in real need, and God values the saving of even a con artist above your dignity. Don't be taken advantage of, but engage with these wayward children of the Lord.

Then there are the ones who hurt us, people we trusted once and can never forgive for their betrayal. They weren't born cruel and callous. They were hurt, so they inflict hurt. God wants *you* to break that chain, to replace hurt with love.

It's a big task and one we might never be able to live up to, but we will be nearer to God for having tried!

God, sometimes it's hard acting in a Christlike way, especially
toward those who are not my friends. Help me, please, to love
everyone, and not just those who love me back. Amen.

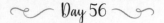

Day 56

If your enemy is hungry, give him food to eat; if he is thirsty, give him water to drink. In doing this, you will heap burning coals on his head, and the L ORD will reward you.
PROVERBS 25:21–22 NIV

This verse defies human nature. The world's way is to bless one's friends and curse one's enemies. Forgiveness and mercy are foreign concepts. However, God's thoughts and ways are higher than man's (Isaiah 55:8), and this passage directs Christians to provide their enemies with subsistence and care.

God desires that believers resist carnal thinking and embrace the message of the cross. Namely, "Love your enemies. . .and pray for them which despitefully use you, and persecute you" (Matthew 5:44 KJV).

The end result of our humanitarianism is that we will heap burning coals on our enemy's head. This isn't backhanded benevolence intended to impose affliction on our enemies; it's a metaphor.

In Bible times, burning coals were placed below and heaped above metals placed in a furnace. In this way, the metal was liquefied and the dross fell to the bottom. In the same manner, loving our enemies will either melt them into repentance and lead them to God or aggravate their condemnation, making their malice even more inexcusable.

The above verse presents an interesting paradox: those who seek revenge are the *conquered,* and those who forgive are *conquerors.*

O mighty God, help me to be forgiving and merciful toward my enemies. Even if they hate me, teach me to bless them by showing them love. Amen.

～ Day 57 ～

In those days, as King Ahasuerus sat on his royal throne in Susa the citadel, in the third year of his reign he provided a banquet for all his officials and his servants. The army of Persia and Media was present, as well as the nobles and the officials of the provinces. Drinks were served in golden containers, all of which differed from one another. Royal wine was available in abundance at the king's expense. There were no restrictions on the drinking, for the king had instructed all his supervisors that they should do as everyone so desired.

ESTHER 1:2–3, 7–8 NET

Ahasuerus is also known as Xerxes I. History records that this party was the planning meeting for the disastrous invasion of Greece in 490 BC. At the battle of Thermopylae, Ahasuerus was delayed and embarrassed by fierce Spartan resistance, and then at Salamis, Athens crushed his fleet.

The Bible condemns drunkenness (Proverbs 20:1; 23:29–35; 1 Corinthians 6:10; Ephesians 5:18) and teaches moderation in drink (1 Timothy 5:23). Ahasuerus and his advisers learned what happens when people drink too much. Maybe with less partying they would have planned better. Let's be sure we learn from Ahasuerus's bad example!

I pray for those living a lifestyle of too much partying and not enough focusing on You. Help them, Lord. Lead them away from that way of life. Amen.

Jesus looked at them and said, "With man this is impossible, but with God all things are possible."
MATTHEW 19:26 NIV

The rich young ruler's conversation with Jesus had not gone as expected. Instead of learning that he had fulfilled all the requirements of the law—which he thought would admit him to heaven—the young man was told to sell his possessions and give to the poor. Dejected, he gave up and went home.

This turn of events prompted much discussion between Jesus and His disciples, centering on the difficulties of being admitted to heaven. Frustrated with the impossible scenario Jesus was painting, complete with camels going through the eye of a needle, the disciples finally asked: "Who then can be saved?" (Matthew 19:25 NIV).

With the question finally asked, Jesus zeroed in on the heart of the matter: no one can be saved by their own efforts! The rich young ruler had tried everything humanly possible, and still he came up short. Man's greatest efforts pale in comparison to the requirements of a holy God.

But grace, freely offered by God and accepted by individuals, will admit us to heaven. With God, all things *are* possible—especially His enabling of forgiven sinners to live eternally. Realizing we can do nothing is the key to gaining everything.

Dear Father, I appreciate Your grace—Your loving-kindness that I don't deserve. I have done nothing to earn it. Grace is Your gift to me, and I thank You. Amen.

～ Day 59 ～

Go to the ant, O sluggard, observe her ways and be wise.
PROVERBS 6:6 NASB

Each species of ants—over ten thousand—consist of one or more queens, a few males, and numerous female worker ants.

The queen ants do not lead or rule. They simply spend life laying eggs to populate the colony. The workers perform the bulk of the labor necessary for the colony to survive and diligently carry out their tasks without any leadership.

In some species, worker ants keep aphids the way people keep cows. The ants care for the aphids over winter and in spring place them outside on plants. When rubbed, these aphids secrete a sweet liquid used as a beverage by the ant colony.

In leaf-cutting species, worker ants cut leaves to grow fungus underground while other workers tend these subterranean gardens. Larger workers patrol the colony, keeping a sharp lookout for enemy insects.

Proverbs contrasts the hardworking ant with a sluggard.

The term *sluggard,* as used in this verse, implies irresponsibility and the lack of ambition to be successful, while the ant's ability to accomplish a task without oversight is applauded.

Do you procrastinate or feel overwhelmed by certain tasks? Break the chore into smaller segments and celebrate each completed part. Become wise by anticipating future needs and planning for them. Study the ant and learn from her.

When a task seems big and overwhelming, remind me, Lord, that You will help me to accomplish it one small step at a time. Amen.

Jesus did many other things as well. If every one of them were
written down, I suppose that even the whole world would
not have room for the books that would be written.
JOHN 21:25 NIV

The Bible contains four Gospels, but it doesn't have a single biography of Jesus.

Aren't the Gospels biographies?

Not exactly. Two of the Gospels ignore Jesus' birth completely, and only Luke makes any mention of His childhood years.

Carl Sandberg needed six volumes to write a biography of Abraham Lincoln. The apostle John said that to write a definitive biography of Jesus would require more room than is available in the whole world. So he chose which details of Jesus' life to include—and with great care.

All of the Gospel writers did. They each had a particular purpose in writing their accounts of Jesus' life. John spells his out clearly: "that you may believe that Jesus is the Messiah, the Son of God, and that by believing you may have life in his name" (20:31 NIV).

Jesus' story continues to be written—in us. May our lives lead others to faith in Him.

Jesus, the Gospels inspire me. They make me want to
know more about You. Teach me to become more like
You and to grow nearer to You as I learn. Amen.

∼ Day 61 ∼

Never stop praying.
1 THESSALONIANS 5:17 NLT

Several passages of the Bible tell us clearly that God listens to us when we pray. He hears every word and is compassionate.

Sometimes the answer to our request is "not yet." Sometimes the answer is even a flat "no." But when we come before the Lord and lay what is in our hearts at His feet, He always finds a way to bless us and make everything work out for the best. He does this even when we don't get exactly what we want.

God is so much smarter than we could ever hope to be. He knows what is best for us and provides it each time. All we have to do is share our concerns with Him and wait faithfully for what He will provide.

God wants to be involved in our daily routines. He wants to hear from us and waits for us. God never promised an easy life to Christians. If we will allow Him, though, God will be there with us every step of the way. All we need to do is to come to Him in prayer. With these three simple words from 1 Thessalonians 5:17, our lives can be fulfilling as we live to communicate with our Lord.

Father, when I pray, remind me that prayer is not only about talking to You, but also about listening to You. Open my heart to Your words. Amen.

Fix these words of mine in your hearts and minds; tie them as symbols on your hands and bind them on your foreheads.
DEUTERONOMY 11:18 NIV

Have you ever seen a person of the Jewish faith wearing a small box attached to his forehead? Phylacteries or frontlets are tiny leather boxes worn by Orthodox Jews, tied to the forehead and left arm and worn at prayer times.

Each box holds scrolls of parchment containing key Old Testament verses. The frontlets provide a method of carrying God's Word with them all the time. When they cross their arms, they draw the scriptures closer to their hearts. They believe this practice helps them fulfill the commandment in Deuteronomy.

How can we as Christians carry God's Word with us all the time? This verse provides the answer: fix it in our hearts and minds.

Memorizing Bible verses isn't a fashionable trend in today's world, but learning key verses plants the Word of God deeply in our hearts.

We draw strength and nourishment in dark times from remembering what God has told us in the Bible. In times of crisis we recall God's promises of hope and comfort. In our everyday moments, repeating well-known verses reminds us that God is always with us—whether we feel like it or not.

What an awesome gift You have given me, God—the Bible! I will fix Your words in my mind and heart and carry them with me wherever I go. Amen.

Day 63

"Where is your faith?" he asked his disciples. In fear and amazement they asked one another, "Who is this? He commands even the winds and the water, and they obey him."
LUKE 8:25 NIV

It was calm on the lake that day when the disciples and Jesus set out in their boat to sail across to the other side. It was such a leisurely boat ride that Jesus fell asleep as they went along. Then it happened.

Calmness was replaced by a squall. The boat began taking on so much water that it was going under. The disciples woke Jesus up and pleaded with Him to do something because they were going to drown.

Jesus got up and spoke to the wind and the powerful water. The storm ceased and calmness was restored. After Jesus stilled the storm, He questioned His followers about where their faith was. Stunned at this new aspect of Christ they had seen, they could only marvel at His ability to control nature.

Jesus used the terrifying boat ride that day not only to display His power over all creation but to provide an opportunity for the disciples to look at the depth of their faith.

We would be wise to do likewise, for the question "Where is your faith?" is one Jesus still asks today.

Jesus, increase my faith. Teach me to trust even more in Your power and Your ability to calm the storms that come into my life. I love You, Lord Jesus. Amen.

Do not answer a fool according to his folly, lest you also be like him.
Answer a fool according to his folly, lest he be wise in his own eyes.
Proverbs 26:4–5 nkjv

Skeptics love to point out what they believe are contradictions in the Bible. Well, here's one if ever there was one. The only problem is, of course, that this is no contradiction. Solomon gave these two contrasting pieces of advice, deliberately stating one right after the other, to make it clear that we are to respond differently in different circumstances. Solomon later pointed out, "There is a time for everything," and "The wise heart will know the proper time and procedure" (Ecclesiastes 3:1; 8:5 niv).

The kind of answer you give a fool (the word here means a "self-confident person") depends on how caught up in his self-confident opinions he is, what the circumstances are, and who's standing around listening. God may lead you to give him a serious answer (in contrast to his proud chatter) or a humorous, foolish answer (to show him how foolishly he's talking).

With a full-blown fool, it's best to bite your tongue and refrain from saying anything at all (Proverbs 23:9). No matter what you say, it won't persuade him.

Dear God, when I don't know how to respond to a foolish opinion, show me. Give me the proper answer, or lead me to keep still. Amen.

Jesus wept.
JOHN 11:35 KJV

If you've attended church for any amount of time, you probably recognize John 11:35 as "the shortest verse in the Bible."

For accuracy's sake, we should actually say John 11:35 is the shortest verse in many English translations of the Bible, including the venerable King James Version. But some modern translations, such as the New International Version, have an even shorter verse, Job 3:2: "He said."

Wherever it stands statistically, John 11:35 is a memorable and powerful verse. Jesus, the Son of God, Creator of the universe (John 1:1–3), actually *cried* when He saw the pain caused by the death of His friend Lazarus.

John 11 goes on to say that Jesus raised Lazarus back from the dead, restoring him to his grieving sisters, Mary and Martha. That showed Jesus' power as God—but before that, in a moment of pure humanity, He wept over the loss of a friend.

These days, those of us who obey Jesus' commands are His friends (John 15:14), and He still feels our pain, sorrow, and temptations (Hebrews 4:15). This is no cold, aloof, angry God we serve!

How might John 11:35 change your outlook today?

Jesus, when things in life make me weep, remind me of Your compassion and Your tears. Embrace me, Lord. Hold me in Your arms and comfort me. Amen.

~ Day 66 ~

"Then you will know which way to go, since you have never been this way before. But keep a distance of about two thousand cubits between you and the ark; do not go near it."
JOSHUA 3:4 NIV

We have numerous items these days to help us navigate through a place we're unfamiliar with. Maps, GPS systems, and cell phones give us confidence that we won't get lost. The Israelites didn't have such tools; instead they had something better for guidance, the ark of the covenant.

The time had come for Joshua to lead the Israelites across the Jordan River into a new land. The people hadn't journeyed in this direction, so the plan was for them to follow the ark, which the priests would be carrying. When they saw the direction the ark was going, they would know which way to go.

The Israelites could safely travel into the unknown only by believing in what was known: that God was leading them. Earlier in scripture it was their ancestor Abraham who had taken a walk of faith into unknown territory under God's guidance (Genesis 12).

Many times in our lives we're going to find ourselves heading in a direction we're not familiar with. When God's the one who has brought us to that unknown territory, we can be sure He'll guide us through it.

Sometimes You lead me into unfamiliar places, Father, but You always bring me through them. You know the way. You stay with me, guide me, and love me. Thank You, God! Amen.

Day 67

*"But I tell you, do not resist an evil person. If anyone slaps
you on the right cheek, turn to them the other cheek also."*

MATTHEW 5:39 NIV

There was one four-letter word Jesus hoped would forever be on the tips of our tongues: love.

The Lord had more to say about love than almost any other topic. His advice was straightforward: Jesus said we should love God (Matthew 22:36–37), love our neighbors (Matthew 22:39), and love our enemies (Matthew 5:44)!

Our enemies? Now that's called "pushing the envelope"!

In theory, it sounds wonderful. But in reality, it can feel impossible. Take the disciple Peter, for example. For years, he had heard Jesus' teachings on love, but when the high priests came to arrest Jesus (John 18:10), Peter resisted love and defensively cut off the enemy's ear. Jesus corrected him, saying, "Put your sword away" (v. 11). Then He healed the man's ear.

God knows we live in a world where walking away is often judged as spineless. That's why He sent Jesus to really "push the envelope" and become the definition of love.

Because God extended us His grace, we too can courageously accept the enemy's strike and "turn the other cheek."

*Heavenly Father, when someone does wrong to me,
please quiet my anger and soothe my hurt. Help me to
love my enemies with Your kind of grace. Amen.*

Do everything without grumbling or arguing.
PHILIPPIANS 2:14 NIV

Pollyanna is a classic children's story about a young orphan whose sunny outlook on life fueled an unstoppable optimism. Regardless of the challenges she encountered, Pollyanna met each circumstance with a commitment to look for the best. Her "Glad Game" reached out to others and encouraged her community.

The apostle Paul knew of hardship and challenges long before the character Pollyanna appeared in a novel. Having endured shipwrecks and imprisonment, Paul's life circumstances were far from a carefree existence. Surely there were moments when he wanted to argue and complain at the harsh circumstances he was experiencing. And yet, after asking the difficult questions, he held to his faith in the God who knew him by name and who had called him to take the Gospel to the Gentiles.

Try this experiment today: Every time you notice you are complaining or arguing, switch your watch (or bracelet, or rubber band) from one wrist to the other. When the day is over, reflect on how many times you made the change. How often did you catch yourself in a negative pattern?

Paul's instructions to do everything without complaining or arguing are a central component in Pollyanna's Glad Game. Perhaps we would all do well to play it daily.

Lord, I argue and complain, and often I am not even aware. Remind me to look on the bright side and to share a little sunshine with others. Amen.

While Paul was waiting for them in Athens, he was deeply
troubled by all the idols he saw everywhere in the city.
ACTS 17:16 NLT

While exploring Athens, Paul discovered the appalling truth of a common Roman saying, "It's easier to find a god at Athens than a man."

Burdened for the Athenians, Paul began proclaiming Christ in the Jewish synagogue and every day in the agora (marketplace). As a result, Epicurean and Stoic philosophers met Paul and brought him to Mars Hill to hear his teachings.

Previously, Paul had noticed an Athenian altar to *agnostos theos*, "the unknown god." In his address on Mars Hill, Paul used this unknown god as a bridge from the Athenian idols to God and His Son, Jesus. He also quoted Epimenides and Aratus, poets familiar to the Athenians.

Rather than condemning the people and spouting dire warnings, Paul looked for common ground and built his case for Christ from there. As a result, several men and women believed his message.

Are you around people whose beliefs differ greatly from yours? Do you sometimes feel lost as to how to turn a conversation to Christ? Copy Paul's approach. Look for a shared viewpoint or familiar truth and slowly build from there.

Father, when I encounter people whose opinions differ
greatly from mine, help us to find common ground.
Then show me the way to lead them toward You. Amen.

Turn my eyes from worthless things,
and give me life through your word.
PSALM 119:37 NLT

How's your spiritual eyesight? Are things in focus, or is your life a little blurry? Are worthless things impeding your vision?

The psalmist recognized that many things in life vie for our attention. Some have little value and take us farther away from God's transformational power—hence the "worthless" designation. Myopic distractions may foster a selfish, nearsighted focus. A farsighted focus can keep us so busily distracted with others that we have no time to reflect and grow in our own lives. Astigmatism reflects the struggle for balance between the two extremes.

But some things bring us closer to God and preserve our life— life that comes through God's Word. To turn away from worthless things, let's focus our eyes on Jesus, "the pioneer and perfecter of faith" (Hebrews 12:2 NIV). Let's allow our lives to be changed by the power of His Word as we encounter Him each day.

What are the things in your life that you need to bring into focus in order to restore 20/20 spiritual vision?

Jesus, there are so many distractions in life, things
that get in my way. Help me to make them less
important and to center my focus on You. Amen.

Day 71

Do not get drunk on wine. . . . Instead, be filled with the Spirit.
EPHESIANS 5:18 NIV

On the day of Pentecost, when those gathered together saw and felt the presence of God's Holy Spirit, they became hilarious. There was a nonalcoholic response to the exciting Third Person of the Trinity. The only hangover experienced was lingering joy.

There was a day when Spirit-filled believers gave expression to their joy in Christ. It was impossible to be blasé about God's transforming work. He is still making "all things new"! Nothing is different today: when one has a brand-new start in life, well, that's to be celebrated!

While the doctrine of the Holy Spirit varies slightly from denomination to denomination, all Christians understand the great influence He has in the life of God's children. In New Testament Greek He is described as the Paraclete, the one who is beside us. Celebrate that!

When Jesus returned to the Father, God gave the Holy Spirit to the world (Acts 2), with responsibility for the comfort, guidance, direction, and empowerment of believers. Celebrate it!

The Comforter has come! The Comforter has come! The Holy
Ghost from Heav'n, the Father's promise giv'n! O spread the
tidings 'round, wherever man is found; The Comforter has come!
FRANK BOTTOME

Mighty God, I celebrate Your Holy Spirit. How wonderful
it is that the Helper has come! The Comforter has
come, and my heart is filled up with joy! Amen.

*"For by your words you will be acquitted,
and by your words you will be condemned."*
MATTHEW 12:37 NIV

Remember when you realized that a certain childhood expression—"Sticks and stones may break my bones, but words will never hurt me"—was a lie?

Words can act as a gentle spring rain or a thunderous storm. Words can stir things up or settle things down. Our words are so important that James spent most of a chapter in his book detailing the nature of the tongue and its power. The book of Proverbs warns us repeatedly to give careful thought to the way we speak.

Before telling a crowd that their words would prove their guilt or innocence, Jesus said that people would someday give account of all the careless words they'd ever spoken (Matthew 12:36).

According to Jesus, our words are a reflection of what we've stored up in our hearts. Good brings out good; evil brings out evil. Other people, who can't see into our hearts, clearly learn what's there by the way we speak.

What is your heart saying today?

*Dear God, please give me wisdom to choose saintly
words. I want each and every word that comes from my
mouth to be pleasing to You and to others. Amen.*

~ *Day 73* ~

You shall not steal.
EXODUS 20:15 NET

The concept of copyright law was unknown to Moses, and indeed throughout most of recorded history. Rights encumberment of the concrete expression of ideas did not occur until the English copyright Statute of Anne in 1709. Even today, it is a civil, not a criminal issue. But using sizable portions of a modern writer's work without permission is theft. Therefore, the public-domain King James Version is widely available online, but more modern translations are available on only a handful of sites.

Still, modern law does not give an author unlimited rights. "He who steals my apple deprives me of a meal," but an idea alone cannot be copyrighted. As Thomas Jefferson so eloquently wrote to Isaac McPherson, "He who receives an idea from me, receives instruction himself without lessening mine; as he who lights his taper at mine, receives light without darkening me."

Jesus said, "The worker deserves his pay" (Luke 10:7 NET), and creators certainly deserve remuneration—no one should steal from them. But nothing in the Bible guarantees any specific law, other than God's Law, will last forever. Plenty of good books and music were written before copyright, and plenty will be written after copyright is obsolete. And even modern copyrights have an end!

To follow the lawmakers' rules, I first must hold fast
to the Law You set in stone. Help me, Father, to obey
Your commandments. In Jesus' name, amen.

*Paul looked straight at the Sanhedrin and said,
"My brothers, I have fulfilled my duty to God
in all good conscience to this day."*

ACTS 23:1 NIV

After his arrest, Paul, a Jew and Roman citizen, stood before the Sanhedrin and chief priests to plead his case. The apostle declared—with a clear and good conscience—his commitment to God, his fervent determination to serve and please Him, and his faultless life even before his conversion to Christ.

Before Christ, Paul lived according to the Jewish law and ordinances and remained true to those teachings. He was void of hypocrisy or dishonesty and acted from his conscience. After Paul's conversion, he was a warrior of faith resolute to serve the Lord with all holiness and zeal, ever mindful of his call to God and service to others.

The translation of the Latin word *conscience* is "what one knows with oneself." The conscience is the inner faculty that decides the moral quality of our thoughts, words, and actions. Our consciences are seared with remorse when we do wrong and endowed with peace and satisfaction when we choose right. All of us must live with our own consciences, whether good or bad.

In another passage Paul said, "So I strive always to keep my conscience clear before God and man" (Acts 24:16 NIV). May we all do likewise!

*God, I am determined to serve and please You. Help
me to live a moral life so that I can stand before You
and others with a clear conscience. Amen.*

There is a way that appears to be right,
but in the end it leads to death.
PROVERBS 14:12 NIV

Why do we love a glorious last stand? General Custer's final defeat is a revered part of American history. The poet Tennyson glorified the Light Brigade for charging into rows of Russian cannons. Butch Cassidy and the Sundance Kid will forever be remembered in freeze-frame just before the Bolivian soldiers shoot them down.

Each time you watch the film, don't you wish Butch and Sundance could find another way out? Don't you still hold your breath to see if Steve McQueen will make it over the barbed wire to freedom in *The Great Escape*? And if only those reinforcements had reached Little Bighorn in time!

Why does the last stand appeal to us so much? Because we know our stubbornness could easily put us in the same position. Our insistence on going the "way that seems right to a man" (NKJV) might satisfy our rebel souls, but we weren't made to be rebels.

Despite our insistence on going our own way, we still long for a last-minute rescue. No matter how far into the Valley of Death we ride, there is one we can count on to save us! Jesus pulls off more rescues than the US Cavalry ever has, and His way leads to life!

Lord, come rescue me from my enemies. Lead me
out of anger and hurt. I put my trust in You. I stand
waiting, knowing that You will save me. Amen.

Consider it pure joy, my brothers and sisters, whenever
you face trials of many kinds, because you know that
the testing of your faith produces perseverance.
JAMES 1:2–3 NIV

This verse comes from a letter written by James, the oldest brother of Jesus. If you remember, James did not always believe Jesus was the Messiah (John 7:5). Perhaps he was speaking from experience when writing these words.

God spoke through James to encourage Jewish Christians who were worn out from persecution for their faith. Likewise, through these same words, God encourages us when we're tired and beaten down by life's challenges.

Initially, the suggestion that we consider trials as "pure joy" doesn't feel encouraging. Enduring difficulties in order to achieve a stronger faith seems futile. But the apostle Peter says, "Trials. . .have come so that the proven genuineness of your faith—of greater worth than gold, which perishes even though refined by fire—may result in praise, glory and honor when Jesus Christ is revealed" (1 Peter 1:6–7 NIV).

God promised that He will never leave nor forsake us (Hebrews 13:5). So when we feel the heat, may we call on God's power to help us persevere. And may we consider it pure blessing to have faith that's refined, genuine, and honorable to Jesus Christ our Lord.

Father God, when I face hard times, refine my faith.
Show me Your mercy, gentleness, and love. In You
I find pure joy, and I praise You! Amen.

Return unto me, and I will return unto you, saith the LORD of hosts.
MALACHI 3:7 KJV

After God spoke through His prophet Malachi, the Lord went silent for about four centuries. Then John the Baptist appeared, preparing the way for the ultimate expression of God's truth—His Son, Jesus Christ.

So what was the Lord's final Old Testament spokesman saying? What message did "My messenger" (the meaning of Malachi's name) have for God's people?

As with all the prophets, Malachi warned the people of Israel about their sin. But he also reminded the chosen ones of the love of their heavenly Father. They had wandered far from God, been punished by Assyrian and Babylonian invaders, and been restored to their homeland. Sadly, their hearts still strayed from true worship.

So Malachi appeared with God's final word before the "Word" finally appeared. "Return unto me, and I will return unto you," the Lord said.

It was a promise to the people of ancient Israel, but also a glimpse into the heart of a loving heavenly Father. It's a promise we can still count on today.

Whenever I stray from You, Lord, I feel empty and alone.
So many times I've returned and asked Your forgiveness,
and always You've embraced me. Thank You, God! Amen.

Day 78

So then, just as you received Christ Jesus as Lord, continue to live your lives in him, rooted and built up in him, strengthened in the faith as you were taught, and overflowing with thankfulness.
Colossians 2:6–7 niv

How do we live as disciples of Christ? This verse gives us four simple guidelines to follow.

First, we reach out to Jesus in daily prayer, as He is now living within our hearts. Living with Him means spending time together so we can learn His ways.

Second, we nourish our roots to grow deeper for a strong foundation. Mighty trees have deep roots to support them in turbulent winds and terrible storms. Our roots are nourished with the waters of prayer and the food from studying the Bible. This stabilizes us to face the storms in life.

Next, we draw strength by remembering what we have learned in the past and what we have been taught by others. Their words or the example of how they lived fortifies our faith.

Finally, we give thanks in all circumstances. Gratitude flows easily during good times. But even in difficult circumstances, expressing appreciation renews our spirits.

How do we live for God? He guides our lives through prayer and study, fellowship with others, and the practice of daily gratitude.

*Guide me, Lord. Nourish and strengthen the roots of my faith.
Lead me to those who will teach me Your ways, and then,
Lord, keep me mindful of what I have learned. Amen.*

Oh, the joys of those who do not follow the advice of the wicked,
or stand around with sinners, or join in with mockers.
PSALM 1:1 NLT

There is no joy greater than that of having done the right thing, even if those around you have not.

God knows what is in our hearts and minds. He loves us and cares about us so much that He takes an intimate interest in everything we do. May He never see us making bad decisions or following those who are obviously making bad choices!

Unfortunately, this is exactly what He occasionally sees. Christianity is not just for intelligent people. It is available to everyone. It is a party to which everyone is invited. But not everyone chooses to make smart decisions. Sometimes it is so much easier to simply go along with the crowd.

This seems to take pressure off us and makes us feel better at the moment. Later, though, we realize what we have done and how we have pushed ourselves away from God.

The next time we are tempted to follow the crowd, may we remember the very first verse of Psalms. What a joy it is to do the right thing!

There is joy in my heart when my actions please You.
But sometimes, God, I give in to temptation. Thank You for
being a forgiving God, a God of second chances. Amen.

Jesus turned and said to Peter, "Get behind me, Satan!
You are a stumbling block to me; you do not have in mind
the concerns of God, but merely human concerns."
MATTHEW 16:23 NIV

That was a bit harsh, wasn't it? Poor old Peter meant well.

But, of course, Jesus was right. He knew death was waiting for Him. He also knew it was an important part of His Father's plan.

Peter was acting out of love, but it was human love with a fair proportion of self-interest. He didn't want to lose his friend.

We forget sometimes how far above us God really is. Our version of love is nothing compared to His, and while we see the death of someone close to us as a tragedy, to God it's surely a glorious homecoming by one of His own.

This is a beautiful world and we, understandably, hate the thought of losing some of the people in it. Satan relies on that. He takes our attachments and weaknesses and uses them as stumbling blocks between us and heaven.

But, wonderfully, Jesus turns stumbling blocks into stepping-stones. When, thanks to Him, we arrive in heaven, hopefully we will find, like Paul, that we didn't really lose anyone after all.

I miss them, Lord, those who have gone to heaven.
Bring me comfort knowing that they are with You and
that, in a little while, we will all be together again. Amen.

～ Day 81 ～

*And Jehovah said unto Satan, Behold, all that he hath is
in thy power; only upon himself put not forth thy hand.
So Satan went forth from the presence of Jehovah.*
JOB 1:12 ASV

Many people picture God and Satan as opposing forces locked in eternal combat. When the good times roll, then God must be having the upper hand. When things go south, Satan is winning.

This fascinating verse opens a window to the inner workings of God's day-to-day administration. In Job 1, Satan first gave an account to God of his travels through the earth. Then God informed Satan of Job's uprightness. Satan replied that Job was on God's side because the Lord had blessed him so much: "Just take away his goods and watch what happens then." At that point, God allowed Satan to test Job but issued a strict charge not to touch his person.

Clearly, Satan is under God's complete authority. The devil can't work without God's permission. No matter how bad things may get, they are never out of control. And a day is coming when God will rid the universe of Satan, casting him into eternal fire.

One final thought: Job was blessed more at the end of his life than the beginning (Job 42:12).

*Job—I feel like him sometimes. I ask, "Why do bad
things happen to good people?" Father, remind me that
You are always in control and You love me. Amen.*

*Who is he who condemns? It is Christ who died, and
furthermore is also risen, who is even at the right hand
of God, who also makes intercession for us.*

ROMANS 8:34 NKJV

When Jesus Christ died on the cross, He paid the price for our sins, and when He rose from the dead, He broke the power of death in our lives. If that wasn't enough, now that He's in heaven, sitting at the right hand of God, He constantly intercedes to God for us.

So who is he who condemns us? The devil does, of course. He's called "the accuser of our brethren," and day and night he accuses Christians before God. But we can overcome him with the blood of Jesus Christ—the same blood that paid the price for our sin (Revelation 12:10–11).

People sometimes condemn us, but Paul said that we shouldn't pay attention to them (1 Corinthians 4:3). And we, in turn, are commanded not to judge others (Matthew 7:1).

We often condemn ourselves, but even "if our heart condemns us, God is greater than our heart, and knows all things" (1 John 3:20 NKJV).

How can anyone really condemn us when Christ Himself took away our sin and never ceases to intervene with God His Father on our behalf?

*If I don't feel good enough, Jesus, You lift me up. If others
condemn me, You are on my side. Indeed, Lord, You
are my treasured friend, and I love You. Amen.*

∼ Day 83 ∼

*"If anyone asks you, 'Why are you doing this?' say,
'The Lord needs it and will send it back here shortly.'"*
MARK 11:3 NIV

The Lord Jesus knew the triumphal entry awaited Him when He borrowed a donkey.

David worshipped this same Jesus, God the Son in the flesh, saying, "The heavens are yours, and yours also the earth" (Psalm 89:11 NIV). As God said to Job, "Everything under heaven belongs to me" (Job 41:11 NIV). Yet the one who owned the world told His disciples to borrow a colt and to tell the owner, when asked, "The Lord *needs* it" (italics added).

The Greek word *chreia*, translated elsewhere as "business," appears forty-nine times in the New Testament. Its primary use refers to things humans need: the sick need a physician (Matthew 9:12). John needed to be baptized by Jesus (Matthew 3:14). God supplies all our needs (Philippians 4:19). Twice, John uses the word to describe Jesus' omniscience (John 2:25; 16:30).

Only in the passages about the triumphal entry do we read that Jesus needed something from us: something as simple as a ride into town, on loan, to be returned shortly.

Everything belongs to God by right. But He grants us the privilege of sharing out of our poverty to join Him in conducting His business.

*Everything I have is Yours, Father—everything.
Show me how to bring You glory and honor by making
good use of what You have loaned me. Amen.*

Now there happened to be a Jewish man in Susa the citadel whose name was Mordecai. He was the son of Jair, the son of Shimei, the son of Kish, a Benjaminite, who had been taken into exile from Jerusalem with the captives who had been carried into exile with Jeconiah king of Judah, whom Nebuchadnezzar king of Babylon had taken into exile.
ESTHER 2:5–6 NET

We should never forget that the Bible tells the story of real people, set in real history.

The book of Esther takes place in 460 BC, against the backdrop of Persian military aggression against Greece. Ancient tablets found by archaeologists confirm that Mordecai was a scribe or minister at the royal court of King Xerxes in Susa, where Nehemiah also served and Daniel had prophesied. Over and over again, the Bible is shown to be true and trustworthy.

"Now there happened to be. . ." Isn't it amazing how God's providence works, even in secular places where He isn't welcomed by name? The book of Esther never once mentions God directly, yet His hand is clearly at work throughout the story.

In the same way, we should be a light in our world, even where we can't discuss God openly.

How can it be, Lord? There are places where I am prohibited from mentioning Your name. When I go there, shine Your light. Make those in need aware of Your presence. Amen.

And he said: "Truly I tell you, unless you change and become like little children, you will never enter the kingdom of heaven."
MATTHEW 18:3 NIV

On the road to Capernaum, Christ's disciples were arguing among themselves about which of them was the greatest. When Jesus asked what they had been arguing about, they kept quiet (Mark 9:33–34). Maybe they were embarrassed to say.

Matthew 18 provides more insight into this story. It says that the disciples asked Jesus, "Who is the greatest in the kingdom of heaven?" (Matthew 18:1 KJV). In other words, "What do we have to do to attain greatness when we get there?"

In Matthew 18:3, Jesus answers their question by using little children as examples. He tells His disciples that they need to change their attitudes and think with the righteous heart of a child.

Very young children approach the world with innocence. They are free from selfish ambition, are humble and dependent on their parents. This simple, meek spirit is what God requires of us. Instead of worrying about being great here on earth or when we get to heaven, Matthew 18:3 indicates we should be concerned about whether we will enter His kingdom at all.

Dear Lord, make me like a little child, innocent and humble in Your company. Take away my selfish ambitions and point my sight in the direction of heaven. Amen.

*When they had crossed, Elijah said to Elisha, "Tell me,
what can I do for you before I am taken from you?" "Let me
inherit a double portion of your spirit," Elisha replied.*
2 KINGS 2:9 NIV

What a bold request.

Elijah offered a blessing to Elisha. Elisha responded, "Let me inherit a double portion of your spirit."

Elijah filled the role of leader, prophet, and miracle worker. Why would Elisha want the heavy responsibilities and difficulties involved in this type of work?

Elisha could have asked for wealth, unlimited power, or a life with no problems. Even the ability to live each day in peace was within his reach.

Yet Elisha asked for Elijah's spirit. He did not ask to have a larger ministry than Elijah—he was only asking to inherit what Elijah was leaving and to be able to carry it on.

What might God give us if we asked boldly for the impossible? God deeply desires to bless us. If our hearts line up with His will and we stay open to His call, He will surprise us. God takes the ordinary and through His power transforms our prayers into the extraordinary—even double-portion requests.

*Bless me, Lord. When my heart aligns with Your will
and when I ask for the impossible, bless me. Show me
beyond my expectations that You are my God. Amen.*

Don't be ashamed of me.
2 TIMOTHY 1:8 NLT

Who could be ashamed of the apostle Paul—especially his almost-son Timothy?

Speculation about the younger man's background includes a sickly childhood, a doting Jewish mother and grandmother, and an absentee Greek father. Perhaps, as the only child in a wealthy family, he was shielded from many of life's vicissitudes; he was timid and undisciplined. Yet Paul saw in Timothy the potential for servanthood.

In this "farewell letter," the apostle is introspective, remembering the boy Timothy used to be. He reminds Timothy that "the Spirit God gave us does not make us timid, but gives us power, love and self-discipline" (2 Timothy 1:7 NIV). *Don't let my present condition deter you from proclaiming Jesus.* Implied: do not be ashamed of our Lord.

Older people can be a great influence on the younger generation, but as the apostle Paul illustrates, it remains the child's task to "fan into flame" the sparks lit by others (1:6 NIV).

Let's all live up to our spiritual responsibilities—whether we're fanning the flame ourselves or igniting the spark in others.

Heavenly Father, You have given me the responsibility of being a responsible Christian. Open my heart to wise teaching and lead me to share You with younger generations. Amen.

*He has made everything beautiful in its time. He has
also set eternity in the human heart; yet no one can
fathom what God has done from beginning to end.*
ECCLESIASTES 3:11 NIV

Our souls know there is a God. The souls of unbelievers know it
too. By setting "eternity in the human heart," God gave us a longing
for Him. That deep desire is fulfilled in those who accept Jesus, but
those who deny Him have to find something else to scratch the
itch. That unfulfilled longing is the best explanation for abuses of
alcohol, drugs, and power.

Of course, earthly desires are traps, but sometimes they are even
used by believers to bolster faith weakened by a lack of understanding.

Our human nature needs to understand. It's a problem that holds
many a believer and unbeliever back. No one can completely "fathom
what God has done." That's what makes Him God. And yet, still we try.

Thankfully, our hearts don't need to understand; neither do they
need earthly "fixes." They just need to be set free, to find God and
revel in the beauty of His never-ending creation. Believers, stop
letting unanswerable questions prevent you from loving Him more
completely. And unbelievers, ask yourself, if you had every material
thing you could want, wouldn't your heart still be reaching out for
eternity?

*I have questions, God—so many unanswered questions about life
and about You. Increase my trust in You. Help me to set aside my
uncertainty and find delight in Your never-ending love. Amen.*

He existed before anything else, and he holds all creation together.
COLOSSIANS 1:17 NLT

Jesus holds our world together in both the spiritual and the physical realm. It's not that He wraps His arms around our universe to keep it from falling apart. Rather, Jesus fine-tuned planet Earth for life and continually preserves those conditions.

Earth's precise distance from the sun is essential to life. If Earth were 5 percent closer, rivers and oceans would evaporate from a strong greenhouse effect. Move 5 percent farther away, and both water and carbon dioxide would freeze. Too cold or too hot means no life.

Even our sterile moon makes life possible by stabilizing the tilt of Earth's axis. Without the moon's steady pull, Earth's tilt could randomly swing over a wide range, resulting in temperatures too hot and too cold for life and erratic seasons.

Astronomers are also discovering how other planets in our solar system actually help Earth. For example, the huge planet Jupiter deflects many comets from entering the inner section of the solar system, where they could easily hit Earth with devastating results.

Through science we discover the physical laws Jesus designed for our universe. Through Bible study we unearth the spiritual laws Jesus designed for us. Look to Jesus to hold your life together.

You knit the heavens and Earth together perfectly. You blessed me with spiritual laws to help me live abundantly here on Earth and forever with You in heaven. I praise You, Lord! Amen.

"When they were discouraged, I smiled and that
encouraged them and lightened their spirits."
JOB 29:24 TLB

This verse prompts a question: If, without the luxury of words, we communicated solely through our actions or mere presence, what message would our lives convey?

It is said that a smile is the light of one's countenance. Job was a righteous, well-respected man of God. His friends and countrymen lauded him for his wisdom, and all men listened to him, heeding his instruction. Prior to Job's afflictions, the people sought his favor. Consequently, his smile was enough to encourage and lighten their loads (vv. 21–24).

Our preoccupation with words often obscures a simple truth: *what we say is not as important as who we are.* Job's smile made a difference because of the life he led.

Our most authentic forms of communication occur without a word. Rather, they flow from an understanding smile, a compassionate touch, a loving gesture, a gentle presence, or an unspoken prayer.

God used Job, an ordinary man with an extraordinary amount of love and wisdom—a man whose only adornment was righteous living and a warm smile. And He wants to use us too. So keep smiling. Someone may just need it.

Remind me, Jesus, to bless others through my actions. A warm
smile, a simple act of kindness, a loving touch might be just
what someone needs today. Remind me, please. Amen.

"My sheep listen to my voice; I know them, and they follow me."
JOHN 10:27 NIV

Sheep graze in large flocks. They often spread out, finding the best spot for some tasty grass or cool water to drink. They wander down gullies and ruts, oblivious to dangers such as pits or wild animals.

Sheep are not very smart animals. They need someone to watch over them and lead them to the best places.

But sheep do know one thing quite well: the sound of the shepherd's voice. They hear him call, even from great distances. His voice directs them back to safety. They know to plead for his help when they get into trouble.

We humans aren't always smart, either. We get lost as we seek the glittering attractions of the world. We wander off our spiritual path, distracted by our own desires and ignoring the dangers.

We also have a Good Shepherd to watch over us and gently call us to safety. If we listen, we can hear His voice even when we drift away.

Jesus wants us to hear Him and to follow His path. What will we choose to listen to? The noisy sounds of the world or His soft whisper to join Him?

Lord, open my ears to Your voice. Shout to me over the noise of the world. Whisper to me in the darkness. Lead me away from trouble and keep me safe. Amen.

*"But Lord!" Moses objected. "My own people won't listen
to me anymore. How can I expect Pharaoh to listen?"*
Exodus 6:12 NLT

The story of the Exodus is familiar to many of us. Called out of the
wilderness, Moses was dispatched by God to rescue the Israelites
from the oppressive Egyptians. Returning to the country he had
fled as a fugitive, Moses no doubt presumed that he would go in,
do what God said, and get out as quickly as possible.

Instead, Moses faced down Pharaoh on multiple occasions,
with the Israelites' oppressive workload doubling as a result of the
negotiations. Instead of smooth sailing, Moses saw circumstances
deteriorate—even as he followed God's instructions verbatim. The
dark hour in Israel's history. . .became even darker!

Moses' discouragement is evident. He was sent to deliver
Israel, and they weren't listening to him. Pharaoh wasn't listening.
Conditions were worsening instead of improving. It would have
been easy for him to say, "Obviously this isn't working, God. Find
someone else who can succeed with this."

Stuck in the middle, Moses didn't give up. Instead, he kept the
lines of communication open between himself and God. Moses chose
to persevere through the hardships of dealing with difficult people.

Who are the difficult people in your life? What impossible
situation is God calling you to persevere through?

*Father, I am tired of life's difficult people and impossible
situations. Still, I promise to persevere because I know You
will lead me out of the darkness and into Your light. Amen.*

~ Day 93 ~

Otherwise, what will those do who are baptized for the dead? If the dead are not raised at all, then why are they baptized for them?
1 CORINTHIANS 15:29 NET

What does this verse mean?

There are over two hundred different theological views of what this verse means! In short, we don't have a clue what Paul meant by this. Those of us who depend for our livelihood upon our specialized skills and education hate the three words "I don't know." But in truth, we don't know.

There is nothing else in all of scripture that even hints at anything related to "baptism for the dead." No great doctrine of the ages has been enunciated by the church about it. In context, Paul refers to it obliquely to illustrate the assuredness of Christ's resurrection. He isn't laying out anything important to salvation.

Many of us take pride in our doctrinal purity. This verse serves as a reminder to all of us that no matter how correct our theology, God is bigger than any of us, and we can never have it all figured out. God cannot be put in a box. Perhaps Paul is just trying to keep us humble!

Shine Your light on the scriptures, Lord. Help me understand them. And when I can't, remind me that Your ideas are sometimes too grand for my human mind to comprehend. Amen.

But Daniel was determined not to defile himself by eating the food and wine given to them by the king. He asked the chief of staff for permission not to eat these unacceptable foods.
DANIEL 1:8 NLT

Of royal or noble descent, Daniel was among the Judean captives taken to Babylon by the armies of Nebuchadnezzar.

Chosen for elite training, Daniel and other select captives were treated luxuriously and given royal cuisine, which included food and drink deemed unclean by Mosaic Law. Determined not to defile himself, Daniel asked his attendant to "test us for ten days on a diet of vegetables and water" (Daniel 1:12 NLT).

When making his request, Daniel illustrated an effective way to present an appeal to others. As the Institute of Basic Young Conflicts points out: First, Daniel sought a solution to the dilemma rather than spreading discontent. Second, he showed concern for the goals of his attendant by offering a time limit along with the unconventional menu. Last, he displayed a humble attitude, approaching his attendant with respect rather than with arrogance or rebellion.

Before presenting an appeal, examine your motives, check your attitude, and try to find a solution that also fits the other person's goals.

However, following these guidelines does not guarantee success. If your request is denied, respond graciously. This keeps communication open and may present an opportunity to introduce someone to our God.

Check my motives and attitudes, Father. Give me the ability to compromise with others and to always be ready with a gracious response. Amen.

*No one who is born of God will continue to sin,
because God's seed remains in them; they cannot go
on sinning, because they have been born of God.*
1 JOHN 3:9 NIV

The Greek word for "seed" in this verse is none other than *sperma*. One born of God has His "seed" in him, a spiritual DNA that marks us as belonging to Him. One of these DNA markers changes our awareness of sin. John repeats his assertion that God's child will not continue sinning twice more in this epistle (3:6 and 5:18).

Paul talked about the constant tension between knowing what is right and yet doing what is wrong (Romans 7:7–25). Only as we live by the Spirit can we put our sinful natures to death (Romans 8). John also acknowledged this tension—and ultimate victory—when he stated that "everyone [who is] born of God overcomes the world" (1 John 5:4 NIV).

People have always been tempted to claim to know God while doing evil. Back in Jeremiah's day, people called the Lord *Father* and *friend*. Jeremiah said, "This is how you talk, but you do all the evil you can" (Jeremiah 3:5 NIV).

In Christ and by the Spirit, we have overcome the world. May our lives reflect this truth in increasing measure.

*Dear God, help me not to give in to sinful temptation.
And when I do sin, thank You for eternal forgiveness—
Your gift to me through Christ. Amen.*

I often think of the heavens your hands have made,
and of the moon and stars you put in place.
PSALM 8:3 CEV

Almost three thousand years ago, the psalmist David looked with awe at the clear night sky. He gazed at the moon and the twinkling stars and marveled at the greatness of God. How could someone so immensely creative care about us lowly humans?

In the summer of 1969, another man wondered the same thing. American astronaut Edwin "Buzz" Aldrin saw the night sky with a new perspective—from the surface of the moon. Aldrin and Neil Armstrong were the first humans to walk on the moon. One can only imagine the thoughts that filled their minds.

For Aldrin, it was a deeply religious experience. As he stood on the moon's surface and gazed up at the sky, he remembered the words of the psalmist David as written in the King James Version of the Bible. He quoted those words in a television interview from space. Aldrin said, "When I consider thy heavens, the work of thy fingers, the moon and the stars, which thou has ordained; what is man, that thou art mindful of him? and the son of man, that thou visitest him?" (Psalm 8:3–4 KJV).

Three thousand years apart, two different men looked up at the sky—and they saw the same God.

Father, I can only imagine what other amazing things lie beyond
Your stars. You created the heavens and the earth, and yet
You know and love me! I am humbled and honored. Amen.

～ Day 97 ～

You will know how to live in the family of God.
1 Timothy 3:15 ncv

Jillian and Robert were twins—obviously not identical. They had been in foster homes since their parents were killed in a car crash on a California freeway.

The kids were raised by three separate foster families. "Nobody wanted the two of us," Robert reported. "Jillian and I didn't see each other for over ten years."

Robert kept a journal through his high school years. In an entry for Thursday, January 15, 2000, he wrote: "When I was a kid, I went to a Sunday school and heard about the family of God. No one will ever know how much I wanted to be a son in that family. Jillian too (a daughter, not a son. lol)."

According to a cable news program, Robert's journal was discovered with his belongings in a war zone in Iraq. It was sent home with his body. A distant uncle remarked, "We never were a close family."

Given the opportunity, Robert could have been a son in the family of God.

He would have learned the things that family life teaches. Things like joy (Psalm 67:4), courage (Deuteronomy 31:6), satisfaction (Psalm 103:5), forgiveness (Ephesians 4:32), togetherness (Proverbs 27:6), and love (1 Peter 4:8–9).

Pray for opportunities to introduce spiritual orphans to God and His family.

Lord, lead me to those who are lost without You. Open my heart to welcome them into my own family and especially into Yours. Amen.

Be merciful to those who doubt.
JUDE 1:22 NIV

Jude wanted to discuss the joys of salvation but first had to warn his readers of the dangers posed by those who follow a more worldly path.

He cautioned the faithful to be cautious—but didn't say, "Stay away from those heathens!" Instead he recommended building ourselves up in "holy faith" because there is work to be done. God doesn't want to lose anyone—and with His help, we might be able to snatch "them from the fire" (v. 23 NIV).

Not all of those faithless folk are intentionally evil or wicked. Many have been fooled into thinking God is for others. Some have doubts and questions and might come to faith if only they could see how it applied to a life like theirs. The world certainly isn't going to show them that—and if we just walk on by, they might never know.

Like Jude, we might want to celebrate our salvation. But, just as he found, there is something more important to be concentrating on. Rubbing shoulders with some worldly people might be a risk worth taking if, in the process, a few doubters can be saved.

After all, if Christianity consisted only of those who never doubted, there would be very few going to heaven—and a lot more feeling the heat.

Heavenly Father, Jesus welcomed unbelievers and led them to You. I want to be like Jesus. Show me how to transform doubt into faith and trust in You. Amen.

"You shall love your neighbour as yourself."
LEVITICUS 19:18 NKJV

Most Christians have never actually read the book of Leviticus. As far as they can see from skimming its pages, it contains endless lists of laws and regulations, tedious, outdated instructions on how to sacrifice animals and stay ritually pure. The book of Deuteronomy, they feel, is almost as irrelevant to life in the modern world.

Yet the two greatest commandments in the Old Testament are found in Leviticus and Deuteronomy.

When a Pharisee asked Jesus, "Which is the great commandment in the law?" Jesus didn't quote any of the well-known Ten Commandments that most of us would have repeated. Instead, he quoted Deuteronomy 6:5: "You shall love the LORD your God with all your heart." Jesus then stated emphatically, "This is the first and great commandment. And the second is like it." He then quoted Leviticus 19:18: "Love your neighbor as yourself" (Matthew 22:35–40 NKJV).

If the two most important commands in the Law are found in these "dull, dry" books, what *else* might be found there that can inspire and guide us? Stray off the beaten path of your scripture reading and explore the remote corners of your Bible. Wonderful gems are hidden there.

Dear God, I confess that I've found some books of the Bible uninteresting, but I will revisit them! Reveal to me what's hidden there. Open my eyes and my heart. Amen.

Herein is love, not that we loved God, but that he loved us, and sent his Son a propitiation for our sins.
1 John 4:10 darby

My Utmost for His Highest points out that we have the wrong theology when we say that God forgives us based on His love. Put it this way. Suppose in court the man on the stand exclaims, "I confess! I killed him!" Then the judge rises up and says, "I love you, sir, so I will pardon your crime. Go free." Well, where would be the justice in that?

God does not forgive based on His love, for then His justice would be unfair. So God sent Jesus to die for our sins. Now God forgives on the basis of the cross. Our sins were punished when Jesus was crucified. Now when God forgives, justice is still satisfied.

Perhaps we are judging God's love based on how much He has blessed us in this life. We forget that we come before Him as sinners in need of a Savior. God in love has provided that Savior—at a great cost to Him. Let's treat sin with the loathing it deserves and God with the love due Him.

Merciful God, I wish I were free of sin! I want to perfectly please You. Thank You for sending me a perfect Savior—one whose sacrifice will wash away my sins forever. Amen.

For as the heavens are higher than the earth, so are my ways
higher than your ways and my thoughts than your thoughts.
ISAIAH 55:9 RSV

God tells us, "My thoughts are not your thoughts, neither are your ways my ways" (v. 8 RSV), and then goes on to describe the vast difference between the way He thinks and the way we mortals think and between the way He operates and the way people try to work things out. God reasons and works on such a higher level that He compares it to the heavens, which are immeasurably higher than the earth.

God has given us intelligence and common sense, and He intends us to use our brains to think through everyday problems and come up with solutions. We are not infinitely smart, however, and sometimes the solution to our problems may be different from anything our minds can envision. A good example is Jesus' command to love our enemies (Matthew 5:44). It runs contrary to normal human logic.

God knows best, and though we may feel certain that God's way won't work or even seems downright foolish, we do well to remember that "the foolishness of God is wiser than men" and that compared to God, "the thoughts of the wise are futile" (1 Corinthians 1:25; 3:20 RSV).

Father, sometimes You send me down a path that I view
as foolish, and then I discover that it leads to something
grand. I praise You for Your perfect wisdom! Amen.

"But I tell you that everyone will have to give account on the day of judgment for every empty word they have spoken."
MATTHEW 12:36 NIV

In the first century, the Pharisees employed the "thinking out loud" method of communication and attributed Jesus' miracle-working to an unholy alliance with Beelzebub, the prince of demons (Matthew 12:24). Jesus responded with, among other things, a warning of coming judgment for thoughtlessly uttered words.

Two thousand years later, we all live in a world of careless speech. An NFL coach's pep talk to his team is broadcast over the airwaves, peppered with profanity. Politicians find it necessary to apologize for comments made when they thought the microphone was turned off. Music is sold with parental advisory warnings about its content.

How easy it is to speak without thinking! Yet Jesus reminds us that our words are powerful—and we will be held accountable for how we use them. Whether we have a public forum or are speaking into the ears of a child, God hears not only the words of our mouth, but the unspoken attitude of our heart that fuels our speech (Matthew 12:34).

What would our world be like if we weighed our words on God's scale and spoke accordingly?

Jesus, every word You spoke had power and purpose. Help me to use my words so that they will always bring You glory and honor. Amen.

*"We saw the Nephilim there (the descendants of Anak
come from the Nephilim). We seemed like grasshoppers
in our own eyes, and we looked the same to them."*
NUMBERS 13:33 NIV

Moses sent spies to explore the land of Canaan. Returning, the men said, "We went into the land to which you sent us, and it does flow with milk and honey! . . . But the people who live there are powerful, and the cities are fortified and very large" (vv. 27–28 NIV).

Compared to Canaan's current inhabitants—especially the Anakims, who were known for their tall and robust stature—the Israelites were grasshoppers. And that shook their faith to its core. But amid the clamor Caleb silenced the crowd, saying, "We should go up and take possession of the land, for we can certainly do it" (v. 30 NIV). And Joshua agreed.

The ten spies believed only in what they saw, while Joshua and Caleb believed God. They dared to oppose the majority with a firm commitment to God and an unwavering confidence in God's promises to them.

Are your trials and problems too overwhelming to face? Like the ten spies, do you feel as if there is no way to conquer them? Stand on God's Word, and He will bring you to the Promised Land. In the process, your faith will transform you from a grasshopper into a spiritual giant!

*Almighty God, when life causes me to feel small
and insignificant, I will stand in faith on Your
promises. I know that You will help me. Amen.*

When you pass through the waters, I will be with you;
and when you pass through the rivers, they will not
sweep over you. When you walk through the fire, you will
not be burned; the flames will not set you ablaze.
ISAIAH 43:2 NIV

This is one of the most comforting verses in the Bible. It is God's promise that when we face trials in our lives, He will not abandon us.

The Bible offers literal examples of this. When Moses and the Israelites approached the Red Sea, with the Egyptian army in hot pursuit, God literally parted the water and allowed the Israelites to escape from their enemies (Exodus 14:10–31). When Shadrach, Meshach, and Abednego were cast into a fiery furnace for refusing to bow down to a golden idol, God brought them out of the fire unscathed. He was literally there in the fire with the three young men, seen as a fourth person (Daniel 3).

Isaiah 43:2 doesn't say "*if* you pass through the waters." It says "when." When we face trouble in our lives, God is with us. Jesus repeats this promise in John 16:33 (NIV), "In this world you will have trouble. But take heart! I have overcome the world."

Jesus, there is still no problem that You cannot
overcome. When I face trouble, I will put my faith in
You and believe that You are with me. Amen.

He was despised and rejected by mankind, a man of suffering,
and familiar with pain. Like one from whom people hide their
faces he was despised, and we held him in low esteem.
ISAIAH 53:3 NIV

Eight hundred years before Christ, the prophet Isaiah was predicting that He would take on the sins of the world for our salvation.

His description of a man we would rather not look at, a man bent under the burden of sin, might apply to lots of people in the world today. We probably all know someone we would rather not talk to: nasty people, evil people, or just plain unpleasant people. But they weren't meant to be like that! Sins, theirs and others, have twisted their lives.

They didn't take that burden on board for us, and they certainly didn't do it for our salvation. But that doesn't mean we should look away or walk around them. We tend to do so because they are dangerous. If we reach out to them, they might well bring us down. People certainly felt the same about Jesus.

But knowing there is a soul God loves in there, knowing that in the least of these the Lord is to be found, we realize our reaching out to them in His name might just be the saving of us—whether they take us down or not.

The world is wrought with trouble, and evil people
seem to reign, but in each of them is a soul worth
winning. Show me how I can help, Lord. Amen.

*"Isn't this the carpenter's son? Isn't his mother named Mary?
And aren't his brothers James, Joseph, Simon, and Judas? And
aren't all his sisters here with us? Where did he get all this?"*
MATTHEW 13:55–56 NET

Can you imagine growing up in the same household with Perfection?
My mother only thinks I'm perfect; Mary *knew* her eldest son was.
But His brothers and sisters were not. The sibling rivalry must have
been intense.

Mark 3:20–21 (NET) says, "Now Jesus went home, and a crowd
gathered so that they were not able to eat. When his family heard
this they went out to restrain him, for they said, 'He is out of his
mind.'" Jesus' own family rejected him. James didn't even come to
the crucifixion; Jesus asked his cousin John to look after Mary.

It was only after the Resurrection that they believed. Jesus
appeared to James (1 Corinthians 15:7). We don't know anything about the meeting, but James quickly became a leader in
the early church. Jesus' other brothers also served in the church
(1 Corinthians 9:5).

Many of us have been praying for our relatives' salvation. Jesus
knows what that's like and cares just as much as we do.

*Jesus, You had parents and siblings. You understand
what it's like to be part of a human family. I'm glad
that You know what it's like to be me! Amen.*

I waited patiently for the LORD; and he inclined unto me, and
heard my cry. He brought me up also out of an horrible pit.
PSALM 40:1–2 KJV

Bible heroes often went through times of great testing. You'd think
that because they were close to God, they would've been spared most
of life's adversities. They weren't. Or you might assume that because
they had great faith they would have been speedily delivered from
whatever pitfalls they fell into. Not so.

David found himself trapped in a "horrible pit" with no apparent
way out, and he cried loudly to the Lord to rescue him. Then he
waited. It took time for God to answer. David undoubtedly learned
more patience in the process and probably had to endure doubts,
wondering if God cared about the dilemma he was in.

Even Jeremiah didn't always get immediate answers to prayer.
One time he and some Jewish refugees were in a dire situation and
were desperate to know what to do. Yet after Jeremiah prayed, the
Lord took ten days to answer (Jeremiah 42:7). But the answer *did*
come. . .in time.

We today sometimes find ourselves in a "horrible pit" as well,
and pray desperately for God to bring us up out of it. He will. We
often just need to be patient.

Why is patience so hard? It's because Your timing is perfect
and beyond my understanding. Help me to be patient
with You, God. I know You will answer me. Amen.

For the word of God is alive and powerful.
HEBREWS 4:12 NLT

The Bible is many things. May we never overlook the fact that of all the things that can be said about it, God's Word is an incredible work of art.

The measure of a good work of art is whether it is fresh and relevant each time it is experienced. Is the work powerful and moving? Certainly the Bible is! Each time we read it, we can discover new things relevant to our current position in life. It is new and different each time we read it. It is alive!

How many books can boast such a property? God does not change, but everything else does. People change, technology changes, schools of thought change. . .but the Word of the Lord does not change. It will be as relevant two thousand years from now as it was two thousand years ago!

The Word of God says several things about itself throughout its pages. As we are reminded in Hebrews 4:12 that God's Word is alive and powerful, we can meditate on just how relevant it continues to be. Even now, we can still communicate with our Lord through prayer and by reading and filling our minds with His words. Let us remember to praise God for this opportunity He has provided us to hear from Him!

I praise You, Father, for Your Holy Word. I've hidden it in my heart. It speaks to me night and day, teaching me and leading me in righteousness. Amen.

～ Day 109 ～

Rather, let the greatest among you become as the
youngest, and the leader as one who serves.
Luke 22:26 esv

Sometimes when we're wrong, we're *really* wrong. We look at the map and turn right, thinking we are headed west. After driving for miles, we find we're going in the opposite direction. It is the same thing when it comes to being great. We think being great involves commanding hundreds of people, of being in a place of authority.

Surprise! If we wish to be great in the kingdom of God, we may have to do a U-turn. Greatness is found in being a servant. The leader is not one who tells others what to do; the leader leads and teaches by example. He doesn't point the way to go; he simply does what must be done.

Jesus did not simply tell His disciples how to live. He humbled Himself to serve, and He never rose above that station. Because He left us an example of humble service, shall we exalt ourselves? We have the promise that as Christ served even to death, and God therefore highly exalted Him, we who serve Him faithfully shall reign with Him.

Jesus, help me to be a servant not only to You, but also to the
world. Teach me to be humble like You were humble. Amen.

"If anyone forces you to go one mile, go with them two miles."
MATTHEW 5:41 NIV

Going the extra mile. The Romans adopted the ancient Persian custom of forcing someone to carry their baggage for them while they traveled. Against their will, people were compelled to lug these conquerors' belongings the length of a mile or one thousand paces.

In the book of Matthew, Jesus said in the Sermon on the Mount to surprise your enemies. Don't just go the minimum distance—be willing to double the effort and walk two miles.

God's love exceeds our wildest imagination. He pours out His blessings, forgiveness, and strength upon us even in our toughest circumstances. He goes the extra mile.

God calls us to do likewise and to live to a higher standard. We choose not to retaliate when we have been wronged. We volunteer for two shifts when others leave early and don't complete their assignments. We help someone without any thought of what we may get in return. We pray for people others ignore. We strive to love the unlovable.

God expects us to go beyond all expectations and to go the extra mile.

God, help me to go that extra mile by giving with
no thought of receiving and by loving those most
in need of Your mercy and love. Amen.

*"If anyone comes to Me, and does not hate his own father
and mother and wife and children and brothers and sisters,
yes, and even his own life, he cannot be My disciple."*
LUKE 14:26 NASB

Jesus must have seriously wanted to discourage people from following Him. He told the crowds following Him, "If you don't hate your family, you can't be My disciple."

Ouch.

But Jesus was using hyperbole to make a point: love Me so deeply that your love for your family will seem like hatred by comparison. When He gave the twelve disciples instructions before sending them out, He repeated the point in less strident terms: "Anyone who loves their father or mother more than me is not worthy of me; anyone who loves their son or daughter more than me is not worthy of me" (Matthew 10:37 NIV).

Jesus applied the same hyperbole to the consequences of loving Him. He told the crowds, *Unless you do this, you will not be My disciples.* He told the Twelve, *You are my disciples; now act in a way worthy of your calling.*

Love for Christ and for others flows in a circle. The more we love Christ, the more we love others. . .and the more we love others, the more we show our love for Christ.

*Jesus, I love You with all my heart; please help me to
love You more. Fill me up with love for You. Then let
Your love shine through me to others. Amen.*

The LORD your God is with you, the Mighty Warrior who saves. He will take great delight in you; in his love he will no longer rebuke you, but will rejoice over you with singing.
ZEPHANIAH 3:17 NIV

God's passion for His people shows itself in many ways.

His mighty power saves us. He delights in us. His love brings peace and quietness to our hearts. And His pleasure is revealed as He rejoices over us with singing.

Angels sang the night Jesus was born (Luke 2:13–14). The Psalms are full of lyrics people have used to praise God over the centuries. And Revelation 5:11–12 paints a glorious picture of heaven, complete with continual songs of praise.

But there is a song that's been written just for you. It has your name as its title. And the composer, God Himself sings your song over you as you go about life here on earth.

Close your eyes. Listen carefully. Do you hear God's melodious voice? He's singing your song. Raise your voice and join Him in the heavenly music!

O Lord, what a lovely image—Your voice singing to me my song: a melodic poem, an encouraging refrain, a gentle lullaby. Open my ears to Your voice! Amen.

Day 113

Jesus replied, "You do not realize now what I am
doing, but later you will understand."
JOHN 13:7 NIV

It was an emotional time for the disciples as Jesus was frequently speaking of His upcoming death. How hard it must have been for these men to believe Jesus would soon be killed, when people had just recently greeted Him with shouts of "Hosanna."

And now another jolt. During dinner, Jesus got up from the table, wrapped a towel around His waist, and began washing the disciples' feet. Peter responded not with humbleness or praise, but with questioning, and then refusal. Peter had a vision for himself, and it didn't include Jesus washing his feet.

Jesus told Peter that he wouldn't understand until later what He was doing. This is a response Jesus could easily give to each of us when we're facing hard or unpleasant events in our lives or seeing them in the lives of others. For which one of us hasn't at least once lifted our eyes to heaven and asked, "Why, God?"

Peter did get his feet washed and eventually came to understand why Jesus did what He did. Until that time of understanding came, Peter had to choose to trust and obey.

Will we make that same choice?

"Why, God?" I ask that question, and Your sweet voice
whispers, "Trust Me. I have it all under control." I trust
You, Father. It is enough that You know why. Amen.

But Moses told the people, "Don't be afraid.
Just stand still and watch the LORD rescue you today.
The Egyptians you see today will never be seen again."
EXODUS 14:13 NLT

On the night of the tenth plague, God brought the Israelites out of Egypt. Under Moses' leadership, God took them across the Sinai Peninsula to the edge of the wilderness. From there they marched toward Pi-hahiroth to camp along the sea.

Meanwhile, back at the palace, Pharaoh regretted freeing the Israelites and ordered his entire army after them. The warriors reached the Israelites as they approached the Red Sea.

According to the historian Josephus, the Egyptian army trapped the Israelites between the Red Sea and a ridge of impassable mountains.

The people panicked, but not Moses. God had promised to deliver the Israelites from the Egyptians, and he believed Him.

God instructed Moses to hold his staff over the water.

In an awesome display of power, God divided the sea. The Israelites walked to the other shore on dry land. When Pharaoh's warriors followed, the walls of water collapsed, drowning the entire army.

Moses acted courageously because he believed God. We too can be fearless when holding on to His promises.

Father, reveal to me the promises in Your Word. Set them
firmly in my mind and heart. When I face my enemies,
remind me of them, and I will be fearless. Amen.

Day 115

*Now I want you to know, brothers and sisters, that what has
happened to me has actually served to advance the gospel.*
PHILIPPIANS 1:12 NIV

Early Christians were mistreated, even tortured and killed, because
of their faith in Jesus Christ. The apostle Paul, author of the book
of Philippians, was no exception. He was stoned, imprisoned, and
shipwrecked during his missionary journeys. But all his sufferings
had a purpose—to advance the gospel he preached.

Paul could have escaped his suffering by turning away from his
faith, but he did not. He endured persecution, boldly shared the
gospel, and grew even stronger in his Christian convictions. More
than preserving his own life, Paul desired to lead others to salvation
through Jesus Christ (Romans 1:16).

After Jesus rose from the dead, He said to His disciples, "Go. . .
into all the world, and preach the Gospel to every creature" (Mark
16:15 KJV). It is our duty as followers of Christ to share the gospel
proudly and without reservation.

Will you share the gospel with someone today?

*Jesus, You've told me to share the Gospel with the
world. Where should I share it today? Lead me to
someone who needs to know You. Amen.*

Better is a dish of vegetables where love is than
a fattened ox served with hatred.
PROVERBS 15:17 NASB

Vegetarians, arise! Lovers of parsnips and broccoli, here is your scriptural approval, but carnivores, never fear, take heart; proverb-writing Solomon is making a point—even the most humble dish on the menu is made gourmet when it includes a certain all-important ingredient.

Most recipes omit that component. Perhaps Christian bookshops need to introduce cookbooks that include this missing ingredient. While there'll never be a cents-off coupon in the Sunday paper for it, it is the secret of all that's good and wholesome. It will always be rewarded.

The ingredient? It's love!

King Solomon, traditional author of this proverb, was considered the wisest of all men. The point of today's fascinating verse is right on the mark. The king was surely aware of romantic love: his poetry collection, Song of Solomon, bears this out. Of all men, Solomon keenly understood the human need for love and friendship.

Check out the nutrition facts on a can of love: Serving size—"All your heart. . .all your soul. . .all your mind" (Matthew 22:37 NIV). Servings per—enough for "whoever believes" (John 3:16 NIV). Calories—May God give you the "fatness of the earth" (Genesis 27:28 KJV).

"The greatest. . .is love!" (1 Corinthians 13:13 NIV).

Heavenly Father, I love You with all my heart,
all my soul, and all my mind. Help me to love You
even more. In Jesus' name I pray. Amen.

Day 117

Immediately [Jesus] spoke to them and said, "Take courage!
It is I. Don't be afraid." Then he climbed into the boat with them,
and the wind died down. They were completely amazed.
MARK 6:50–51 NIV

Imagine being on a big lake during a storm. The waves and the wind seem to be having a contest to see which can overturn the boat first. The fishermen in the boat hold on as tightly as they can. Just as they are sure it will be their final fishing trip, the very Son of God appears outside of the boat, standing on the water! He identifies Himself and reassures the men. At this, He climbs into the boat, and everything becomes calm. The storm is no more, and the danger is gone. Imagine how those fishermen must have felt!

This is what actually happened as described in Mark 6, but Jesus continues to work this same way with us. We occasionally have so much trouble that we see no way out of it. Jesus walks directly across our personal storm and reminds us that He is still there. Then, just as He climbs aboard "the boat," He fills us with His presence and shows us that there is nothing to fear if only we will trust Him. Just as we read in Mark 6:50–51, we have no choice but to be completely amazed.

Jesus, nothing can keep You from me—not fire, flood,
storms, not even a vast expanse of ocean. I trust You to
overcome any obstacles that stand in my way. Amen.

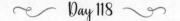

Day 118

Then the manna ceased on the day after they had eaten the produce of the land; and the children of Israel no longer had manna.
JOSHUA 5:12 NKJV

For forty years, while the children of Israel wandered in the deserts of Sinai, God miraculously provided manna—"bread from heaven"— for them to eat (Exodus 16:1–16). This wonder bread continued to appear all around them while they marched south around Edom and through the deserts east of Moab. The manna even continued to cover the ground when they camped in the fertile land near Jericho.

For forty years, or some 14,600 days, day after day, the manna had continued to appear (Deuteronomy 8:2–3). But the day after the Israelites ate the Passover meal in the Promised Land, this continuous forty-year miracle ceased. Before the manna stopped appearing, God had already begun to provide food that grew by natural means.

This same thing happened in the life of Elijah: when the water in the Cherith Brook dried up, God told him it was time to move to Zarephath, where a widow would now provide for him (1 Kings 17:5–9).

This same principle often applies to us today. God provides for us in different ways at different stages in our life, and when one means of supply dries up, He has another means ready.

Thank You, God, for providing for me. You know my every need, and You fulfill it at the perfect time and through Your perfect will. I love You, Father. Amen.

"Blessed are those who mourn, for they will be comforted."
MATTHEW 5:4 NIV

Jesus began His Sermon on the Mount with nine blessings, or "Beatitudes." The Amplified Classic Edition suggests that blessed means "enviably happy [with happiness produced by the experience of God's favor and especially conditioned by the revelation of His matchless grace]" (Matthew 5:4 AMPC).

Apparently Jesus' interpretation of happiness doesn't match ours: Happy are the poor? The hungry and thirsty? The persecuted?

Happy are those who *mourn*?

Yes, for they will be comforted.

Did the religious leaders stand up in protest? With those words, Jesus staked His claim as the awaited Messiah. He would "comfort all who mourn. . .to bestow on them. . .the oil of joy instead of mourning" (Isaiah 61:2–3 NIV).

The psalmist frequently praised God as the source of comfort (71:21; 23:4; 86:17). Isaiah commanded the mountains to burst into song because of the Lord's comfort (49:13). Even Jeremiah, the weeping prophet, called God "my Comforter in sorrow" (8:18 NIV). In Jesus, Christians receive comfort "in all our troubles" (2 Corinthians 1:3–4 NIV).

The earth will experience the final fulfillment of that promise in heaven, when "God will wipe away every tear from their eyes" (Revelation 7:17 NIV).

In this life, tears will come—but so will God's comfort.

We are blessed.

Father God, when life events sadden me and tears
fall from my eyes, I am blessed because You soothe me
with Your continuous, comforting love. Amen.

*He said, "Who are you?" She replied, "I am Ruth, your servant.
Marry your servant, for you are a guardian of the family interests."
He said, "May you be rewarded by the LORD, my dear! This act of
devotion is greater than what you did before. For you have not
sought to marry one of the young men, whether rich or poor. Now,
my dear, don't worry! I intend to do for you everything you propose,
for everyone in the village knows that you are a worthy woman."*
RUTH 3:9–11 NET

In most times and places in history, most people have been married.
But 42 percent of adult Americans are single. It can be a challenging
life. God understands, and He cares for us too. He loves us enough
to devote an entire book of the Bible to us.

Every paragraph of the book of Ruth is full of examples and
wisdom for older single people. It is a beautiful love story between
Boaz and Ruth, a man and woman who didn't fit into their society's
traditional family structure. They both found themselves single when
far older than their neighbors.

God loves us and has not forgotten us!

*Dear Lord, You understand us wherever we are in our
lives—married or single, content or lonely. You remember
us and love us. Oh, what a friend You are! Amen.*

*And now these three remain: faith, hope and
love. But the greatest of these is love.*
1 Corinthians 13:13 niv

In 1 Corinthians 13—known as the "love chapter"—Paul underscores
the role of love in a Christian's life. Throughout this chapter, God
exalts Christlike character more than faith, spiritual gifts, ministry,
or even martyrdom (vv. 1–3). Even so, the church often heralds the
attributes of faith, despite the apostle's mandate to seek love above
those other virtues.

During the late Senator Edward Kennedy's battle with brain
cancer, his family noted that he always had hope. Undoubtedly,
hope is a needed and admirable characteristic. Hope fuels faith
and throws us a lifeline in times of adversity. Hope possesses the
promise of a brighter day.

And who can deny the power of faith? Throughout history,
faith has closed the mouths of lions, opened blinded eyes, and
saved countless lost souls. And the scriptures note that without it,
we cannot please God (Hebrews 11:6).

Yet as wonderful as these qualities are, it is love that God deems
the greatest. Love lasts and never fails. It is patient, kind, unselfish,
and honest; it never keeps a record of wrongs or delights in evil. In
a word, love is God. And there is no *one* greater.

*Father, I strive to love patiently, kindly, unselfishly,
and honestly because in doing so I become more
perfect in love and more like You! Amen.*

Day 122

Be still, and know that I am God.
PSALM 46:10 NKJV

David experienced a great deal of trouble, and the only way he survived was by trusting in the Lord. He had to believe that God was indeed God, the Creator of the heavens and the earth, powerful enough to help him out of his difficulty. To gain such confidence, David had to turn away from his problems, stop fretting, quiet his heart, and focus on God. Only when he was perfectly still and trusting could he know in a very real way that God was God.

David also wrote, "Meditate within your heart on your bed, and be still" (Psalm 4:4 NKJV). Many of us have lost the ability to meditate on God. Either we tell ourselves that meditation is something only Buddhist monks do, or else we cry out frantic prayers while distracted by the careening roller coaster of life. When we lie down in bed at night, instead of meditating calmly and trusting in God, we fret and toss and turn.

When we learn to trust that God can protect us and work out our problems, then we can lie down peacefully and sleep (Psalm 4:8). That same trust gives us the strength to face our days with confidence.

Dear God, quiet my mind. Remove from it all the worldly thoughts that come between You and me. Create stillness within me and turn my thoughts toward You. Amen.

*"I will give them an undivided heart and put a new
spirit in them; I will remove from them their heart
of stone and give them a heart of flesh."*
EZEKIEL 11:19 NIV

When a person has a heart attack, a portion of the heart muscle dies—making the organ less efficient in pumping life-giving blood throughout the body.

A heart of stone—cold, hard, and immovable—cannot pump life and love within us, either. We are born needing a heart transplant. Our naturally divided hearts chase after the glittering desires of the world, jealous of the success of others, harboring deep resentments, bitterness, and anger in their dark chambers. We think the world will satisfy the emptiness we feel inside.

God is willing to give us an undivided heart—a heart that is open and ready to see, hear, and love God. This heart has a single focus: loving God and others with a tenderness that we know comes from someone beyond us.

The good news is we have already had successful surgery, and our donor heart is within us. We received our heart transplant when we invited Jesus to be our Savior, creating new spirits within us.

God's heart changes everything and creates us as new people with living hearts.

*Thank You, Lord, for giving me a new heart, a heart so
perfect in love that it will last me forever. Amen.*

*And it shall come to pass, that all they that look upon thee
shall flee from thee, and say, Nineveh is laid waste: who will
bemoan her? whence shall I seek comforters for thee?*
NAHUM 3:7 KJV

If the Old Testament's prophetic books were movies, Nahum would
be the sequel to Jonah.

You remember *Jonah*, the action/adventure movie with the
anticlimactic ending? The star of the film reluctantly challenges
Nineveh, the world's center of evil, with a message from God:
"Turn from sin, or you're history." Amazingly, the capital of
the brutal Assyrian empire repents and God relents. As the movie
ends, Jonah watches in disappointment as Nineveh lives to see
another day.

Actually, it'll live another century or so. But in *Jonah II*, Nahum
warns Nineveh that it's on God's wrath list again for, among other
things, its bloody victimization of other nations. Though this
movie doesn't show the actual destruction, history records that the
Babylonians flattened Nineveh in 612 BC.

Nahum's "it shall come to pass" does. . .and Jonah's decades-old
wish is fulfilled.

The End.

*Whatever You say, God, will surely happen. Your Word is
perfectly just, solid, and true. When evil seems to overtake the
world, remind me—Your will shall come to pass. Amen.*

"Therefore I tell you, do not worry about your life, what you will eat or drink; or about your body, what you will wear. Is not life more than food, and the body more than clothes?"
MATTHEW 6:25 NIV

This verse is part of Jesus' Sermon on the Mount, which addresses the moral expectations He has for His followers. Jesus' speech consisted of five great dissertations that—if followed—would ultimately give us inner peace.

Picture those gathered on the mountainside, adorned in robes and sandals, nodding their heads as they identified with Jesus' words over two thousand years ago. What's fascinating is the relevance of this verse to our "red carpet"–obsessed society. What if we removed our hunger for possessions and our desire to look a certain way and focused on God instead? What would we be left with?

Jesus said we would be left with a treasure, one that never goes out of style! A treasure that moths and rust can't destroy and thieves don't break in and steal (Matthew 6:20). And the best part is—it's free.

Heavenly Father, I see a world obsessed with money and possessions. Help those looking for happiness in wealth to see that You are what they are searching for. Amen.

The LORD is close to the brokenhearted and
saves those who are crushed in spirit.
PSALM 34:18 NIV

Some versions of the Bible provide a clue about when this psalm was written. They begin with an introduction: "A Psalm of David when he feigned madness before Abimelech, who drove him away and he departed" (NASB). You can read more about this time in David's life in 1 Samuel 21.

Psalm 34 is an acrostic poem. When written in Hebrew, the verses begin with the successive letters of the Hebrew alphabet. It is David's song of praise and thanksgiving for God's redemption. In some ways, it is like the book of Proverbs, because it teaches the reader about the character of God.

"The LORD is close to the brokenhearted and saves those who are crushed in spirit" (v. 18). This reassuring verse guarantees that God is close to us when we are sad. It promises to save us from despair.

Jesus restated these words in His Sermon on the Mount: "Blessed are the poor in spirit: for theirs is the kingdom of heaven. Blessed are they that mourn: for they shall be comforted" (Matthew 5:3–4 KJV).

Are you brokenhearted today? Is your spirit weighted down with despair? Then meditate on Psalm 34:18. Ask God for help. He cares about you! (1 Peter 5:7).

I am never alone, God. When I feel sad, You are with
me. You care for me and comfort me with Your Word.
Oh, what a loving Father You are! Amen.

～ Day 127 ～

I have no greater joy than to hear that my
children are walking in the truth.
3 John 1:4 niv

People speak of what they see others doing and hear them saying. John had received reports that his friend Gaius was living out his faith. So pleased was John over this that he wrote Gaius a letter in order to praise him.

First, John was pleased that Gaius not only was walking in the truth but was faithful to the truth. Second, John was delighted that Gaius was showing hospitality to those who were doing the work of the church. John encouraged Gaius to continue living in such a manner.

John wasn't encouraged, however, about something else he had been hearing. A man named Diotrephes was hurting the church with his bad behavior. He was engaged in gossiping and wasn't welcoming people. John condemned Diotrephes for his actions and wrote that he would hold him accountable.

While John took a few lines of his correspondence to address Diotrephes' situation, this letter really focuses on Gaius and the encouragement others were receiving because of his faithfulness.

Are we living out our faith in such a manner that others are uplifted and encouraged? Do our choices bring God joy? They're questions worth considering.

Lord, search my heart. Show me the ways in which
I am not uplifting others and, more importantly,
not bringing pleasure and joy to You. Amen.

"Take my yoke upon you and learn from me."
MATTHEW 11:29 NIV

The setting is Galilee, where Jesus meets John the Baptist's disciples. Their leader, in Herod's prison, wants verification that Jesus is the Christ of whom he has preached. Besides John's followers, there are many who come out of curiosity as well as need.

Standing with the gathered crowd, Jesus is moved by their burdened spirits. "For my yoke is easy and my burden is light," He adds, after calling them to yoke up with Him (v. 30 NIV). One imaginative writer described a hanging shopkeeper's sign that swung in the breeze, reminding Jesus of the sign outside Joseph's carpentry shop that read, *My Yokes Are Easy.*

A yoke is not worn by one animal—it unites two, to perform a task. For thousands of years the yoke was a symbol of labor and hardship; Jesus turns the familiar implement into a metaphor for uniting oneself with His heavenly Father. Such a union is a light burden.

In verse 28 Jesus tells the crowd that such linkage is available by coming to Him and accepting His way. In a team relationship with Jesus, one discovers His gentleness, humility, and rest.

Jesus, sometimes I try to carry the load all by myself.
I forget that by teaming with You the burden is
light. Together, we can do anything! Amen.

Wanting to satisfy the crowd, Pilate released Barabbas to them.
He had Jesus flogged, and handed him over to be crucified.
MARK 15:15 NIV

Pilate didn't want anything to do with this Jesus fellow. Even his wife had warned him not to get involved. So he stalled. Then he released a murderer and killed an innocent man.

Why? Because Pilate was a bad man? No. To please the crowd.

The people in the crowd, whipped into a self-serving frenzy, chose what they knew—a sinner like them—instead of reaching for something better. That's what crowds do. With few exceptions, most mobs appeal to the lowest in us.

We deal with crowds like that all the time, even though they might not be howling in the street. The "crowd" might be school friends who want to ostracize someone, the party crowd who wants you to get as drunk as them, even fellow church members who focus on earthly traditions above heavenly love.

As sociable beings, we often enjoy being in groups. Usually they're fun and harmless, and because of that, it's often tempting just to go with the flow. But when the crowd laughingly suggests something that makes your soul hesitate, ask yourself: Are you choosing Barabbas or Jesus?

I choose You, Jesus! When the crowd presses in
around me, desiring to drive me away from You and
Your teaching—Jesus, I choose You! Amen.

Surrounding the throne on each of its sides, were four living creatures covered with eyes in front and behind.
REVELATION 4:6 GNT

When John visited heaven, he saw four amazing "living creatures" surrounding the throne of God, almost like the majestic lions some kings used to keep chained near their thrones—only these bizarre beasts were unchained and far more majestic! One creature was like a lion, another like an ox, another like a man, and another like an eagle. Each beast had six wings and was covered with eyes all over its body—even under its wings!

These creatures are also described in the book of Ezekiel, where they are called *cherubim* and are described as having human bodies (Ezekiel 1:5; 10:1). Here too they are covered with eyes, even on their hands, wings, and backs. In Ezekiel's visions, instead of having six wings they have four wings, and *each* creature had all four faces: the face of a man, an eagle, an ox, and a lion (Ezekiel 1:5–10; 10:8–14).

Despite the striking similarities, there are differences. Either this is because the descriptions are symbolic (quite likely), or the living creatures, like other angelic beings, are capable of morphing (*also* quite likely).

These incredible heavenly beings are a testament to the unparalleled imagination and creativity of God.

Creator God, often I marvel at what man has made; but what is man when compared with You? I can only imagine the incredible things that I will see someday in heaven. Amen.

*Physical training is of some value, but godliness has value for all
things, holding promise for both the present life and the life to come.*
1 TIMOTHY 4:8 NIV

Without a dad to give him advice, it stands to reason that young
Timothy turned to his mentor, Paul, for direction in growing up as
a man. Unlike today, he would not have been confronted with the
desirability of a well-toned body and six-pack abs, or the testimonials
of weight-loss gurus.

To Paul, disciplines for athletes—primarily runners—are simple
and direct (see Hebrews 12:1–2). They often become metaphors
for the Christian life: run with patience, lay aside everything that
hinders, no one is crowned "except by competing according to the
rules" (2 Timothy 2:5 NIV).

A gym in the Northwest bears the slogan, "For now and the
future!" In other words, get started while you're young, and you'll
continue caring for yourself into old age. Paul's advice to Timothy
looks beyond today and tomorrow—into eternity.

In a letter to Timothy's home church in Ephesus, Paul wrote,
"Be strong in the Lord and in his mighty power" (Ephesians 6:10).
When he writes to his almost-son, the apostle is more specific—
training for spiritual strength has lasting results. Give consideration
to the "life to come."

*I am a Christian in training. Heaven is my goal, and You
have given me all the training equipment I need: Your Word,
prayer, and faith in You. Thank You, God! Amen.*

> *"But the Advocate, the Holy Spirit, whom the Father will send in my name, will teach you all things and will remind you of everything I have said to you."*
> JOHN 14:26 NIV

Jesus' earthly missionary journey was about to end, and in this passage the Master prepared His disciples for His departure.

The disciples were confused and frightened, so Jesus comforted them with words of assurance, comfort, and hope: "Do not let your hearts be troubled and do not be afraid" (14:27 NIV).

At first, Jesus' followers thought they would be left alone. But Jesus assured them He would send the Father's Ambassador to teach, direct, guide, and remind them of every word He had told them.

Jesus called the Holy Spirit "the Advocate," a translation of the Greek word *parakletos*: "one called alongside to help." It can also indicate Strengthener, Comforter, Helper, Adviser, Counselor, Intercessor, Ally, and Friend.

The Holy Spirit walks with us to help, instruct, comfort, and accomplish God's work on earth. Through His presence inside us, we know the Father. In our deepest time of need, He is there. He comforts and reveals to us the truth of God's Word.

Jesus is always with us because His Spirit lives in our hearts. No Christian ever walks alone!

Strengthener, Comforter, Helper, Adviser, Counselor, Intercessor, Ally, Friend—oh, Holy Spirit of God! Thank You for dwelling within my heart, guiding me, and drawing me near to the Father. Amen.

Even though I walk through the darkest valley, I will fear no evil,
for you are with me; your rod and your staff, they comfort me.
Psalm 23:4 niv

Do a rod and a staff sound comforting to you? These well-known Bible verses bring hope to many people, yet little is mentioned about the shepherd's tools—the rod and staff.

Sheep traveled into valleys for food and water, but the valley also contained danger. The high ridges created perfect places for lions and coyotes to wait to snatch an innocent lamb.

Anticipating new grass, sheep often wandered away where they slipped into swamps or fell down steep cliffs. Tiny flies bit their ears.

But the shepherd was prepared. He constantly watched over his flock for any signs of danger. With his tall staff and its crooked end, he could snare a sheep from a swamp or guide him in fast-moving waters.

His rod, a short stick with leather strips on the end, kept the flies and mosquitoes away—and could be used in cleaning and grooming.

As stubborn, somewhat dumb creatures, we (like sheep) get into dangerous situations in the valleys of life. But the Lord stays with us, protecting us from the nuisances, cleaning us of our sins, and redeeming us when we fall.

Lord, You are my Shepherd. You direct me where I should
go, steer me from danger, and rescue me when I stray.
You never leave me, and I am so grateful. Amen.

*"The blind receive sight, the lame walk, those who have
leprosy are cleansed, the deaf hear, the dead are raised,
and the good news is proclaimed to the poor."*
MATTHEW 11:5 NIV

What did Jesus say when the Pharisees and Pilate asked Him if He was the Son of God? Well, let's just say He didn't give them any answers they understood. Those powerful questioners were left deeply frustrated.

But when John the Baptist sent messengers to ask, "Are you the one who was to come?" Jesus specifically tells them about the work He is doing. Why the difference?

Well, the Pharisees and Pilate were asking for reasons of earthly power. They didn't really want to know the Lord, while John, helplessly chained in a cell, wanted nothing more. Within days of death and with doubts gnawing at his soul, John asked for words of comfort. Jesus' reply must have made the Baptist's beleaguered soul sing. This was what he devoted his life to! His Lord was walking on the earth!

Those ruled by earthly passions will never understand when Jesus speaks. But servants of God, no matter how desperately flawed they are or how foolish their questions might seem, can call on Him and receive an answer. It might be comforting; it might be challenging. You just have to be prepared to listen.

*My heart listens for You, almighty God. I question
You, and I trust that You will answer me. Prepare
my heart to receive Your words. Amen.*

*These commandments that I give you today are to be on
your hearts. Impress them on your children. Talk about
them when you sit at home and when you walk along
the road, when you lie down and when you get up.*

DEUTERONOMY 6:6–7 NIV

God's words in Deuteronomy were originally delivered to the people of Israel from Moses. These verses (Deuteronomy 6:3–9) later became known as "the Shema," meaning "hear" in Hebrew.

The Shema is one of the central points of the morning and evening Judaic prayer services. For Jews and Christians alike, it serves as a spiritual pledge of allegiance.

In verses 6–7, God gives us the ins and outs of His commandments in regard to our families. Check out God's desired time commitment: it's not what you would call hit and miss! These verses in Deuteronomy remind us that, like breathing, our commitment to God isn't haphazard—rather, it's a minute-to-minute lifeline!

Today, as we get up and lie down, may we also remember to commit to this pledge of allegiance as one nation under God.

*Dear God, I promise devotion to You every day of my life,
and I will do my best to honor Your commandments
all day, every day, morning to morning. Amen.*

[Jesus] replied to him, "Who is my mother, and who are my brothers?"
MATTHEW 12:48 NIV

That sounds a bit harsh. Disrespectful, even.

Jesus' family had heard of the crowds of people looking for healings. They were understandably worried. When someone announced their arrival, He asked this question that seemed to deny them.

Part of the importance we place on family comes from the fear of strangers, but each "stranger" is beloved by God. Jesus wasn't excluding His mother and brothers—He was expanding the definition of family. He goes on to say, "Whoever does the will of my Father in heaven is my brother and sister and mother" (v. 50 NIV). That's a pretty wide net to cast—but it goes further. Even those who haven't done the will of the Father can join the family if they repent.

The idea of a universal family sounds very "summer of love." The "flower power" generation grasped the concept of loving humanity, but they sometimes put more faith in sex and drugs than in God.

The idea of a family in which we are all God's children is like G. K. Chesterton's description of Christianity. It "has not been tried and found wanting, it has been found difficult and not tried." A true family of Christ is still possible. It begins when we lay aside fear and hold out a hand.

I am honored to be a member of Your family, God. Allow me to see beyond my own family and to reach out in love to all my sisters and brothers in Christ. Amen.

*After these things God tested Abraham and said to
him, "Abraham!" And he said, "Here I am."*
GENESIS 22:1 ESV

The command that follows this verse boggles the mind: God tells
Abraham to offer his son Isaac as a sacrifice.

Through Isaac, God had promised to give Abraham descendants
as numerous as the stars. Yet at God's word, Abraham prepared to
obey, trusting the Lord to raise his son from the dead (Hebrews
11:17–19). Why would God ask Abraham to do something He
later condemned (Jeremiah 19:5)?

Perhaps the answer lies in the test God was administering to
Abraham.

The word *tested* appears almost thirty times in the Bible. Job
expected vindication after God's testing (Job 23:10). Solomon said
praise tested a man (Proverbs 27:21). Paul told Timothy deacons
must be tested (1 Timothy 3:10).

Our confusion may be due to the use of the word *tempt* in
some versions, including the King James. In contemporary usage,
a temptation invites us to sin; a test proves knowledge we are supposed to possess. God knew the quality of Abraham's faith, but He
demonstrated it for future generations.

We can face life's tests with confidence that God expects us to
pass. He only wants to let us—and others—measure our faith by
our experiences.

*Sometimes, Father, I expect blessings to be showered upon me,
and often they are. But some of Your best blessings have come
through the experiences that tested and built my faith. Amen.*

*All Scripture is inspired by God and is useful to teach us what is
true and to make us realize what is wrong in our lives. It corrects
us when we are wrong and teaches us to do what is right.*
2 TIMOTHY 3:16 NLT

Many versions of the Bible use the phrase "God-breathed" to translate
this version's "inspired by God." We may hear these words and hardly
give them another thought. It is as if God breathed this scripture,
and then it was there. When we consider the Word of God more
deeply, though, we also remember that Hebrews refers to the Bible
as being "alive."

God's Word continues to be God-breathed! It is as relevant
today as it ever was! Scripture speaks to us in our current situations
just as it did to people a few thousand years ago. . .just as it will for
eternity. God speaks to us today through His Word and helps us to
know right from wrong. It is a powerful teacher.

Situations and cultures and languages and technologies have
changed all throughout history, but God has been able to speak to
people exactly where they are through His living Word. There is
certainly no other book, collection of books, or any other thing in
the world that can do that. . .only the living Word, which continues
to be God-breathed.

*Dear God, all things pass into history except for You and Your
Word. How wonderful it is that Your Word transcends time,
is relevant in the present, and will live forever! Amen.*

Precious in the sight of the LORD
is the death of His saints.
PSALM 116:15 NKJV

Benjamin Franklin said, "Two things in life are certain, death and taxes."

We can sometimes escape paying a tax, but we cannot escape death. Every one of us will die someday.

In Psalm 116, the psalmist tells of his cries to God for mercy. He cried out to God because he was afraid. "The cords of death entangled me, the anguish of the grave came over me" (v. 3 NIV). Then he goes on to praise God for saving him. We can't know if the psalmist was literally saved from dying or if his words were a metaphor. But we do know from reading Psalm 116 that God saves our souls from dying (v. 8).

The Twenty-Third Psalm holds the familiar words "Yea, though I walk through the valley of the shadow of death, I will fear no evil: for thou art with me" (v. 4 KJV). Through our belief in Jesus Christ, we know that we are saved; we become God's "saints."

Psalm 116:15 assures us that our transition from this world to heaven is precious in God's sight. God paid the price of our eternal life through the sacrifice of His only Son. In death, we have nothing to fear.

Lord, I must remember that I am not my body. My soul
lives within it with You, and after my body dies I will
live on in heaven as Your precious child. Amen.

*In those days there was no king in Israel; everyone
did what was right in his own eyes.*
JUDGES 21:25 NASB

Reading through the book of Judges conjures up scenes that rival some horror movies produced by Hollywood.

During the era of the judges, the Israelites bounced from one disaster to another while ignoring God's Law, only to be brought back into repentance when oppressed by an enemy. Hearing their cries for help, God would raise up a hero to rescue them.

This hero, or judge, ruled over the people and kept them in line until he died. At that point the Israelites again "did what was right in their own eyes," and the cycle began anew.

This situation is not unlike our own culture. Instead of using God's standard of right and wrong, today's society tells us to determine our own morals. Why? Because it claims there is no lawgiver apart from us, individually.

When each Israelite set his (or her) own criteria for right and wrong, tragedy and heartache resulted.

Ignoring God's standards didn't work for the Israelites, and it won't work for us today. It's wise to periodically examine our personal criteria of right and wrong to keep them in line with God's standards laid out in the Bible. Ask yourself, "Whose standards am I following?"

*Separated from You, Lord, the world is spiraling downward.
We are so in need of redemption! Send Your people to
redeem the lost. Save them from eternal death. Amen.*

Devote yourself to the public reading of Scripture.
1 TIMOTHY 4:13 NIV

Heard too often in some pulpits: "Because of a lack of time this morning, I'll eliminate the reading of my scriptural text and get right to my sermon."

Imagine how the apostle Paul might bristle over those words. He was convinced that the public reading of scripture had spiritual value. Unlike Shakespeare's plays, the power of the Word does not rest in acting or oral interpretation, but in the spirit of the words themselves.

There is nothing "hocus-pocus" about the Bible. Its power comes from divine inspiration (2 Timothy 3:16). Its words, hidden in a believer's heart, are armor against sin and a source of comfort.

These same attributes are ascribed to personal scripture reading, but when the inspired words are delivered aloud in worship with authority and unction, the Holy Spirit uses them to God's glory.

Listen to a reading of Psalm 23. Note how the familiar words can affect you. Observe how fellow worshippers are moved by the passage. Shut your eyes and give over your mind and heart to green pastures and still waters. Allow the spoken Word to lift your spirits and affect your outlook.

Agnostic author Pearl S. Buck commented, "My books will not last many generations, but scripture will be making a difference forever."

Lord, You are my Shepherd, and I want for nothing. You comfort me in lush, green grass beside clear, still water. How blessed I am by Your merciful goodness! Amen.

I pray that the eyes of your heart may be enlightened in
order that you may know the hope to which he has called
you, the riches of his glorious inheritance in his holy people,
and his incomparably great power for us who believe.
EPHESIANS 1:18–19 NIV

This verse is part of a letter written by the apostle Paul to the church in Ephesus. His letter addresses the mystery of God's power, forethought, and purpose.

Here, Paul prays for the eyes of our hearts to be enlightened. Could it be Paul was speaking from firsthand experience when he used the words *eyes* and *heart* simultaneously? Essentially, God performed spiritual surgery on Paul as he walked the road to Damascus. Not only did he receive a heart transplant, but his eyes were literally opened to Jesus (Acts 9:1–19).

Our heart is central when it comes to God. It's vital for not only our physical life but our spiritual life as well. It's the thinking apparatus of our soul, containing all our thoughts, passions, and desires. Why was Paul so anxious for Christians to make heartfelt spiritual progress? Because of the payoff! God freely offers us His incomparably great power along with a rich, glorious inheritance. We just have to see our need for a little surgery.

Instill in me a new heart, God. Fill it with Your unrivaled
power and love. Place within it the priceless gift of Jesus'
sacrifice and the promise of eternal life in heaven. Amen.

*"What do you mean by repeating this proverb concerning
the land of Israel, 'The fathers have eaten sour grapes,
and the children's teeth are set on edge'?"*
EZEKIEL 18:2 RSV

The Jews of Ezekiel's day were basically saying, "Our fathers sinned,
and we're suffering for their sins." They had it wrong. It wasn't just
their *fathers* whom God was punishing for their idol worship and
sins and disobedience. It was *them!* They were suffering for their
own sins because they were just like their fathers (see also Matthew
23:29–32).

The people of Judah were lamenting that they were innocent
but suffering for their ancestors' sins of hating God in fulfillment
of Exodus 20:5. They failed to see that by not loving and obeying
God, they too were part of the "hate God" generation and were
being punished for it.

God told them to stop using that proverb and declared that every
person would be punished for their disobedience or blessed for their
obedience. It didn't matter how bad a man's father had been; if that
man broke the bad habits he'd been taught, loved God, and did what
was right, he'd be blessed (Ezekiel 18:3–18).

We are the products of our upbringing too, but we can break
free of a negative heritage and love and serve God. We can make
the right decisions.

*Father God, You whisper in my heart what is right
and what is wrong. Help me always to make right
decisions that align with Your will. Amen.*

~ Day 144 ~

They were using this question as a trap, in order to have a basis for accusing him. But Jesus bent down and started to write on the ground with his finger.
JOHN 8:6 NIV

The confrontation between the woman caught in adultery and her accusers fascinates us. For one thing, the passage (John 7:53–8:11) isn't found in the earliest manuscripts. Another facet is the response of the Pharisees to Jesus' writing on the ground as they slipped away one by one.

Did the words He wrote convict? Did He remind them of the commandments they had broken?

Or did they recognize the handwriting?

God Himself wrote the Law on two stone tablets—not once, but twice (Exodus 34:1). The prophets later promised that God would write His Law on their hearts (Jeremiah 31:33) and on their minds (Hebrews 10:16).

The Bible refers to a record where "all the days ordained for me" (Psalm 139:16 NIV) are written. Only those found in the Book of Life (Daniel 12:1; Revelation 20:15; 21:27) will enter the New Jerusalem.

Most precious of all, God inscribes His name on those who belong to Him (Revelation 3:12; 14:1).

Praise God. He has written our names in His book.

You know me, Lord. You know even more about me than I know. Thank You for loving me and writing my name in Your Book of Life. Hallelujah! Amen.

Day 145

Now the LORD said to Abram, "Go forth from your country, and from your relatives and from your father's house, to the land which I will show you; and I will make you a great nation, and I will bless you, and make your name great; and so you shall be a blessing; and I will bless those who bless you, and the one who curses you I will curse. And in you all the families of the earth will be blessed."
GENESIS 12:1–3 NASB

Sometimes people say that world missions is a New Testament theme, not foretold in the Old Covenant.

Everything in the Bible should be taken seriously. Anything repeated is worthy of particular attention. Only a handful of verses are repeated three times. But five times in the book of Genesis alone, God says that through Abraham all the nations of the earth will be blessed (Genesis 12:3; 18:18; 22:18; 26:4; 28:14).

In reality, the foreshadowing of good news to the Gentiles is scattered throughout the Old Testament. Psalms is full of references to all the nations singing His glory. Jonah calls a non-Jewish people to repentance, while Ruth is a wonderful testimony to Gentile salvation.

*Heavenly Father, only when the whole world knows You
will our Savior come again. Sing to the glory of God,
all nations! Sing praises to His wonderful name. Amen.*

Then Peter came to Jesus and asked, "Lord, how many times shall I forgive my brother or sister who sins against me? Up to seven times?"
MATTHEW 18:21 NIV

Peter underestimates by some considerable amount in this verse. The Lord's answer is either seventy-seven or seventy times seven, depending on which version of the Bible you read (v. 22). Either way, it seems Peter was looking for an easy way out of the forgiveness question. And don't we all?

Perhaps a better question than "How many times shall I forgive?" would be "How many times would I like to be forgiven?"

If we live the biblical three score and ten years, that's roughly 25,550 days. Now we might be hard-pressed to sin when we are babies, but I'm sure most of us make up for that when we hit the teens. And many of us will live more than seventy years. If we sinned or had a sinful thought only once a day (and many would be glad to get off with that amount), then that's an awful lot to be forgiven for—way more than seven, Peter!

So how many times should we forgive our fellow sinners? Until we have forgiven once more than the number of times we will hope for forgiveness.

It's only fair, after all!

Lord, my heart holds tight to hurt feelings. But You have given me the capacity to forgive even the worst of sins. So help me to forgive those who have hurt me. Amen.

*Yet I will rejoice in the L*ORD*, I will be joyful in God my Savior.*
HABAKKUK 3:18 NIV

Habakkuk had grown weary of the tough times in which he was living. He wanted to know how long this would continue. So he took his complaints to God. When would the injustice stop? Why hadn't God answered his pleas for help?

God answered Habakkuk's grievance. Yes, He was aware of what was going on—and yes, there would be justice, and it would come about in *His* timing. Habakkuk's complaints switched to words of praise, which is amazing because nothing had changed. There still wasn't food in the fields or livestock or even buds on the fig trees.

Habakkuk wasn't the first person in the Bible to face dire conditions. Joseph was unjustly tossed into prison (Genesis 39:20); Daniel was carried off to a foreign land (Daniel 1:1–6); and David was on the run because Saul wanted him dead (1 Samuel 23:7–14). How is it possible that these men could praise God in the midst of such trying situations?

They must have understood as Habakkuk finally did that joy is found in Jesus Christ alone. Situations change and people come in and out of lives, but Jesus is always with us, all the time, all the way.

Sounds like a great reason to rejoice, doesn't it?

Dear Jesus, when blessings don't come when I ask for them, when I wonder if they will ever come, thank You for being the only blessing I need. Amen.

*Wherefore I put thee in remembrance that thou
stir up the gift of God, which is in thee.*
2 TIMOTHY 1:6 KJV

In his letter to Timothy, Paul exhorted his spiritual son to "stir up the gift of God" within. Literally, this directive meant to blow the coals into a flame as one would stir embers under a fire. A similar metaphor in Latin, *excitare igniculos ingenii*, means to "stir up the sparks of genius."

This passage is a reminder to every believer. It demonstrates that our God-given gifts remain strong only through active use and fostering. Gifts left unattended or unused become stagnant and, like an unattended fire, die. But if we continue to exercise the gifts God gives us, as in the parable of the talents, they will increase, strengthen, and even multiply.

Just as wood or coal fuels a fire, faith, prayer, and obedience are the fresh fuels of God's grace that keep our fires burning. But this takes action on our part.

Are you using the gifts God has given you? Can He entrust you with more?

Perhaps today is the day to gather the spiritual tinder necessary to stoke the fire of God within.

*God, You have given me special talents and inspiring gifts.
I pray You would open my eyes to sharing those gifts.
Through faith and obedience I will use them to serve You. Amen.*

*Brethren, I do not regard myself as having laid hold of it yet;
but one thing I do: forgetting what lies behind and reaching
forward to what lies ahead, I press on toward the goal for
the prize of the upward call of God in Christ Jesus.*
PHILIPPIANS 3:13–14 NASB

The apostle Paul possessed an extraordinary résumé. A "Hebrew of Hebrews" (Philippians 3:5 NASB), he traced his lineage back to Abraham, Isaac, and Jacob through both parents.

Highly educated, Paul belonged to the prestigious Jewish sect of Pharisees. Careful to keep the Law, he refused to adopt pagan customs from the surrounding Greek culture.

With misguided passion for his faith, Paul relentlessly persecuted Christians, "breathing threats and murder against the disciples of the Lord" (Acts 9:1 NASB). When confronted by the risen Christ, Paul redirected his religious zeal toward spreading the Gospel.

Although burdened with memories of mistreating Christians, Paul didn't allow his past actions to impede his service for Christ. Neither did he depend on his ancestry or lifestyle for special favors from God.

We cannot allow past failures to keep us from moving ahead with our God-given tasks. Neither can we glide along, resting on past victories and accomplishments or the laurels of family endeavors.

We live in the now. The past is gone forever, the future yet to come. "Press on toward the goal for the prize of the upward call of God in Christ Jesus" (Philippians 3:14 NASB).

*Father, how can I spread Your Word where it is most
needed right now? Tell me, Father! Amen.*

He went away a second time and prayed, "My Father,
if it is not possible for this cup to be taken away
unless I drink it, may your will be done."
MATTHEW 26:42 NIV

If you have a Bible printed in red and black ink, you probably know that the red words are those spoken by Jesus. In this verse, Jesus was in the Garden of Gethsemane, just hours away from His arrest and crucifixion. He prayed, asking God if there was some different way to accomplish redemption. In fact, Jesus didn't just ask it once—He made the request three times in Matthew 26. These red-letter prayers reveal the 100 percent human side of Jesus.

In one of His darkest hours, Jesus was overwhelmed with trouble and sorrow. He asked God for something that God would not provide. But Jesus, perfect and obedient, ended His prayers by saying, *"Your* will be done."

When we face our darkest hours, will we follow Jesus' example? Can we submit to God's perfect will, focusing on how much He loves us—even when His will doesn't match ours?

I wonder why You refuse when I ask for what I think is right.
But Your knowledge is greater than my understanding.
So Thy will be done, God; Thy perfect will be done. Amen.

Remember, it is sin to know what you ought to do and then not do it.
JAMES 4:17 NLT

"The road to hell is paved with good intentions." Wouldn't it be interesting to know what the context was when this proverb was written? It sure sounds like an adaptation of James 4:17.

We've all heard anecdotes about how numerous people stood by and ignored cries for help as a heinous crime was committed. Stories abound on the shocking apathy of human nature, just when it matters the most. And as we learn of them, we think, *I would never stand idly by and do nothing in circumstances such as those.*

And yet, how many smaller opportunities slip right past us as we fail to make the connection? How many times do we think, *It would be really nice if I did something for this person*, and then proceed to talk ourselves out of it? *They'll think this is silly*, or *They won't even notice*, or even *I don't have time.*

James warns us to stay focused on doing what's right. Regardless of our plans, we never know what the future holds. We never know when we will desperately need the intervention of a good deed from someone else.

*Dear God, today make me aware of little ways
that I can brighten the lives of others. Where You
see a need, Father, send me to fill it. Amen.*

"The greatest among you will be your servant."
MATTHEW 23:11 NIV

"If I won the lottery," a certain young boy said, "I'd hire a butler. Someone to do everything for me."

Ignoring the little matter of not being old enough to play the lottery, his father went straight to the more important problem of his son's selfishness.

"Oh!" the boy responded, trying to make his dream sound a little more generous. "Everyone could have one!" After a moment's thought, his fantasy expanded even further. "Wouldn't it be cool if everyone in the world had a servant taking care of them?"

"And whose would you be?" The father answered the son's confused look by explaining that if *everyone* had a butler or maid, then that would include the butlers and maids! The only way everyone could be pampered like that would be if all the people *with* servants also *were* servants!

Everyone taking care of everyone else—doesn't that sound like a Christian paradise? It only breaks down when people think they are too important to serve. But Jesus served us unto His death and beyond. And God has already done everything for us by giving us this world, this life, and the next.

We have already been served by the greatest. None of us is more important than that!

So whose servant will you be?

Jesus, I sometimes miss opportunities to serve You and others. Open my heart to the possibilities. Teach me to be a good servant. Amen.

Day 153

"You are my Son; today I have become your Father."
HEBREWS 5:5 NIV

No one knows who wrote the letter to the Hebrews. But one sure thing, its writer understood the supremacy of God's Son, Jesus.

The epistle's target readers were Jewish Christians who accepted Jesus as more than human but less than divine. Many were flirting with a return to Judaism, thus the description of them as "those who are ignorant and are going astray" (Hebrews 5:2 NIV).

As proof of Christ's sonship to God, Hebrews takes unusual effort to point out that Jesus wasn't assuming such a position; He was in God's great heart from the very beginning. He was the fulfillment of a prophecy recorded in the Psalms (2:7), reiterated in Hebrews 5:5.

Well-meaning witnesses may tell you that Jesus matured into sonship. Others feel He was a local kid from Nazareth who made good. Still others ignore Him completely—they couldn't care less. None of these are scriptural teachings.

Some of the most poignant passages in the Bible are when Jesus talks to His Father (Luke 22:42; 23:34, 46).

To a Roman centurion standing on Calvary that day, there was no question that the Man on the center cross "was the Son of God" (Matthew 27:54 NIV).

In the heart of every believer is the unshakable truth that Jesus is God's "only begotten Son" (John 3:16 KJV).

Son of God, You are so wonderful! How amazing
that God sent You to save me from sin. Jesus, You are
in my heart. I love You. I praise You. Amen.

"I sent the hornet ahead of you, which drove them out before you—also the two Amorite kings. You did not do it with your own sword and bow."

JOSHUA 24:12 NIV

Throughout the book of Joshua, Israel's armies fought the Canaanites in one battle after another. You could certainly get the impression that their swords and bows had a great deal to do with the conquest of Canaan. But wait! Almost every battle was accompanied by a miracle: collapsing walls, divine hailstorms, prolonged daylight—even God inspiring them to go on night marches and launch surprise sunrise attacks.

In addition, just before Israel showed up, God drove the Canaanites crazy and sent many of them fleeing from Canaan, driven out by massive plagues of hornets. No surprise. God had forewarned Moses *twice*, forty years earlier, that He would do that (Exodus 23:28; Deuteronomy 7:20). So when Israel entered the Promised Land, Canaan's armies were already depleted and weaker.

Why did God do these miracles? He wanted Israel to understand very clearly that only He could give them victory, and that they should therefore fear and serve Him (Joshua 24:8–14; 2 Chronicles 20:12, 15). God still does miracles to help us achieve our goals today, and His reasons are the same.

You are always present in life's big moments—those times when humans can only wait for You to give them victory. Thank You, God, for Your greatness and Your love. Amen.

So Jesus, when he began his ministry, was about thirty years old.
He was the son (as was supposed) of Joseph, the son of Heli, the son
of Matthat, the son of Levi, the son of Melchi, the son of Jannai,
the son of Joseph, the son of Mattathias. . .the son of Shem,
the son of Noah, the son of Lamech, the son of Methuselah, the son
of Enoch, the son of Jared, the son of Mahalalel, the son of Kenan,
the son of Enosh, the son of Seth, the son of Adam, the son of God.
LUKE 3:23–25, 36–38 NET

Have you ever wondered why God included such long and boring genealogies intertwined with the exciting account of Jesus' birth? To our Western ears they seem so dry and lifeless. But the Bible isn't just for modern Americans. It is a book for all humankind.

In many developing world cultures, one hasn't been properly introduced until a person's family lineage is known. It places a person into the context of both family and people. The genealogies aren't boring to them. Instead Jesus, Mary, and Joseph are revealed in their proper family setting. Isn't it great that Jesus is properly introduced?

Father, You have given me a lineage here on earth, but
more importantly a heavenly lineage. I am a child of God,
a daughter of the King of kings. Hallelujah! Amen.

"Heaven and earth will pass away, but my
words will never pass away."
MATTHEW 24:35 NIV

That's quite a claim for the penniless son of a carpenter. Listeners must have struggled to believe such an outrageous statement.

Since then, the world has changed with frightening speed. We live in an age where words zip around the globe in seconds, and opinions voiced by ordinary folk can be broadcast to millions via television and internet.

So how do the words of a "faith healer" from centuries before the printing press hold up to all that?

It's a safe assumption that if all the Bibles ever printed were still available, there would be one for every human being alive today—with plenty left over. The New Testament has been translated into half of the world's languages, but some 90 percent of the world's population can read those languages. The Bible can be accessed in Braille, downloaded from the internet, heard via audiobooks, and carried around in a cell phone. One hundred million copies are sold each year, and the average American home is estimated to contain four Bibles.

Heaven and earth are still around, but with many fearing that "pass away" thing. Meanwhile, Jesus' words go from strength to strength. It's time to accept that Jesus wasn't showing off. It's really time to commit.

Jesus, Your words are a priceless offering to the world.
I pray for the lost to come to believe in them as the
truth and receive Your gift of eternal life. Amen.

We do not make requests of you because we are
righteous, but because of your great mercy.
Daniel 9:18 niv

Many people know that Daniel saw visions of the end-times, writing dramatic prophecies in a Bible book that bears his name. Few probably realize that Daniel read the earlier writings of a fellow prophet, trying to understand exactly what was happening to his homeland.

Daniel lived most of his life in Babylon, having been kidnapped as a youth from a ransacked Jerusalem. But he faithfully served Israel's God in a pagan land—for which he was once thrown into a den of lions. (God, of course, protected Daniel from harm.)

When Daniel "understood from the Scriptures, according to the word of the Lord given to Jeremiah the prophet, that the desolation of Jerusalem would last seventy years" (Daniel 9:2 niv), he prayed a long prayer of confession for his people, who had sinned so badly and persistently against God that He had allowed heavy punishment to fall upon them. And in the midst of that prayer, Daniel uttered one of the great truths of scripture, the verse we know now as Daniel 9:18.

Let's understand, with Daniel, that we bring absolutely nothing to God. But let's also know, like Daniel, that in God's great mercy, He chooses to hear, love, and forgive us

Powerful God, Your great mercy is beyond my understanding.
I have nothing to bring You, yet in my sinfulness You hear
me, love me, and forgive me. Thank You, Father. Amen.

Finally two came forward and declared, "This fellow said, 'I am
able to destroy the temple of God and rebuild it in three days.'"
MATTHEW 26:60–61 NIV

What an impossible claim! Destroy the temple and rebuild it in three days? Accusations spread like wildfire.

The chief priests and Sanhedrin sought false evidence against the Lord to put Him to death (v. 59). They couldn't find any, so several accusers stepped up and told the assembly that Jesus claimed He could destroy and rebuild the temple in three days. The innuendo was unfair and inaccurate; the men clearly embellished the truth to give their accusations credibility.

The truth is, John 2:19 (NIV) records Jesus saying, "Destroy this temple, and I will raise it again in three days." Jesus spoke of His death and resurrection. The temple He referred to was His physical body, not the physical structure (John 2:21). He said this in response to the moneychangers who refuted Jesus' authority to cleanse the temple. So the Jews took what Jesus said literally (v. 20) and used His words to create unfounded accusations against Him.

Making a few minor modifications, we often take the most holy things or innocent people and build a case against them. But we are to seek and speak the whole truth, void of personal biases or prejudices.

The Bible says to add nothing to Your Word; the entirety of
Your Word is truth. When sharing Your Word with others,
God, may I speak only Your words and Your truths. Amen.

*I love the L*ORD *because he hears my voice and my prayer for mercy.*
PSALM 116:1 NLT

So many verses in the book of Psalms are songs of lament. Hurting, pain, struggle. . .certainly God understands these things. Some of these verses can be outright depressing if you really consider them for very long.

Psalm 116:1, though, is a wonderful short verse that should not be missed. It is neither lament nor praise, as are many of the other psalms. But it is a strong assurance of hope. Whether we are offering our praise to God or falling at His feet with our struggles, we know from these few words that God hears us. Isn't that mind-blowing? The almighty God of the universe who created and assembled every particle in existence hears us when we come before Him.

Maybe we go to the Lord, praising him in song. Maybe we spend some time reading and thinking about God's Word. Maybe we are praying to Him as we reach out for His comfort. Whatever we do, God hears us and is interested in what we have to say. Isn't that a great reason to love the Lord? May we never forget to give thanks to God daily for the opportunity that He provides us simply to be heard.

I have so many reasons to love You, Lord, so many
reasons to worship and praise You. How grateful I am
that You hear my voice! I love You, Lord. Amen.

∽ Day 160 ∽

*Herod feared John and protected him, knowing him to
be a righteous and holy man. When Herod heard John,
he was greatly puzzled; yet he liked to listen to him.*
MARK 6:20 NIV

John the Baptist was at Herod Antipas' mercy. Herodias, Herod's wife, wanted the Baptist dead, so her husband threw the prophet in prison. John shouldn't have lived as long as he did, but Herod "liked to listen to him."

Why? Because there is something in each of us that yearns for God. Our souls came from Him and long to be reunited with Him—even the souls of the "bad guys."

A tiny part of Herod must have hoped John would answer his questions and show him salvation. Sadly, Herod's trust in earthly power meant that would never happen.

John's was a voice "in the wilderness," not in a lush garden (Matthew 3:3 NIV). He didn't talk only to those who wanted to hear; he was compelled to address those who claimed they couldn't care less—people like Herod.

God wants the faithful, but He also wants the "godless." They'll struggle and fight against it, of course—but their souls cry out to be saved.

Look around you. Whose wilderness might you speak His love in?

*Dear God, lead me to the godless ones whom You know
I can help. Give me the perfect words and actions to
lead them to You and Your salvation. Amen.*

Do not be yoked together with unbelievers.
2 CORINTHIANS 6:14 NIV

History doesn't reveal much of the apostle Paul's social life. There is a tradition that claims he'd been married once and that his wife was not sympathetic to the demands of the Christian lifestyle. The Bible is silent on this phase of Paul's personal life.

What Holy Writ is not silent about is the difference between believers and unbelievers. Paul was fully aware of the world. He knew how pernicious worldliness can be. As oil and water do not mix, so too the attitudes of the worldly and born-again believers.

The apostle's warning is not necessarily limited to courtship and marriage. He was aware that the Corinthian church was infiltrated with unbelievers and troublemakers. The weekly love feasts and observances of the Lord's Supper were misused, and spurious philosophies were being advocated by not-yet-grounded newbies.

In no uncertain terms, Paul compares believers flirting with life outside of Christ as light to darkness, righteousness to wickedness, and Christ to Belial (6:14–15). His solution is this direct advice: "Come out from them and be separate" (6:17 NIV).

God, give us believers separate from the crowd!
A time like this demands strong minds, great hearts,
true faith, who need not the approval of the crowd.
JOSIAH GILBERT HOLLAND

I know it is possible for worldliness to turn believers away
from You, Father. Give me the strength to steer clear of worldly
perspectives and turn my thoughts toward You. Amen.

*"The foundations of law and order have collapsed.
What can the righteous do?" But the LORD is in his
holy Temple; the LORD still rules from heaven.*
PSALM 11:3–4 NLT

What does daily life look like when an earthquake rocks a third-world country, killing hundreds of thousands and leaving an already-desolate nation in ruins? When a tsunami sweeps away entire villages? When a hurricane flattens all within a one-hundred-mile radius of the shore?

Law and order collapse when natural disasters strike. The struggle for basic survival eclipses all else and creates a tremendous need for strong leadership. All too often, corrupt or inept governments are unable to meet the needs of their citizens when a catastrophe strikes.

Where is God when it hurts? Where is God in the midst of injustice? Does God care? These timeless questions never lose their relevance. The entire book of Job wrestles with these questions. The psalmist also picks up the lament and only responds that God is still on the throne.

We may never understand why bad things happen or why God seems to be silent. But we can know that regardless of the way things appear, our loving God is still in control—even when things appear to be spiraling out of control. How will you trust God today?

*Heavenly Father, I am always increasing my trust in You.
When bad things happen, I learn to trust You without
understanding. It is enough that You are in control. Amen.*

I am Alpha and Omega, the beginning and
the end, the first and the last.
REVELATION 22:13 KJV

Who said that Jesus is not deity? Over and over we find that the titles God gave to Himself in the Old Testament are being applied to Jesus Christ as well. In the Old Testament, the Lord God called Himself a shepherd, the Alpha and Omega, the Beginning and the End, and the Almighty. He is called the First and the Last. In the New Testament, we find the same titles given to Jesus.

This makes our God unique among the religions of the world. No other religion has a God whose Son is equal to the Father. The Jews and Muslims reject the idea of God having a Son. Only Christianity has a triune God—three persons in one God.

The Bible is unique, because in it God fully reveals who He is. Since Jesus is fully God, let this truth renew our hope and faith in our Savior. He who created all things out of nothing will re-create this world into a paradise without sin.

Jesus, I learn how to live by Your human example, and I
trust in You as my God—Father, Son, and Holy Spirit—
three persons, one God, one perfect You! Amen.

We love because he first loved us.
1 John 4:19 niv

Where does love begin? Love—that unselfish and unconditional emotion that drives us to our knees in worship, to forgiveness when broken, and to give to others beyond where common sense ends.

The Bible tells us we love because God loves first. Our love flows from God's bottomless well of devotion to us. He initiates the relationship He wants with us, drenching us with His love as He adopts us as His children.

We worry when we can't love others as He told us in the greatest commandment—to love Him and to love others. We can't do this on our own. But God loves with an everlasting love.

The power of His love within us fuels our love when human love is running on empty. He plants His love within our hearts so we can share Him with others. We draw from His endless supply.

Love starts with God. God continues to provide His love to nourish us. God surrounds us with His love. We live in hope and draw from His strength, all because He first loved us.

Dear Lord, the human love I know on earth cannot compare with Your love. When I feel empty, Your love fills me up. Your love is perfect. It never fails. Amen.

Sacrifice and offering you did not desire—but my ears you have opened—burnt offerings and sin offerings you did not require.
PSALM 40:6 NIV

Psalm 40 is a messianic psalm. The writer of Hebrews applied this verse to Jesus, saying, "We have been made holy through the sacrifice of the body of Jesus Christ once for all" (Hebrews 10:10 NIV). In quoting the psalmist, he said, "a body you prepared for me" (v. 5 NIV), instead of "my ears you have opened." That wording reflects the Septuagint (Greek) translation of the Old Testament.

However, Psalm 40 also applies to us. In saying God didn't desire sacrifices and offerings, David reflected a truth found elsewhere throughout the Bible. Rather than ritual religion, God wanted obedience (1 Samuel 15:22) and a broken spirit (Psalm 51:16–17).

God also wanted a willing slave. The Law allowed one Israelite to buy another with the understanding he would release him in the seventh year (Exodus 21:2). It recognized that the slave might choose to remain with his master. In that case, the command was "He shall take him to the door or the doorpost and pierce his ear with an awl. Then he will be his servant for life" (Exodus 21:6 NIV).

God wants to pierce our ears. After that, sacrifice and offering will come naturally.

Father, help me to be a willing slave to Your commandments and Your Word. In serving You, I will learn to sacrifice my own will and become accepting of Yours. Amen.

A Canaanite woman from that vicinity came to him,
crying out, "Lord, Son of David, have mercy on me!"
MATTHEW 15:22 NIV

One day Jesus and His disciples traveled north out of the borders of Galilee into the region of Tyre. When a non-Jewish woman, a Syrophoenician, heard that He was there, she repeatedly cried, "Lord, Son of David"—a common name for the Messiah—and begged Jesus to drive a demon out of her little daughter (Mark 7:24–30).

Many Christians are mystified by how Jesus at first ignored the woman, finally informing her that He was "sent only to the lost sheep of Israel," then comparing her to a dog—simply because she was non-Jewish (Mark 7:24–27 NIV). Mark clarifies this by stating the children of Abraham, the Jews, had to eat their fill first before the dogs could expect to share the food.

Jesus loves Gentiles; He was simply taking the Gospel first "to the lost sheep of Israel" (Matthew 10:5–6 NIV), "first to the Jew, then to the Gentile" (Romans 1:16 NIV).

The astonishing thing is that this woman was not simply a Gentile, but a despised Canaanite, yet Jesus even had mercy on her and answered her prayers. This gives hope to all of us.

Dear Jesus, You love us no matter where we come from,
who we are, or where we live. You give everyone the
hope of eternal life. Oh, what a Savior! Amen.

"As soon as you began to pray, a word went out, which I have come to tell you, for you are highly esteemed."
DANIEL 9:23 NIV

Daniel was an upright Jewish man, carried off into captivity as the Babylonians conquered Jerusalem. Enrolled in King Nebuchadnezzar's indoctrination program, Daniel spent three years learning the culture of Babylon before becoming one of the king's most trusted advisers. Living in exile for most of his life, Daniel nevertheless remained faithful to God, and his heart broke for the cumulative sins of the people of Israel.

In the middle of pouring out his heart to God one day, Daniel was interrupted by the appearance of the angel Gabriel. Bringing insight and understanding (v. 22), Gabriel's message contains the interesting concept that in the instant that Daniel began to pray, the answer was already on its way.

Before Daniel got past his salutation, God knew Daniel's heart and had already set in motion the response to Daniel's unfinished prayer.

As He did for Daniel, God knows our needs even before we give voice to them in prayer. We can rest in the knowledge that even before the words leave our lips, God has already heard them, and He has already answered them.

Thank You, God, for answering my prayers. Before the words leave my lips, You already have the answer. How great You are, God! I praise You. Amen.

Day 168

So Judas threw the money into the temple and left.
Then he went away and hanged himself.
MATTHEW 27:5 NIV

Judas has become known as the archbetrayer, but two people betrayed Jesus on the night He was taken. The other was Peter.

Judas identified Jesus in front of His enemies; Peter denied he ever knew Him, not once but three times. In terms of betrayal, both acts were horrible—yet Peter went on to do great works while his fellow member of "the Twelve" died in torment and disgrace. What made the difference?

Perhaps Judas sold the Lord for greed, or maybe he wanted to provoke Jesus into defeating Rome's rule over the Jews. Either way, he took matters into his own hands. Even after admitting his mistake, Judas still assumed control of his own life by ending it.

Peter, on the other hand, owned his shame—it appears in all of the Gospels—and stayed with the Twelve. He trusted in the Lord's redemption and was given great responsibility by the risen Jesus.

Judas betrayed the Lord but also himself, as we do when we take our lives into our own hands. There are more loving and capable hands awaiting, as a repentant and saved Peter learned.

I forget sometimes and try to control my own destiny. Forgive me, Father. Once again, I give You control of me, and I put my life journey into Your capable hands. Amen.

~ Day 169 ~

At this, Job got up and tore his robe and shaved his head. Then he fell to the ground in worship.
JOB 1:20 NIV

Grief expresses itself in different ways. When troubles come, some people spill copious tears, others burst with fits of anger, and a few simply shut down in silent numbness. In Western cultures, black is the color of grief. People wear white in oriental countries.

How did Job express his grief? He worshipped.

Job followed the traditional ways of mourning in his culture by tearing his clothes and shaving his head.

But Job also worshipped.

Despite the overwhelming darkness of shock and grief, he turned to God. He lay prostrate on the ground in front of the Lord, submitting his entire self. In his time of overwhelming loss and overpowering helplessness, he opened his heart to the only one who fully understood and could help him in his time of deepest need—God.

When everything in life seems gone, lost, or out of reach, God is waiting. God understands our sorrow and stays with us while we grieve. As we turn our hearts to Him in worship, His healing Spirit will provide comfort.

Sadness is a powerful emotion, Lord, but not nearly as powerful as Your love. I worship You for understanding, for comforting me, and for sharing my pain. Amen.

The person without the Spirit does not accept the things that come
from the Spirit of God, but considers them foolishness, and cannot
understand them because they are discerned only through the Spirit.
1 CORINTHIANS 2:14 NIV

In this passage, Paul divides humans into two classes: the natural
(the unbeliever, unrenewed through the new birth) and the spiritual
(the born-again believer, walking in full communion with God).

The natural man and woman may be extremely intelligent yet
fail to understand God's Word because it is spiritually discerned.
Consequently, the basic truths of scripture are hidden from them.
Natural instincts and worldly desires dictate their hearts, and spiritual things make little sense. So they are unable to comprehend the
magnitude of God's love and the power of His promises.

On the other hand, the spiritual person is focused on the thoughts
and will of God. The indwelling presence of God's Spirit leads,
guides, comforts, and speaks to the believer.

Jesus said, "Very truly I tell you, no one can see the kingdom of
God unless they are born again" (John 3:3 NIV). Only through the
new birth can we attain true spirituality. The moment we repent of
our sins and accept Jesus into our hearts, we become God's own.
And from then on, we begin to understand.

Heavenly Father, I know people whose hearts are closed to You.
They trust in absolutes and certainties. Open their hearts to
be born again, to understand, and to trust in You. Amen.

Then Jacob gave Esau bread and lentil stew; and he ate and drank, and rose and went on his way. Thus Esau despised his birthright.
GENESIS 25:34 NASB

The birthright, traditionally conferred on the oldest son, transferred the estate and management of the entire household to this son upon the death of the father. Esau's birthright, unlike others, also carried the lineage of the promised Messiah.

But Esau didn't care about God or spiritual matters. He loved hunting and often roamed the countryside looking for game.

One day Esau came in from a hunt totally famished. His brother Jacob had a pot of lentil stew simmering on the stove, filling the room with delicious aromas. Esau grabbed for a bowl.

Jacob shook his head. "First sell me your birthright" (Genesis 25:31 NASB).

Esau felt faint from hunger. The stew bubbled in the pot. He watched Jacob cut a thick slice of bread.

His stomach growled. "What use then is the birthright to me?" (Genesis 25:32 NASB). Esau sold his birthright for stew and bread.

What did God think of all this? "Make sure that no one is immoral or godless like Esau, who traded his birthright as the firstborn son for a single meal" (Hebrews 12:16 NLT).

At times it's so easy for us to trade eternal treasures for temporary comfort or pleasure.

I'm tempted sometimes, Lord, to desire worldly things that for a short while bring me comfort, joy, and peace. You are all those things now, always, and forever. Help me to remember. Amen.

> *"For the king knows about these things, and I am speaking*
> *freely to him, because I cannot believe that any of these things*
> *has escaped his notice, for this was not done in a corner."*
> ACTS 26:26 NET

Paul could speak boldly, because what had occurred twenty-six years earlier at the crucifixion was widely known, even among non-Christians such as the Jewish historian Josephus. He records in *Antiquities of the Jews:*

> *Now, there was about this time, Jesus, a wise man, if it be lawful to call him a man. . . . He drew over to him both many of the Jews and many of the Gentiles. He was the Christ; and when Pilate, at the suggestion of the principal men amongst us, had condemned him to the cross, those that loved him at the first did not forsake him, for he appeared to them alive again the third day, as the divine prophets had foretold these and ten thousand other wonderful things concerning him; and the tribe of Christians, so named from him, are not extinct at this time.*

Most in the first century accepted the historical fact of Jesus, but then, as now, many refused to accept His lordship.

Jesus, You are my Savior and also my Lord. I worship
and praise You, believing that You are the Risen Son
come to earth to save me. Thank You, Jesus! Amen.

He found a fresh jawbone of a donkey, reached out his
hand and took it, and killed a thousand men with it.
JUDGES 15:15 NKJV

God used Samson to provoke and judge the Philistines, who were ruling harshly over Israel. At one point, Samson set their fields on fire, and the Philistines responded by burning his wife. His own people, fearful of further violence, came to arrest Samson and hand him over to the Philistines. He agreed, but at the moment of handoff, the Spirit of God came upon Samson. He grabbed a jawbone of a donkey and wiped out a thousand Philistines.

How could that be? It was certainly the power of God that allowed one man to take down a legion of others. Sadly, though, Samson was dismissive of the things of God. He was a man of the flesh, a womanizer who never rose to his true potential—and he ended up praising his own strength and a lowly jawbone for the victory, rather than the empowering Spirit of God.

That's common for human beings. We'll all worship something—either the stuff of this world or the one who gave us this world by His power.

Which will you choose today?

Spirit of God, You empower me to make the right
choices and to do well. I worship You above all else!
All glory, praise, and honor belong to You. Amen.

*For we brought nothing into the world,
and we can take nothing out of it.*
1 TIMOTHY 6:7 NIV

Paul preached that "you can't take it with you" long before those words became a familiar saying.

In this letter, Paul addressed the issue of falling into the trap of believing that riches bring about a contented life. Paul reminded Timothy that one day people would leave their things behind. In addition, Paul warned that spending their time chasing after wealth was going to lead his flock into temptations that would have a domino effect in their lives. Soon they'd be more dedicated to their money than they would be to their faith.

Jesus also preached about the struggle the wealthy face when it comes to thinking about the kingdom of God (Matthew 19:16–30). The book of Ecclesiastes is full of the despair that comes from seeking after the wrong things.

Though we don't take anything out of the world, we do leave things behind, and not just material items. We leave behind the people whose lives we have touched for better or for worse. We leave behind the words we've spoken, which may or may not have been encouraging.

Finally, we leave behind the comments that others say about us, remarks that can show either our love for possessions or our love for God.

*When I leave this world, I want others to remember
me as a disciple of Christ who led others to Him.
Help me to live out that legacy, Lord. Amen.*

*"Circumcise yourselves to the L*ORD*, circumcise your hearts,*
you people of Judah and inhabitants of Jerusalem."
JEREMIAH 4:4 NIV

The ancient people of Egypt, Edom, Ammon, and Moab all practiced circumcision (Jeremiah 9:25–26), but God gave the rite to Abraham as a sign of the covenant between the two of them (Genesis 17:9–14).

Although circumcision is a physical thing, the Bible also speaks of it in metaphorical terms. When God called Moses to confront Pharaoh, he replied that he was "uncircumcised of lips" (Exodus 6:12, alternate NIV reading). Jeremiah accused the Israelites of having uncircumcised ears, incapable of hearing the Lord's message (Jeremiah 6:10, alternate NIV reading).

Moses pointed to a day like Jeremiah's, when the people would need to repent of their uncircumcised hearts (Leviticus 26:40–42). In Deuteronomy, God expanded on the concept of "circumcised hearts" by commanding the people to stop being stiff-necked (10:16) and to love the Lord with all their hearts and souls (30:6).

For Christians, the Holy Spirit circumcises our hearts at the new birth (Romans 2:29). He replaces our hearts of stone with a new heart and a new spirit (Ezekiel 36:26).

Everyone—including us—is prone to a stubborn persistence in our own ways. But if we renew our commitment to love God with all our hearts, souls, minds, and strength, we can "circumcise our hearts" and live.

Father, today I renew my commitment to love You with
all my heart, soul, mind, and strength. Your Spirit
dwells within my heart, and I am redeemed. Amen.

For in him dwelleth all the fulness of the Godhead
bodily. And ye are complete in him.
COLOSSIANS 2:9–10 KJV

Paul wrote the epistle to the Colossians to counter two forms of heresy that were making inroads into their church: on the one hand was an ultrastrict form of Judaism emphasizing tradition, circumcision, and ritualistic ceremonies (Colossians 2:8, 11, 16–17). On the other hand, an early branch of Gnostics were promoting philosophy, "secret knowledge," and asceticism (Colossians 2:4, 18, 21, 23).

Paul insisted that both of these extremes were missing the point. "Secret wisdom" and philosophical arguments were exalting themselves against the knowledge of God (2 Corinthians 10:5), and an insistence on keeping rituals and traditions was an attempt to say that faith in Christ was not enough.

Paul stated clearly that the fullness of deity lives in bodily form in Christ. He is God the Son, and when you have God in your heart, you are complete. You don't need anything added—whether ceremonies or so-called secret knowledge—to make you more complete. If the Spirit of Jesus Christ dwells in your heart and you are connected to God, you've got it all! Don't let anyone persuade you otherwise (Colossians 2:8). Don't settle for substitutes.

Jesus, You complete me. Since You dwell in my heart, I am
forever connected with God and heaven. I have all that I
need—salvation and Your perfect, eternal love. Amen.

Do not forget to show hospitality to strangers, for by so doing some
people have shown hospitality to angels without knowing it.
HEBREWS 13:2 NIV

Hebrews 13:2 is a verse about hospitality. This is just one of many illustrations of hospitality in the Bible.

Jesus and His disciples often relied on the hospitality of others for shelter and food. They traveled light, and they had few possessions. In the New Testament, Paul, Timothy, Peter, and John all wrote about the importance of hospitality (Romans 12:13; 1 Timothy 5:10; 1 Peter 4:9; 3 John 1:8). The author of Hebrews 13:2, possibly Paul, reminded Christians to extend hospitality to strangers. He suggested that some strangers might even be angels sent from God.

In Genesis 18:2–6, Abraham entertained three angels who appeared in the form of men. Daniel also wrote about seeing an angel who looked like a man (Daniel 10).

Today, most strangers to whom we extend generosity and hospitality are probably not angels, but we can't know if someday God will allow us to entertain an angel without our knowing it.

When you practice hospitality, God might be using you to minister to others. What are some other ways you can extend hospitality to strangers?

Lord, teach me to be wise when extending hospitality to
strangers. Enlighten me. Teach me new ways to minister
to others and show them Your amazing love. Amen.

"Power belongs to you, God, and with you, Lord, is unfailing love."
Psalm 62:11–12 niv

Sammy, the little boy next door, has begun school for special-needs kids. The other morning he was out front waiting for the bus with his mom. Sammy didn't want to leave his home, so his mom, Paula, was attempting to lift his apprehension: "I love you, Sammy. Just remember that all day long."

Today's fascinating verse is from a psalm of David, who was fully aware of his powerful and loving God.

His testimony? On a battlefield with a slingshot and five smooth stones: "The whole world will know that there is a God. . . . All those gathered here will know that it is not by sword or spear that the LORD saves" (1 Samuel 17:46–47 niv). Facing the end of his life: "If my house were not right with God, surely he would not have made with me an everlasting covenant. . .he would not bring to fruition my salvation and grant me my every desire" (2 Samuel 23:5 niv).

So, David, what makes you so optimistic? "Because our strong God loves me!"

Next-door neighbor Paula, why do you care so much? "Because I love Sammy and want him to be a strong man."

Reader, are you aware of our loving Father's strength? It's available to "whosoever believeth" (John 3:16 kjv).

*Father, strength isn't about muscles and physical power;
it's about the power You give me to conquer all of life's problems.
You are my strength. Without You, I am weak. Amen.*

Always learning and never able to come to the knowledge of the truth.
2 TIMOTHY 3:7 NASB

Beginning with the year AD 1, it took until 1500 for mankind's knowledge base to double one time. Currently it's been estimated that this base doubles every one or two years, and some claim this happens in less than twelve months.

Today we have 24-7 access to the internet, TV, and radio.

Medical breakthroughs have provided us with artificial knees, transplanted organs, and laser surgery. Modern medications treat conditions ranging from an annoying headache to an irregular heartbeat. New technologies have unveiled the complexities of the microscopic cell and peered deep into outer space.

Scientific discoveries have revealed the design and order of our world as never before. God's fingerprints are everywhere. Nonetheless, our culture spurns God along with His Son, Jesus.

Learning is good, but knowledge divorced from God is incomplete and leaves us vulnerable to false teachings and intellectual fads. The apostle Paul warns people "will turn away their ears from the truth" and "will turn aside to myths" (2 Timothy 4:4 NASB).

What are we to do? "Be diligent to present yourself approved to God as a workman who does not need to be ashamed, accurately handling the word of truth" (2 Timothy 2:15 NASB).

Beware of embracing any teachings that clash with God's truth in the Bible.

*All-knowing God, make me wise in Your Word. Give
me a discerning heart, and help me to filter false
teaching from Your faultless truth. Amen.*

As Jesus was getting into the boat, the man who had
been demon-possessed begged to go with him.
MARK 5:18 NIV

Almost all the Gerasenes wanted Jesus gone. The only one who
thought differently was a man who'd been living in tombs, someone
chains couldn't hold, an outcast from whom Jesus had driven a "legion"
of demons. This Gerasene had just been handed his life back, and
his response was to give that same life back to Jesus.

Jesus said no—and yes!

The man faced an all-too-modern dilemma. Letting Jesus save
our lives often involves a separation from the people around us,
the people who played such a big part in our "earthly" lives. In this
instance, these were people who valued their pigs above the new
believer's redemption.

Seems he wanted to turn his back to them, going instead where
he knew he was loved. But Jesus sent him back into their midst. It
must have been a lonely walk. Faith doesn't always put us where we
want to be—it puts us where we are most needed.

Left on his own, among people who didn't want to know Jesus,
this redeemed soul spread the word to ten cities—and "all the people
were amazed" (Mark 5:20 NIV).

Look around yourself—at your workplace, your friends, your
family—and ask, "Who could I amaze today?"

God, sometimes I feel uncomfortable with nonbelievers.
Teach me not to be shy about sharing Your Word.
Show me what to do and say. Amen.

"For I know the plans I have for you," declares the LORD, "plans to prosper you and not to harm you, plans to give you hope and a future."
JEREMIAH 29:11 NIV

When God promises something, He is sure to deliver.

Due to their sin and rebellion, the Jews were held hostage by Babylon. At the end of Israel's seventy-year captivity, Jeremiah prophesied that their deliverance was near. God promised that if the people would pray and seek Him with all their hearts, He would listen and be found (vv. 12–14).

In Jeremiah 29:11, the prophet's reassuring words of hope must have soothed and refreshed like cool water on parched lips. The same is true today.

Sometimes hope comes in the form of a second chance, easing our sense of failure. Other times it's clothed in the words of a doctor who informs his patient that a full recovery is near. Hope thrives in the fertile soil of a heart restored by a loving gesture, a compassionate embrace, or an encouraging word. It is one of God's most precious gifts.

God *wants* to forgive our sins and lead us on the paths of righteousness—just as He did for the Israelites of old. He has great plans for us. That's His promise, and our blessed hope.

Father, You provide hope when all seems hopeless. Trusting in Your plans for me brings me joy. My future is in Your hands, so how can it be anything but good? Amen.

Miserable comforters are ye all.
JOB 16:2 KJV

Those familiar with Job's story recognize this plaintive cry.

It was Job's description of three friends—Bildad, Eliphaz, and Zophar—who had originally come to sympathize with him. Days before, Job had lost everything but his wife in a series of freakish "accidents" orchestrated by Satan. The "perfect and upright" Job (1:1 KJV) lost all seven thousand of his sheep, three thousand camels, five hundred yoke of oxen, five hundred female donkeys—and worst of all, ten children—when Satan tried to break his faith. Shortly, again with God's permission, Satan would also take Job's health.

When the friends came to commiserate, they wisely sat in silence for seven days. But then they began to question *why* Job had suffered—ultimately concluding that Job had committed terrible sins. It wasn't long before Job uttered his "miserable comforters" quotation.

Many modern Bible translations have kept the King James Version's phrasing, while the New American Standard uses "sorry comforters" and the New Century Version "painful comforters."

Of course, none of those adjectives—*miserable, sorry,* or *painful*—actually go with the word *comforter.* When our friends are going through trials, let's make sure we're true, loving, and godly comforters.

*Father God, Comforter of my soul, when I am suffering
You know the perfect ways to console me. Please teach
me to comfort others with true, godly love. Amen.*

"Therefore, in the present case I advise you: Leave these men alone! Let them go! For if their purpose or activity is of human origin, it will fail. But if it is from God, you will not be able to stop these men; you will only find yourselves fighting against God."
ACTS 5:38–39 NIV

Peter and the apostles were preaching Christ. This didn't sit well with the Sadducees, who arrested them. They escaped from jail, were arrested again, and were brought before the Sanhedrin. They were sentenced to die after Peter boldly spoke of Christ's resurrection and said he would continue to preach about Christ because "we must obey God rather than human beings" (Acts 5:29 NIV).

Gamaliel, a highly respected Pharisee, addressed the Sanhedrin. He reminded them of the other men who had started movements or preached. Once those men were killed, their followers fell away. Yet Gamaliel's advice was to set Peter and the others free. Gamaliel believed that if Peter's actions were man-inspired, they would eventually fail. If, however, what Peter was doing was by God's hand, nothing would stop them. The Sanhedrin, realizing they'd lose in a fight against God, released the men.

When we face obstacles while doing the work God has called us to, we can press on, reassured in the knowledge that God's plan for our lives will always triumph.

Dear God, why should I worry when obstacles get in my way? You have a plan for me. It is a perfect plan, and nothing can stop it. Amen.

"See, I have engraved you on the palms of my hands."
ISAIAH 49:16 NIV

Have you ever had a bad day turn into a bad week. . .turn into a bad month. . .turn into a bad year? Judah was in the middle of one of those times. The storm clouds of impending judgment had begun to gather, and God was preparing to hold His people accountable for forsaking Him. Assyria and Babylon were growing in power, and it wouldn't be long before living in exile became the new reality for God's people.

In the middle of tumultuous times, it's tempting to proclaim that God has forgotten us. Both Israel and Judah struggled with the idea that God had abandoned them. But God took steps to contradict this notion. In an image that prefigures Jesus' crucifixion, God boldly proclaimed that His children were engraved on the palms of His hands. The nail-scarred hands that His Son would endure bear the engraved names of all of us who call upon Him as Savior and Lord.

God does not forget us in the midst of our troubles! It is His nail-scarred hand that reaches down and holds our own.

*Jesus, the scars on Your hands are because of me—a testament
to my salvation. My name is engraved on Your hand as
a child of God. Oh, thank You, dear Jesus! Amen.*

*"You have let go of the commands of God and
are holding on to human traditions."*
MARK 7:8 NIV

Despite this warning from Jesus to the Pharisees, very little has changed. Since then the church has been split by the traditions of men countless times.

One takes communion while another abhors it. One will ordain women priests, and that causes a walkout elsewhere. Some churches adhere to strict dress and moral codes, while others are open to addicts and criminals in whatever state of dress they can attend. Some prefer guitars, others prefer organs. And who do these divisions help?

Before we pass judgment, we might consider what Moses would make of the average American church service. He actually walked with God! Would he recognize our style of worship as correct?

Let's face it. If Jesus visited our place of worship, He wouldn't stop to see what the minister or priest was wearing. He wouldn't check if the cross was real gold or plate. He, frankly, wouldn't be interested in which prayer book we read from. He would want to know one thing: Do we hold on to the commands of God, loving the Lord our God and our neighbor as ourselves? It's a question that is much more important than any tradition—and one we should be ready to answer at any time.

*Lord, are You happy with my church? Is it a place that
honors and promotes You and Your commands? If not,
Lord, show me what to do and where to go. Amen.*

"Whoever hits his father or his mother is to be put to death."
EXODUS 21:15 GNT

Many find it difficult to love God after reading of the extreme violence in the Old Testament. The chapter where we find this verse gives us insight behind this violence. Here we find that God is not sending violence upon His people randomly. Rather, the people have agreed to the consequences outlined in the Mosaic Law in the chapters in Exodus and Leviticus. All the consequences of turning away from God and disobeying Him were laid out in advance, and the Israelites had agreed to abide by the contract.

We have a legal system of laws with their consequences too. If we apply for a driver's license, we agree to the laws and legal consequences regarding driving and the rules of the road. If we violate those rules, such as speeding through a stop sign, then we know we will bear the consequences if we get caught.

God was not being unfair when the Israelites suffered extreme hardships. It was all laid out in the Law. Let us not be surprised that what we sow, we shall also reap.

God, You are always fair and just in Your punishments.
I want to please You. Father, help me to sow wisely
so that I might reap Your favor. Amen.

Now standing beside Jesus' cross were his mother, his mother's sister, Mary the wife of Clopas, and Mary Magdalene.
JOHN 19:25 NET

The Gospels frequently overlap and record the same event from different witnesses' perspectives. Comparing this verse with the parallel verses in Matthew and Mark shows us something very interesting!

Many women who had followed Jesus from Galilee and given him support were also there, watching from a distance. Among them were Mary Magdalene, Mary the mother of James and Joseph, and the mother of the sons of Zebedee.
MATTHEW 27:55–56 NET

There were also women, watching from a distance. Among them were Mary Magdalene, and Mary the mother of James the younger and of Joses, and Salome.
MARK 15:40 NET

All three are essentially identical accounts, but compare the names of the women. By deduction, we learn that Salome was the mother of James and John. We cannot be absolutely certain, but it seems Salome was the sister of Mary, Jesus' mother. In other words, James and John were Jesus' cousins.

Isn't it cool that Jesus was a real person with an extended family just like us?

Dear Jesus, I love that You understand my human ways and my connections with family. Amen.

Love covers. . .a multitude of sins.
1 Peter 4:8 niv

It used to be a saying attributed to Shakespeare, but then someone discovered it in the Bible, and it's become a bit of a way out of a sticky situation—"Just love 'em to death!"

Commentaries vary in their interpretation of this verse. One writer quotes a *Life* magazine letter to the editor using that verse as a remedy for our wartime treatment of American Japanese: "We must learn to eat sushi." Bad hermeneutics!

The inspired writer of this chapter confronts the reader with suggested behavior for these "last days." It's an operations manual for godly behavior within the body, as well as toward those who have persecuted us.

In this particular scripture, the need for forgiveness and love is held up as a necessity for the times. These are the marks of a Christian: love each other deeply, understand that love forgives over and over again, and accept another's love and forgiveness.

Prayerfully read these verses: 1 Thessalonians 4:9–10; 2 Peter 1:7; 1 John 4:7. When these truths have sunk in, read Matthew 18:21–22; 1 Corinthians 13:5; Ephesians 4:32.

Now transfer these concepts to your family, to your place of employment, to your church. Talk them up. Believe them. Practice them.

Heavenly Father, teach me to love. I want to love in the best and worst of times and especially love those who are difficult to love. Please show me how. Amen.

For my people have committed two evils; they have forsaken
me the fountain of living waters, and hewed them out
cisterns, broken cisterns, that can hold no water.
JEREMIAH 2:13 KJV

God's people committed two fundamental sins: they turned away
from God, and they sought pleasure in idolatry and idolatrous living.

Through the voice of Jeremiah, God used the illustration of a
broken cistern to describe the fruitlessness of idolatry and the sinful
life. In ancient times, the people spent much time and effort digging
pits into the earth or rock to receive rain. Yet these cisterns cracked
with changing temperatures, leaving mud and filthy sediments at best.

Similarly, the world—even some Christians—hew cisterns of
wealth, pleasure, and prominence, thinking these elements contain
the waters that will sustain them and bring them happiness. Instead,
their unprofitable efforts leave them void and empty; or as the Lord
said, "Hath a nation changed their gods, which are yet no gods? but
my people have changed their glory for that which doth not profit"
(Jeremiah 2:11 KJV).

Jesus said, "For what is a man profited, if he shall gain the whole
world, and lose his own soul?" (Matthew 16:26 KJV). Living waters
flow from a personal relationship with Christ, for only He can quench
our thirst. Man-made cisterns become cesspools, but God's waters
are pure, sparkling with new life.

My Savior, Jesus, fill me up with Your living water. Quench
my thirst for You. Your water is refreshing, infinitely pure,
and always available. Thank You, Jesus! Amen.

And the word of the LORD came to him:
"What are you doing here, Elijah?"
1 KINGS 19:9 NIV

Isn't it surprising when God, who knows everything, asks *us* a question?

At the time God asked Elijah this question, He already knew what had brought Elijah to the point of such despair that he prayed to God to take his life.

God knew Elijah had just been victorious over the prophets of Baal. He knew too that Elijah had been threatened by Jezebel and was running in fear for his life. Despite knowing all this, God still asked Elijah why he was hiding out in a cave.

Elijah isn't the first person God has asked a direct question, knowing the answer. God asked Adam and Eve where they were even though He knew they were trying to conceal themselves from Him (Genesis 3:9). In their case as well as Elijah's, fear and despair had driven them to a place of hiding and shame.

Sometimes we live in a manner that causes God to ask us the question He posed to Elijah. Whether we're in a literal place we shouldn't be or our emotions have led us to a place of captivity, God wants us to stop and consider where we are.

Aren't you thankful He cares enough to ask?

Father, You always see me. To protect me from evil,
sometimes You ask me, "What are you doing here?" Help
me to stop, think, and act according to Your will. Amen.

*Jesus, full of the Holy Spirit, left the Jordan and
was led by the Spirit into the wilderness.*
LUKE 4:1 NIV

Jesus had just been baptized and received the ultimate accolade from His approving Father, God. Then He went into the desert. But He wasn't just wandering—He was deliberately led there by the Holy Spirit.

Forty days' worth of temptation! What would have been the point if there weren't at least a possibility that Jesus' human nature might have rebelled against His mission? In Luke we read of a few instances of Jesus resolutely defying Satan during this time, but He was out there for almost six weeks. Jesus already knew what awaited Him, and part of Him must have been sorely afraid—so the Holy Spirit immediately put Him to the test.

Those forty days, when Jesus might have struggled to remain resolute, give hope to the rest of us. He would have been scared, perhaps tempted—and there would have been doubts and the possibility of failure. But because of that experience, the Lord is able to stand right beside us, empathizing, when we face *our* testing times.

Turn to Jesus, because He knows what it's like—and He knows the way out of the desert!

*Jesus, You understand what it's like to be human and face
worldly temptations. Sometimes it's hard to resist! Please give
me strength to stand up to Satan. Thank You, Jesus. Amen.*

Your eyes saw my unformed body: all the days ordained for me
were written in your book before one of them came to be.
PSALM 139:16 NIV

The psalmist states it in a dozen poetic ways: God knows everything about us. He knows where we are at all times. He knows what we are going to say before we open our mouths. In fact, He knows every one of our days and has since before our conception.

The Bible talks about several people God set apart from birth: Samson, the first candidate for the "world's strongest man"; Jeremiah, prophet to the nations; John the Baptist, called to prepare the way of the Lord.

But God also knows the days of ordinary people. Job said, "A person's days are determined; you have decreed the number of his months" (Job 14:5 NIV). The same knowledge applies to our new birth. He created us anew in Christ Jesus for good works "which God prepared in advance for us to do" (Ephesians 2:10 NIV).

The God who knows everything about us still loves us. With the psalmist, let us declare, "Such knowledge is too wonderful for me, too lofty for me to attain" (139:6 NIV).

God, how can You know all about everyone who has lived or
ever will live? Your ways are so far beyond my understanding,
and yet You love me. You are so wonderful! Amen.

Our "God is a consuming fire."
HEBREWS 12:29 NIV

Fire signifies the presence, judgment, and holiness of God. Fire is a powerful image throughout the entire Bible, causing worshippers to approach the throne of the Lord with awe and reverence.

An Israelite, ready to make the perfect offering to the Lord, would bring the best lamb to sacrifice on the altar. The holy ritual of spilling blood and burning the fat of the animal in an all-consuming fire symbolized the cleansing of the worshipper's sin.

A consuming fire destroys everything. The massive destruction observed in fierce forest fires at first looks like complete annihilation. But soon signs of rebirth appear with shoots of green growth and the return of life. What was destroyed soon brings forth new life.

God's fire burns away our self-centeredness, ego, and sinful nature when we place our hearts on His altar. His love melts away our selfishness, pride, and anything that blocks His light from shining through our lives. Let the passion of God burn away our old lives, allowing His life to be reborn within us.

Lord, cleanse me of my sin. Burn away my old ways, and redeem me from the ashes. Create in me a new and holier life. Amen.

*He began by saying to them, "Today this
scripture is fulfilled in your hearing."*
LUKE 4:21 NIV

At the start of a mission that would change the world, Jesus declared Himself the anointed one in front of a hometown audience. More than a few jaws would have dropped, but the listeners were quite civil about it—until He wouldn't play the game the way they wanted. Then they tried to throw Him off a cliff!

These folk knew Jesus' parents, and they had known Him as a child. Now He was shaking their world.

People who come to faith later in life or Christians who find themselves in a faithless environment (perhaps in the workplace) face the same dilemma. It's difficult to stand up in front of people who know your shortcomings and say, "I am a child of God." Some will think you've flipped; others will poke fun. Who needs the hassle? It's much easier just to do good works and keep quiet, isn't it?

But that isn't what it's all about. God wants to be heard. Jesus spoke up—now God wants us to do the same.

Face others and tell them who you are. It won't be easy, but God will provide the courage. When you proclaim "the Lord's favor" (v. 19), the scripture is fulfilled in you!

*Dear God, take away any shyness I have about sharing
You with my family and friends. You are my Father,
and I am proud to let others know. Amen.*

He will not let your foot slip—he who watches
over you will not slumber.
PSALM 121:3 NIV

Have you ever stayed up all night studying for a major test, waiting for a loved one to come home, or rocking a sick child? The next day or two your mushy brain barely functions, and your body, drained of all energy, finds it difficult to focus even on the most important decisions.

You'll regain your balance and energy only after several nights of refreshing sleep. The human body requires regular periods of rest in order to thrive.

The Psalms tell us that God does *not* sleep. He watches over us, never once averting His eyes even for a few quick moments of rest. God guards our every moment.

The Lord stays up all night, looking after us as we sleep. He patiently keeps His eyes on us even when we roam. He constantly comforts when fear or illness makes us toss and turn.

Like a caring parent who tiptoes into a sleeping child's room, God surrounds us even when we don't realize it.

We can sleep because God never slumbers.

Dear God, how grateful I am that You never sleep. When
weariness overtakes me, You guard me like a mother who
watches over her child. I love You, Father! Amen.

"Very truly I tell you, unless a kernel of wheat falls
to the ground and dies, it remains only a single
seed. But if it dies, it produces many seeds."
JOHN 12:24 NIV

Jesus compared Himself to a grain of wheat to emphasize the necessity of His death, the power of His resurrection, and the incalculable regenerated souls gleaned from His sacrifice.

In nature, before a seed is sown, it lies on the barn floor seemingly lifeless. The grain of wheat is entombed within itself until—buried in proper soil—chemical agents begin to penetrate its waterproof coating. Soon, roots emerge downward as tiny fronds jet upward. And before long, the seed blossoms into towering stalks filled with innumerable grains of wheat.

This parable applies not only to Christ but to every believer. The apostle Paul stated, "I die daily" (1 Corinthians 15:31 NASB). Death to self means life to the Spirit. Jesus first had to die in order for God to raise Him from the dead. Similarly, we must die to self to experience resurrection life.

If we nurse our selfishness and refuse to deny self and all its trappings, we will never reach spiritual fruitfulness and maturity or win souls to Christ. But if we allow God to cultivate the soil of our hearts and minds, one seed will turn into many.

Lord, aid me in keeping selfishness from creeping into
my heart. Only when I am selfless can I experience the
fullness of Your love and Your teaching. Amen.

"But the one who stands firm to the end will be saved."
MATTHEW 24:13 NIV

In Matthew 24, Jesus describes signs of the end-times. His comments come just after His triumphal entry into Jerusalem and His condemnation of the scribes and Pharisees.

While the disciples admire Jerusalem's temple and the fine things inside, Jesus is unimpressed. When He tells them that the temple will be completely destroyed, the disciples are shocked. The temple is the center of their universe—its destruction equals the end of the world.

Later, on the Mount of Olives, the disciples ask Jesus when the temple will be destroyed and what signs will indicate the end of the age. Jesus warns them of deceit and wars, famine and earthquakes. Then He says, "You will be handed over to be persecuted and put to death, and you will be hated by all nations because of me" (Matthew 24:9 NIV). Imagine how the disciples felt about that—but in Matthew 24:13, Jesus gave them hope, saying, "But the one who stands firm to the end will be saved."

During troubled times, we too can find hope in Matthew 24:13. When we stand firm in Christ, we will certainly receive His promise of eternal life.

Father, only You know when the end will come, but until then I will stand firm in Christ and His promise of eternal life. Amen.

*The cows headed straight for the road to Beth Shemesh,
and went along the highway, lowing as they went, and
did not turn aside to the right hand or the left.*
1 SAMUEL 6:12 NKJV

In one battle, the Philistines defeated the Israelites and captured the ark of the covenant, which symbolized the very presence of God. Soon multitudes of terrified Philistines were dying from a plague, and the Philistines reasoned that they must have angered God and decided to send the ark back to Israel.

They built a new cart and hitched it to two milk cows that had never been yoked or pulled a cart before. They took their calves away and set the cows on the road to Israel. They knew that normally nursing cows would never leave their calves behind, so this was the final test: if the cows acted contrary to their nature and pulled the cart all the way to Israel, then God was the one who had sent the plagues.

Sure enough, the cows took the ark straight down the road, "lowing as they went." They were distressed at leaving their unweaned calves behind, but still they obeyed God. Sometimes, as Psalm 126:6 says, we too go forth weeping to do God's work—but when we return, we will be rejoicing, glad that we obeyed.

*God, sometimes You tug me in a direction I don't want
to go. Teach me to trust that You know the right way.
Show me that obedience leads to joy. Amen.*

*If anyone thinks they are something when they
are not, they deceive themselves.*
GALATIANS 6:3 NIV

Constantine the Great probably thought he was something special.
As Roman emperor, he was the most important man in the world.
Much as she loved him, though, his mother, Helena, may have had
a different view.

Constantine was the first Christian emperor, but he was often
more "emperor" than "Christian." His mother was a powerful influence in his life, and in the 1950 novel *Helena*, Evelyn Waugh portrayed her praying for help for her son. Her request would have
surprised many.

"May he, too, before the end," she said, "find kneeling space in
the straw. Pray for the great, lest they perish utterly." The "straw" she
mentioned was the straw around the manger, and by "perish utterly,"
she didn't just mean physically. Helena knew that being ruler of the
known world didn't guarantee a place in heaven.

Let's not deceive ourselves, thinking that money or position
makes us anything in the eyes of God. Some who are "nothing" by
the standards of the world might be everything in the heart of the
Lord. What matters in the end won't be the time we spent trying
to be something special. It will be the times we saw ourselves as
nothing without Him, the times we spent "in the straw."

*Heavenly Father, You have blessed me with accomplishments
here on earth—but what I have achieved is nothing without
You. All the glory and honor belong to You, my Lord! Amen.*

Pharaoh got up in the night, along with all his servants and all Egypt, and there was a great cry in Egypt, for there was no house in which there was not someone dead. Pharaoh summoned Moses and Aaron in the night and said, "Get up, get out from among my people, both you and the Israelites! Go, serve the LORD. . . ." Now the Israelites had done as Moses told them—they had requested from the Egyptians silver and gold items and clothing. The LORD gave the people favor in the sight of the Egyptians, and they gave them whatever they wanted, and so they plundered Egypt.

EXODUS 12:30–31, 35–36 NET

Skeptics claim there is no Egyptian evidence of the Exodus. Dating the Exodus is difficult. It probably occurred around 1500 BC, but perhaps several centuries earlier or later.

However, dating anything in Egyptian records is a mess. Each pharaoh had five official names, and subsequent dynasties would destroy records as political winds shifted. The Ipuwer Papyrus (about 1200 BC) records that the poor became rich, the rich became poor, "the River is blood," and famine and death were widespread. This seems convincing evidence of the Exodus, seen from Egyptian eyes.

I believe the Bible as truth, Lord. I need no evidence of the Exodus or any other biblical event. My proof is in You, the one who cannot lie. Amen.

Day 201

Woe to you who are complacent in Zion.
AMOS 6:1 NIV

"Call me what you will, but never call me lazy!" So said a local bank president whose enterprise was in shambles. The nightly news exposed his so-called laid-back and self-centered mode of operation. While bank investigators warned the bank's board that they were in trouble, Banker X brushed it off with, "Whadda they know?"

Ironically, a restaurant has opened in the space once held by that savings and loan organization. Its name is "At-EZ."

The prophet Amos pronounced a woe on all who were "at ease" and complacent in Zion. Later in this verse, Amos identifies those smug persons as "notable men of the foremost nation," but he declares that their ungodly, less affluent neighbors are better off than they are.

Complacency and laziness are not synonymous. The lazy person wants his comfort, to the detriment of responsibility. The complacent individual doesn't even care; he's self-satisfied—unconcerned.

Remember the old sermon story about the preoccupied bird pecking at a morsel on an ice flow headed for a massive waterfall? He waited too long to lift off, his feet froze to the ice, and over he went.

To you who are self-satisfied and complacent, Amos might say, "Wake up! Get with it! There's a waterfall ahead!"

*Lord, it means nothing when I am satisfied with
myself but everything when You are satisfied with me.
Wake me up! Send me out to work for You. Amen.*

Day 202

Lot lifted up his eyes and saw all the valley of the Jordan,
*that it was well watered everywhere—this was before the L*ord
*destroyed Sodom and Gomorrah—like the garden of the L*ord*.*
GENESIS 13:10 NASB

The available pastureland no longer could support the massive flocks
and herds of both Abram and his nephew, Lot. As a solution, Abram
offered Lot first choice of the surrounding areas. Abram would
relocate in the opposite direction.

Eyeing the best land, Lot moved onto the lush and beautiful
plains of the Jordan Valley.

But the inhabitants of this fertile area were "wicked exceedingly
and sinners against the L*ord*" (Genesis 13:13 NASB). When their
evil ways escalated to the point of no return, God destroyed the place
with fire and brimstone. Only Lot and his two daughters escaped
the destruction.

The ashen ruins of ancient cities dot the Jordan Valley. Still-
recognizable city walls and buildings have been transformed into
calcium sulfate and calcium carbonate ash, both by-products of
intensely burning limestone and sulfur.

Lot took what looked like the best. But he ended up losing
everything except what he and his daughters carried while fleeing
their city.

Sometimes there's wisdom in holding back.

Father God, help me to carefully weigh what looks
too good to be true. Before I make a decision, remind
me to hold back and seek Your will. Amen.

Then he turned to his disciples and said privately,
"Blessed are the eyes that see what you see."
LUKE 10:23 NIV

What would you give to have been down by the Sea of Galilee when Jesus was calling His disciples? "The Twelve" were blessed men to have been in the right place at the right time. It wasn't that they were particularly special—not until Jesus chose them—but no man or woman before them or since them has been as blessed.

The disciples were fortunate enough to see Jesus in the flesh, to live, eat, and walk with Him as a human being, something none of us will get to do. And they paid dearly for the privilege.

But Jesus' mission wasn't finished once the flesh was left behind. He would appear to the disciples and guide them as they spread the Good News in foreign lands, and He had also taught them to look for Him in "the least of these."

We didn't get to be part of the Twelve, but that doesn't mean we don't get to see Jesus. We just have to look in different places. Until we join Him in His eternal kingdom, we will see the Lord in the humble, the hungry, the lonely, the destitute—and our eyes will be blessed too!

Jesus, allow me to see Your divine self through the
world's humanity. Open my eyes to Your gentle
compassion, the truths of Your teaching, Your profound
forgiveness, and Your deepest love. Amen.

*"Look at the nations and watch—and be utterly
amazed. For I am going to do something in your days
that you would not believe, even if you were told."*
HABAKKUK 1:5 NIV

The prophet Habakkuk cried out to God, "Our Lord, how long must I beg for your help before you listen? How long before you save us from all this violence? Why do you make me watch such terrible injustice? Why do you allow violence, lawlessness, crime, and cruelty to spread everywhere? Laws cannot be enforced; justice is always the loser; criminals crowd out honest people and twist the laws around" (Habakkuk 1:2–4 CEV).

Do Habakkuk's words sound familiar? They were written about 2,600 years ago, yet they echo the cries of Christians today. "Lord, why won't You do something about the injustice and violence in the world?"

God answered Habakkuk: "If I told you how I'm going to fix this, you wouldn't believe Me." Then God allowed an evil army to cause even greater injustice and violence, but He promised to punish them in the end. This was not the answer that Habakkuk expected—or wanted.

When you become discouraged with the state of the world, meditate on Habakkuk 1:5. God is in control. He works all things together for the good of His people (Romans 8:28).

*Dear God, I worry that nothing seems to be going right,
but then I remember—You are in control, working it
all out for my good. I trust You, Father. Amen.*

The Lord turned and looked straight at Peter. Then Peter
remembered the word the Lord had spoken to him: "Before
the rooster crows today, you will disown me three times."
LUKE 22:61 NIV

What do you think Peter saw when he looked into the eyes of the Lord he had just abandoned? Remember, he lived in times when to betray your king was seen as treason, a crime that almost always brought a sentence of death.

In His time of greatest need, this particular King turned to His man and heard him lie, heard him put his own safety before his previously declared loyalty. The expression on Jesus' face made Peter run away. Not to hide or go into voluntary exile, but to weep bitterly, because, undoubtedly, he would have seen only love and understanding on Jesus' face.

In a way, it is necessary that we fail, necessary that we are broken down. How else do we come to realize that the things of this world will not sustain us? How else do we come to the place where God can build us back up?

Like others who betrayed their king, Peter died. Those bitter tears signaled the death of the man he thought he was. But the love of Jesus allowed him to be reborn as the Peter his Lord knew he really was.

Mighty God, I leave my old self behind. I shed my sinful
past and give my life to You. Shape it into something
grand, something that will bring You glory. Amen.

Whatever your hand finds to do, do it with all your might.
ECCLESIASTES 9:10 NIV

This verse is a call to excellence. Ecclesiastes 9:10 admonishes us to summon—with unwearied diligence—all of our strength and effort in whatever we have the opportunity or ability to do. Our first and best efforts should be made to turn away from and repent of our sins, to depend on God's wisdom above our own.

But this passage involves far more than spiritual determination. In a similar verse, Paul exhorted Christians to regard all work as a service to the Lord (Colossians 3:23). In essence, we are to think of God—not our earthly boss—as our employer. When we give, we give our best; when we work, we do so as if we were working for God Himself; when we pray, we pray with all of our hearts.

Meanwhile, God's eyes are open to our efforts. In biblical times, Paul admonished slaves to obey their masters and respect them, just as they would Christ. In doing so, the Lord promised to reward them for their obedience (Ephesians 6:5–9).

The call to excellence is clear: "So whether you eat or drink or whatever you do, do it all for the glory of God" (1 Corinthians 10:31 NIV). Do your best—and leave the rest to God.

Lord, please keep the thought fresh in my mind that whatever I do, I am doing it for You. Then help me to do my best. Amen.

We are therefore Christ's ambassadors, as though
God were making his appeal through us.
2 Corinthians 5:20 niv

Jesus is for everyone. There is plenty of room in the kingdom of heaven for everyone ever born; and to say that Jesus went out of His way to reach people wherever they were is an understatement. Jesus did everything that could have been done to offer hope. He performed miracles one after another. He healed the sick. He made the blind see and the lame walk. His teaching caused enormous crowds to gather as word of who Jesus was spread from region to region. He showed compassion to people, whether or not there were others around to witness it. Certainly Jesus knew how to reach people!

It may seem difficult to imagine that anyone could relate to the Son of God. How amazing it is to consider that while He was so far above everyone else, He humbled Himself and was able to relate to all people on a level that no one else in history ever could. Today as representatives of our Lord, let us never forget to be at peace with everyone so that they can see that love of Jesus shine through us.

Jesus, let Your perfect love shine through me.
Especially in turmoil and difficult situations,
allow me to be a beacon of Your love. Amen.

Day 208

Show me your unfailing love in wonderful ways. By your mighty power you rescue those who seek refuge from their enemies.
Psalm 17:7 NLT

David certainly wasn't feeling love and adoration from humanity as he penned these words—he was on the run! His prayer cries out to God for vindication and protection. And yet, in the midst of fleeing his enemies, David calls out to his God of unfailing love. Giving in to despair and frustration must have been tempting, but David kept his focus on God in the midst of a dangerous situation.

We may never find ourselves running from murderous enemies, but all of us have moments when the cards seem to be stacked against us. Sometimes the situation is a direct result of our actions, and other times we are left to struggle with the injustice of circumstances beyond our control. Whatever the scenario, we have a choice—like David—to remember God's unfailing love.

Today, look for the ways God reveals His love for you. It may be in a sunrise that takes your breath away, the scenery you encounter on your commute to work, or in an unexpected comment by a stranger. God's unfailing love is at work in your life in wonderful ways.

*Father God, remind me today of all the little ways
that You love me. Show me what I have missed, and
I will respond with worship and praise. Amen.*

*Gracious words are a honeycomb, sweet to
the soul and healing to the bones.*
PROVERBS 16:24 NIV

Remember this old nursery rhyme? "Sticks and stones may break my bones, but words will never hurt me."

It may be a classic poem, but it's simply not true. Harsh words spoken by another person do hurt, cutting deep into our spirits. They churn in the pit of our stomachs like undigested food.

But how sweet the taste of pleasant words. Encouraging and loving remarks give renewing energy that revitalizes the whole person.

Honey is a symbol of delight and health in the Bible. This proverb contradicts the old nursery rhyme—words coated with honey bring health throughout the body and soul. They provide healing to our wounds.

We often forget the immense power of our words in soothing another person's spirit—or in injuring with deep cuts. Passing on an overheard compliment, saying, "I love you," or writing that long-overdue note of appreciation transmits God's love through our words.

Choose your words carefully—and coat them with honey.

*Lord, words slipped from my lips that I wish to take back,
words that hurt You and others. From now on, I will think
before I speak and measure my words wisely. Amen.*

*And with your feet fitted with the readiness
that comes from the gospel of peace.*
EPHESIANS 6:15 NIV

Paul included footwear in his description of the armor of God. A Roman soldier's sandals were spiked to assure good footing. The spikes that allow God's warrior, "after you have done everything, to stand" (v. 13) stem from a strange place: readiness from the Gospel of peace.

Christians serve in the army of the Prince of Peace (Isaiah 9:6), and Isaiah also brings attention to their feet. "How beautiful on the mountains are the feet of those who bring good news, who proclaim peace" (Isaiah 52:7 NIV). In his exposition of the spread of the Gospel, Paul started with the feet of those sent with the Good News (Romans 10:15).

Here are some of the benefits of digging the spikes of our shoes into the Gospel of peace:

- Our minds are steadfast, firm, and unwavering (Isaiah 26:3).
- God is the driving force for all our accomplishments (Isaiah 26:12).
- God's love and peace will remain when everything around us falls apart (Isaiah 54:10).

Next time we face a spiritual battle, let's be sure to lace up our shoes.

God, I want my feet to be steadfast and swift. I want my feet to help me carry the Good News and to always be ready to defend it. Amen.

*Take away the dross from silver, and it will
go to the silversmith for jewelry.*
PROVERBS 25:4 NKJV

Silver is rarely found in the earth in a pure state. Generally when silver is dug out of the rocks, it's mixed with the sulfide ore of lead or other less valuable minerals. It then must be put through a refining process to remove the dross (the cheaper or worthless alloys).

There are a number of ways of doing this, but one ancient method was to melt the ore containing the silver in a furnace and add lead to the mix; the lead oxidized and worked as a flux to draw out the cheap alloys. The result was pure silver, which could then go to the silversmith to be made into articles of beauty and value.

The Bible describes God's people as silver and the Lord as a "purifier of silver" who puts them through the refiner's fire to remove the impurities (Malachi 3:2–3 NIV). If we endure the fire and allow God to purify us, we will be vessels fit for the Master to use (2 Timothy 2:20–21). If we resist the process, then the refining process is in vain, and we will be "rejected silver" (Jeremiah 6:27–30 NIV).

The choice is up to us.

*Almighty God, refine my sinful heart. Remove its
impurities and make it a place of cleanliness and
beauty, a place suitable for Your presence. Amen.*

∽ Day 212 ∽

Jesus said, "Father, forgive them, for they do not know what they
are doing." And they divided up his clothes by casting lots.
LUKE 23:34 NIV

They never accepted Christ; they worshipped pagan gods; they weren't
even very nice guys. There were many reasons why the soldiers who
drove nails through Christ's hands and feet and then hoisted His
cross high never should have met God personally. But Jesus asked
His Father to forgive them, even as they killed Him. If ever anyone
felt the full force of forgiveness, it would be those guys.

We will never be as forgiving as Jesus. That's a given. But we
are called on to try.

Take a few minutes to recall the people who've hurt you or
betrayed your trust. . .the ones you refuse to talk to, whose hands
you determinedly refuse to shake. Then ask how their sins stack up
against those of the men with the hammer and nails.

Forgiveness is one of the biggest tests we face in this life—and
one of the blessings we need the most. Can't bring yourself to do
it? Try imagining the faces of those arriving up above—like those
soldiers—to find your prayers have preceded them and they're
already forgiven!

Aren't those expressions worth the effort?

Father, as best as I am humanly able, I forgive those who have
mistreated me. I resolve to live with them in peace. I forgive
them because You have so generously forgiven me. Amen.

*"For I am the LORD your God who takes hold of your right
hand and says to you, Do not fear; I will help you."*
ISAIAH 41:13 NIV

Fear not! Do not be afraid! I am with you!

Hundreds of Bible verses address our emotions of fear, anxiety, and worry. Fear never discriminates and has held all of us captive at one time or another. Perhaps that's why verse after verse, God continually reassures us of His presence and offers us peace, as He has done for countless others.

God gave Moses and Jeremiah the right words (Exodus 4:12; Jeremiah 1:9), David the strength (1 Samuel 30:6), Solomon the wisdom (1 Kings 3:12), and Mary the courage (Luke 1:30) to rise above fear. But when we're clutched by fear, how do we follow their lead to trust God and rise above it?

Look at Isaiah 41:13. God is so tender here. He holds our hand and says four precious words: "I will help you." It's a direct invitation to hold on to God's hand and accept His help—or we can let it go.

*Take my hand, precious Lord, and help me. Allow Your
strong, yet gentle, touch to take away my fearfulness.
Hold my hand and lead me on. Amen.*

On an appointed day Herod, having put on his royal apparel, took his seat on the rostrum and began delivering an address to them. The people kept crying out, "The voice of a god and not of a man!"
Acts 12:21–22 NASB

Herod Agrippa was known for his eloquence and gracious manners, along with extreme vanity. Although he was Jewish, Herod's faith hinged on outward show rather than inner conviction.

Desiring to honor Caesar, Herod assembled a festival of exhibition games in Caesarea.

On the morning of the second day, Herod entered the theater wearing a garment woven from silver. As he spoke, sun rays illuminated his royal attire, spawning cries of "The voice of a god and not of a man!" from the audience.

Ascribing god status to the ruling class was nothing new. The Caesars often demanded worship.

However, Herod was familiar with Mosaic Law. He knew the Lord's command, "You shall have no other gods before me" (Exodus 20:3 NIV). Nevertheless, Herod accepted the adulation. As a result, God's angel infected him with parasites, and he died five days later, according to the Jewish historian Josephus.

Deliberately breaking God's commands is serious indeed. Heartache always follows, though not necessarily right away. Are you dabbling with something you know to be wrong? If so, there's danger ahead. Change course before it's too late.

Lord, please forgive me for those times when I've done what I know is wrong. Help me in the future to listen to Your warnings and resist temptation. Amen.

Sarah lived 127 years. Then she died in Kiriath Arba (that is, Hebron) in the land of Canaan. Abraham went to mourn for Sarah and to weep for her. Then Abraham got up from mourning his dead wife and said to the sons of Heth, "I am a foreign resident, a temporary settler, among you. Grant me ownership of a burial site among you so that I may bury my dead."
GENESIS 23:1–4 NET

As long as the Lord tarries, death will come to all of us and to our loved ones.

Abraham had to ask a stranger for land to bury Sarah. He purchased the Cave of the Patriarchs in Hebron for four hundred pieces of silver. Later, Abraham, Isaac and Rebekah, and Jacob and Leah were buried there too. Hebrews says Abraham died in faith without seeing the fulfillment of God's promise in his lifetime.

When we have the sad duty of burying a loved one, we know that God has something better in store: "And these all were commended for their faith, yet they did not receive what was promised. For God had provided something better for us, so that they would be made perfect together with us" (Hebrews 11:39–40 NET).

Heavenly Father, thank You for the promise of eternal life. I look forward to the day when I will be reunited with my family and friends in heaven. Amen.

When he had said this, he showed them his hands and feet.
LUKE 24:40 NIV

Promises are easy to make—and to break. If you don't manage to keep one (and you don't care about your word), you can retroactively change the conditions to make it seem that wasn't what you meant in the first place. There's always "wiggle room."

Think about Jesus, though. He could have summoned legions of angels to His defense, but instead He walked to a humiliating, awful death. After the Resurrection, He could have slipped the bonds of human flesh and returned in all His glory. But He didn't come to terrify or overwhelm—He came to keep a promise. Jesus was the embodiment of a promise of redemption foretold by prophets of bygone times. He was the promise that God would never forsake His creation, that He loved us all despite our failings.

The torn flesh of His hands and feet spoke without words. "Do you see how much I love you?" it asked.

Let's live the promise of our faith in such a way that when we get to heaven, God will say, "I saw how much you loved Me." Remember, when it came to keeping the most important promise of all, Jesus may have writhed, despaired, and cried out . . .but He didn't wiggle.

Jesus, You were true to Your word. You never backed out.
You always did what You promised. Help me to show my love
for You by faithfully honoring my commitments. Amen.

Day 217

A voice of one calling: "In the wilderness prepare the way for the
LORD; make straight in the desert a highway for our God."
ISAIAH 40:3 NIV

An ancient custom in the Near East required that a representative be sent ahead of a dignitary to prepare the road. He removed obstacles like rocks and boulders and filled in the potholes. Travel was easier when the crooked road became straight and even.

People wanted to get through the hot, parched desert quickly. Travelers were prone to injury while walking on the rocky ruts in the road. If they found the straightest route, they arrived quicker at their destination, often an oasis. Here they found cool, refreshing water and much-needed rest to regain their strength to complete their journey.

Our journey in life often veers into the valleys of spiritual dryness. We crave God's living water to quench our thirst, yet feel we are alone on a long, winding highway. We want to do what is right, but stumble over the uneven terrain.

God prepares our way for us and, through Jesus' death and resurrection, removes the obstacles and makes straight our paths. We may still have dry times, but we journey onward, relying on God's strength.

Dear God, like the pillar of fire in Moses' time, You go
before me and light my way. You make for me a straight
and even path. Thank You, Father God! Amen.

Be anxious for nothing, but in everything by prayer and supplication, with thanksgiving, let your requests be made known to God.
PHILIPPIANS 4:6 NKJV

The above verse is a clear echo of Christ's teachings. In the Sermon on the Mount, Jesus told us, "Do not worry about your life," and went on to explain that we shouldn't worry about where our food and drink are coming from or where we'll get the money to buy new clothes. Jesus concluded with "Do not worry about tomorrow" (Matthew 6:25–34 NKJV).

"Be anxious for nothing" sounds like great advice, but at times most of us have the feeling that it only works for highly mature saints and is not practical for the average Christian, who is, frankly, quite often anxious about today's problems and worried about today's troubles, such as upcoming bills and looming deadlines.

Yet the key to making it work is found in the same verse: we can "be anxious for nothing" if we are continually taking those problems to God in prayer, thanking Him for solving past problems, and trusting Him to work the current situation out. Praying about things, of course, shouldn't keep us from doing what God inspires us to do to solve the problems. But we should trust and pray instead of fretting and worrying.

Father, anxiety makes me weary. Today I ask You to take all my problems and work them out for my good. Show me the way, Lord, and I will obey You. Amen.

The light shines in the darkness, and the darkness has not overcome it.
JOHN 1:5 NIV

There is a belief that the natural inclination of the universe is to fall apart. The "law of entropy" states that everything ultimately fades and breaks down. Even the stars will go dark eventually. According to entropy, darkness wins.

The same thing, people say, happens in society—the general trend seems always to be downward. But that's not universally true. There is an alternative interpretation of John 1:5 (ESV) that says "the darkness has not overcome."

The enemy of darkness is God. He shines His life and light into each of us. With His help, we can banish the darkness from our families, our workplaces, and our neighborhoods. It's up to us to make things better rather than worse.

In space, the Herschel Telescope showed that fading stars are actually hurling bits of themselves out into the universe—stardust that coalesces to make new stars.

So maybe entropy and darkness don't win after all. Let's make sure they don't here on earth. As we pass through this world, let's spread as much "God dust" as we can so that new Christians will grow and shine—and the darkness will be more confused and confounded than ever!

Lord, I want to be a light in the world. I want to be a light for the lost and shine my light on the road to heaven. Amen.

God sets the lonely in families, he leads out the prisoners with
singing; but the rebellious live in a sun-scorched land.

PSALM 68:6 NIV

God understands what it's like to be lonely. If your biological or adoptive family has let you down, your circle of friends and your church family are also a part of God's plan for your life.

God knows what it is to be imprisoned under false pretenses. Sometimes our own rebellious choices lead us into a prison of our own making, and sometimes we find ourselves falsely accused by others. Regardless of how we arrive there, God promises to deliver us from our captive state, and He leads the way in song.

Most of the Bible's musical citations refer to humanity worshipping God through song. But in this verse (and also in Zephaniah 3:17), God's voice sings over us.

Close your eyes. Listen carefully. Do you hear God's song of freedom and salvation? He's singing to you. Consider that for a moment: God is singing to you. His musical voice calls you from captivity into freedom and from loneliness into loving community. Will you join Him in His song?

Dear God, how sweet Your song is for me! It takes
away the loneliness I feel. It reminds me that I am
Your daughter and that You love me. Amen.

He went there to register with Mary, who was pledged
to be married to him and was expecting a child.
LUKE 2:5 NIV

You probably recognize Luke 2:5 from the story of Jesus' birth. It's
an unassuming verse, one we might read without much thought.

Caesar Augustus decreed that a census be taken of the entire
Roman world, and everyone went to his own town to register. Joseph
and Mary traveled from Nazareth to Bethlehem, where she gave
birth to Jesus (Luke 2:1–7). Those are the simple facts.

The Bible doesn't tell us that the journey from Nazareth to
Bethlehem was almost a hundred miles. The route would take the
couple through rugged terrain, up and down steep hills. That must
have been a concern for the two, since Mary was nearing the end
of her pregnancy. The trip would take a minimum of five days on
foot; and at night, Joseph and Mary would need safe places to camp.
That Mary completed the trip is in itself a miracle.

Mary and Joseph aren't the only ones who have faced life's ups
and downs. Most people—spouses, friends, coworkers—experience
"rugged terrain" in their relationships. God understands! This entire
life is a journey of faith. When we're tired and face steep hills to
climb, He'll give us strength to persevere.

Lord, life's journey is sometimes like trudging up a steep
hill. I know that You understand. Take my hand and
walk with me. Give me strength to go on. Amen.

Though an army besiege me, my heart will not fear; though war break out against me, even then I will be confident.
PSALM 27:3 NIV

Although King David was a man of many faults, his love for and confidence in the Lord were undeniable. His assurance and faith were birthed from an intimate and ongoing relationship with God.

In Psalm 27, the psalmist-king bemoaned the actions of those who hated him and tried to kill him. Yet in the same pass of the pen, he acknowledged God's presence and power at work in his life. Undaunted, David pledged that no matter the circumstances, he would trust God—because he knew it was safe and wise to do so.

Overconfidence can be a problem, but godly confidence is essential in our walk with God. Without it, our faith falters. Trusting God with heartfelt assurance is an expression of that faith and indispensable to persevering despite the odds.

The more we seek God, the more our faith grows. We can be confident of that.

Father God, my confidence is in You. My faith grows stronger as I learn to trust You not only with big things, but also with the small details of my life. Amen.

The temptations in your life are no different from what others experience. And God is faithful. He will not allow the temptation to be more than you can stand. When you are tempted, he will show you a way out so that you can endure.
1 Corinthians 10:13 NLT

There have been times that we have looked around and wondered if anyone else has struggled with a particular temptation. The Bible says that Satan is the father of lies. He wants us to believe that we have extraordinary temptations, or maybe extraordinary weakness against certain temptations. But God's Word paints a different picture.

Sometimes we may be incredibly tempted to give in to sin. We may have weaknesses, and we may feel as if we fall flat on our faces in front of God way too often. But the Word of God assures us that there is nothing extraordinary about what tempts us.

Satan works very hard to tempt God's children. All of us! But we know from 1 Corinthians 10:13 that God has stepped in on our behalf and drawn a line that cannot be crossed. No matter how weak we may feel, with God on our side we can endure anything. It is so reassuring to know that God is there for us!

"Lead me not into temptation but deliver me from evil." Familiar words—but Lord, I rarely meditate on their deeper meaning. You are my leader, my deliverer, and my strength. Amen.

But they that wait upon the LORD shall renew their strength; they shall mount up with wings as eagles.
ISAIAH 40:31 KJV

Alternative medicine has entered the mainstream. Yoga, acupuncture, chiropractic—medical remedies that were scorned only a decade ago are now readily available in many communities. Unfortunately, one well-known verse in the Bible that's guaranteed to relieve stress is not getting the widespread use it deserves.

This thirty-first verse of Isaiah 40 is God's alternative medicine. As with any other cure, we must use it according to the doctor's orders. When we have lost the strength to go on, it's because we were not waiting on God. We did whatever the flesh wished to do. The flesh cannot give; it can only take away.

God's remedy is simple: wait on Him. Make time to sit and be quiet, to read the Word and reflect on it. Cut out the distractions and let God give you a message.

There's nothing quite as exhilarating as finding the Creator of the universe taking the time to encourage you to trust Him. To discover again that God is for us, not against us. We gather strength again because God has confirmed that He is with us on the journey. Now that's good medicine!

Dear God, quietly I wait for You. Remove all distractions that might keep me from hearing Your voice. Speak to me, Father. I'm listening. Amen.

Day 225

"We have come to believe and to know that
you are the Holy One of God."
JOHN 6:69 NIV

Jesus had just been deserted by many followers who found His teachings difficult. And though He already knew their answer, He asked the disciples where *they* stood. Simon Peter gave this simple but profound statement of faith.

The disciples were rough, realistic, working men, guys like Peter the fisherman and Matthew the tax collector, who otherwise would have had little in common. They had earned a hard living in a hard land and then walked away from those jobs to follow Jesus.

In doing so, they set themselves against their society's rulers—and made themselves enemies of the greatest military empire the world had yet known. They left their homes and families, and in many cases walked willingly down a road that would lead to execution.

These were ordinary men, like those you might find on a construction site, in an office building, or on a farm. What would cause them to walk away from all that they knew? What would make any twelve people you know do that? Only something very convincing.

Belief will take you only so far. But *knowing* will take you all the way. The disciples *knew*—and through this verse, we know they knew. That certainty is something to hold on to in moments of doubt.

Lord, do away with every sliver of my doubt, and
teach me to know that You are God—real in every way,
my Creator, my Savior, and my Hope. Amen.

*"Yet a time is coming and has now come when the true
worshipers will worship the Father in the Spirit and in truth,
for they are the kind of worshipers the Father seeks."*
JOHN 4:23 NIV

Our culture has created catchphrases with the word *worship*. "Worship
form," "worship function," and "worship songs" have permeated our
vocabulary in the church. We seem always to be looking for the next
best thing in our quest to worship God.

Straight out of His encounter with the woman at the well, Jesus
focused the discussion on the kind of worshipper God desires. Isn't
that an interesting idea: God has a specific concept of what true
worship should look like, and He has already defined it. There is a
certain kind of worshipper who captures God's heart!

True worshippers worship in spirit and in truth. We know that
Jesus *is* truth (John 14:6), and we know that the Holy Spirit lives
in us when we accept Christ as the truth (Ephesians 1:13). Worship
fulfills God's design as it acknowledges the "worth-ship" of God, as
revealed by Jesus and prompted by the Holy Spirit. This worship
captures His attention. No doubt it makes Him smile.

Does your own worship reflect spirit and truth? How have you
experienced God's smiling approval during your times of worship?

*When I worship You, send the Holy Spirit to lead me
in worshipping You in truth. Accept my gift of praise,
Lord, my Redeemer and my King. Amen.*

And ye now therefore have sorrow: but I will see you again, and
your heart shall rejoice, and your joy no man taketh from you.
JOHN 16:22 KJV

Knowing that Jesus is your Savior, do you ever get sad? With the promise of heaven ahead of you, do you ever get down and depressed?

Of course you do—and nonbelievers will use that as a weapon against you. "If you really believed you were saved," they say, "you would be singing and dancing all the time!" Churchgoers, while avoiding addressing their own failings in the matter, will tell you that joy comes—if only you believe harder!

One of the devil's most effective weapons is to make you believe your lack of joy is due to your own shortcomings.

But we are sad because we are broken. The Fall separated us from Love, and ever since then, in many and various ways, that sadness has been seeping through.

Here Jesus makes the beautiful promise, "I will see you again, and your heart shall rejoice." Our hearts will rejoice because Jesus is the Physician who will heal our wound. He is the Counselor who will restore us to Love.

Until then, if you feel a bit down, don't beat yourself up. Remember, there's a good reason for it—and it's all going to get much better soon.

It is part of being human, Lord, for sadness to seep
into my heart. But You are my joyful promise. I smile
when I remember that I will see You again. Amen.

For you have been my hope, Sovereign LORD,
my confidence since my youth.
PSALM 71:5 NIV

Internal clues suggest that the psalmist wrote Psalm 71 during a troublesome time. In the midst of recounting his situation, he asserted that God had been his hope and confidence since his youth. As Paul later outlined in Romans 5, his previous experiences built that hope.

Psalm 71:5 is an example of synonymous parallelism in Hebrew poetry. The two lines express nearly the same thought, the second expanding on the idea expressed in the first.

"You have been my hope": I have a trustful expectation that You will fulfill Your promises.

"You have been my confidence": I not only expect You to fulfill Your promises; I am certain You will.

Although translations alternate between "trust" and "confidence" in this verse, either translation is appropriate. Confidence makes a slightly stronger, in-your-face statement of trust. It's like looking at today's news in tomorrow's newspaper. The game is fixed and the outcome predetermined.

Confidence in the Lord allows us to face disasters without fear (Proverbs 3:25–26); to live in peace (Isaiah 32:17); and to approach God (Ephesians 3:12).

In an unpredictable world, we serve an unchanging God who has earned our confidence.

Father, in this ever-changing, fast-paced world, I find
comfort knowing that You never change. My confidence
is in You with a good outcome guaranteed. Amen.

～ Day 229 ～

"For David, after he had served the purpose of God in his own generation, fell asleep, and was laid among his fathers."
ACTS 13:36 NASB

The youngest of eight sons, David began life as the annoying baby brother to his siblings and the underrated child to his dad.

When the prophet Samuel invited Jesse and his sons to a special sacrifice, Jesse didn't think to include David until Samuel asked if there were other sons.

While delivering food to his brothers on the battlefield, David became incensed when he heard Goliath's boasting. But his oldest brother chided him, telling David to get back to his few sheep, a real put-down.

But God had a divine purpose for this boy's life.

God designed him with a natural talent for music and poetry, which David used to write many of the psalms. His God-given leadership abilities gave him success on the battlefield and later as king of Israel.

David desired to obey God but failed miserably at times. Yet God looked deep within David's soul and saw "a man after My heart, who will do all My will" (Acts 13:22 NASB). Despite the ups and downs, David accomplished God's plan for his life.

God has a tailor-made purpose for each of us too, and He's designed us with the talents and abilities needed to complete it. Exciting!

Thank You for the talents and abilities You have given me, Lord. I know they are part of Your plan for me. Help me to use them wisely and according to Your purpose. Amen.

Then the disciple whom Jesus loved said to Peter, "It is the Lord!" As soon as Simon Peter heard him say, "It is the Lord," he wrapped his outer garment around him (for he had taken it off) and jumped into the water.
JOHN 21:7 NIV

"As soon as Simon Peter heard"—in other words, he hadn't actually recognized Jesus Himself at that point. But he didn't need the evidence of his eyes. He only needed the merest possibility.

Peter had been stripped down for work, but he grabbed his coat or robe before launching himself into the water. Why? It wasn't going to help him swim faster. In fact, a heavy woolen garment was more likely to drag him down. So why did he take it with him? Because, there and then, Simon Peter had no notion of ever returning to the boat. He was *all* about getting to his Lord!

After the Resurrection, the disciples never knew when or where they might meet Jesus—and that's pretty much the situation today. The question of how we respond is still an important one. Will we be hesitant, asking for all kinds of assurances and looking around to see who is watching? Or will we follow Simon Peter's example, casting our so-called dignity to the wind, grabbing our coats, and diving in headfirst?

Jesus, call to me, "Here I am," and I will come to You. I come in faith, wanting to be near You, wanting to learn all that You have to teach me. Amen.

*The LORD said to him, "Who gave human beings their
mouths? Who makes them deaf or mute? Who gives them
sight or makes them blind? Is it not I, the LORD?"*
EXODUS 4:11 NIV

In Exodus, God asked Moses to complete some pretty hefty jobs.
Throughout chapter 4, we repeatedly hear Moses tell God why
God's plan won't work, finally stating, "Uh, Lord, You've picked
the wrong guy for the job. . . . You see, I'm not eloquent enough"
(see Exodus 4:10).

Did Moses really think this was news to God? God's response
in Exodus 4:11 is fairly chastising.

Often when God asks us to do something, we have a similar
response. We doubt, ignore, get angry, or even laugh (like Sarah in
Genesis 18:10–14). In our attempts to tell God why He's wrong,
God's response would surely be something like "I know you better
than you know you, so get on with it. . . . Oh, and don't forget. This
isn't a solo mission" (see Exodus 3:12).

Ironically, what *we* label impossible and imperfect is often God's
perfect way to execute His plans. It's up to us to make ourselves
available, remembering we're not alone.

*Father, I know that the impossible is possible when You
and I tackle it together. If You think I'm good enough,
then I am. I'm ready. I'm willing. Let's go! Amen.*

What is more, I consider everything a loss because of the
surpassing worth of knowing Christ Jesus my Lord, for whose
sake I have lost all things. I consider them garbage, that I may
gain Christ and be found in him, not having a righteousness
of my own. . .but that which is through faith in Christ.

PHILIPPIANS 3:8–9 NIV

Paul had room to boast. His Jewish heritage was unprecedented. He was a Pharisee and son of a Pharisee, raised under Gamaliel, the renowned teacher of the law (Acts 22:2–5). He was a zealous and devout "Hebrew of Hebrews" (Philippians 3:5 NIV), yet he surrendered his very birthright for the sake of Christ's kingdom.

This passage reveals the apostle's heart and the heartbeat of Christianity. Namely, when we surrender what we once treasured, admired, and highly esteemed for the sake of the kingdom, we gain far more. In verse 7 Paul explained, "But whatever were gains to me I now consider loss for the sake of Christ."

When the things of this world lose their luster and no longer compete for the throne of our hearts, we will attain all the privileges and blessings of a child of the King. But to know Christ's resurrection, we first must die to self. To gain the righteousness through faith in Christ Jesus, we first must consider our own righteousness worthless.

Lord, everything I have is worthless compared to You.
But I am the wealthiest woman on earth because I have
You in my heart and the promise of eternal life. Amen.

*Don't let anyone look down on you because you are
young, but set an example for the believers in speech,
in conduct, in love, in faith and in purity.*
1 TIMOTHY 4:12 NIV

In almost every aspect of life, age has its privileges. If we have any intelligence at all, we can't help but accumulate wisdom as we pass through this world. An older person will not necessarily be better educated than a young person but certainly *ought* to be wiser.

It doesn't work that way with faith. How did Jesus ask us to come to Him? Like little children! A long life can provide a longer walk with God, but we could live to be 150 and still not understand Him the way a child instinctively does. Much of the wisdom we gain comes through experiences we try to shed in an effort to get back to a purer, more innocent state. The poet Thomas Hood wrote, "I'm farther off from heaven than when I was a boy."

Young believers can be a reminder to the older generation of the joy and enthusiasm a pure faith can generate. And they have another important task; after all, "peer pressure" doesn't always have to be negative. The young are best positioned to bring other young folk to God, and that is work fully deserving of respect.

*Dear God, help me to rediscover childlike innocence,
the simplicity of faith without doubt. It is in that purest
form of belief that I am nearest to You. Amen.*

When Jesus heard this, he was amazed at him, and
turning to the crowd following him, he said, "I tell you,
I have not found such great faith even in Israel."
LUKE 7:9 NIV

It's hard imagining Jesus being amazed. Yet in the Gospel of Luke, that's exactly what happened.

A centurion had sent for Jesus to come to his house and heal his dying servant. Before Jesus could arrive, however, the centurion sent another message. He told Jesus he wasn't worthy to have Jesus come to his home and that he believed Jesus had the power to heal his servant from where He was. Jesus was moved by the centurion's faith. He was moved so much, in fact, that He spoke of it to the crowd gathered around Him.

The centurion wasn't the only one whose faith Jesus commended. There was the Canaanite woman who begged Jesus to heal her daughter (Matthew 15:22–28); the four men who tore through the roof of a house in order to get their paralyzed friend inside to see Jesus (Mark 2:1–5); and a woman who'd been bleeding for twelve years, who believed that by touching Jesus' cloak she'd be healed (Matthew 9:20–22).

Each one approached Jesus in a different manner, but all came to Him with a faith that He applauded.

Could Jesus praise our faith?

O Jesus, I have faith in You, but I want even more.
Increase my faith! Show me how to have faith
without doubt. Answer me, Jesus. Amen.

When I am afraid, I put my trust in you. In God, whose
word I praise—in God I trust and am not afraid.
PSALM 56:3–4 NIV

King David was forced to fight many wars. First King Saul's armies
hunted him. Then he was arrested by the Philistines. After David
became king, his land was attacked, first by the Philistines, then
by the Ammonites, then by the Arameans. In his later years, after
David had conquered all his outside enemies, his land was troubled
by civil war—think of Absalom and Sheba's rebellions—and other
conspirators were eager to end his life (Psalm 56:5–6).

David had many powerful enemies, and he was often tempted
to despair. David didn't say that he was *never* afraid, because that
wasn't true. There were times, when war loomed and his armies
were vastly outnumbered, when he *was* afraid. But David's key to
success was this: "When I am afraid, I put my trust in you." When
he trusted that God would be with him, David's courage returned
and he could declare: "I will not be afraid."

Most of us today don't have enemies out to kill us, but the
principle that helped David survive decades of opposition three
thousand years ago works just as well for us today.

God, in You I trust, and I will not be afraid. Trusting You
is the key to overcoming my fear. Trusting You makes
me strong. Yes, God, I put my trust in You. Amen.

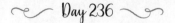

*When they saw the courage of Peter and John and realized that
they were unschooled, ordinary men, they were astonished
and they took note that these men had been with Jesus.*

ACTS 4:13 NIV

The priests and the Sadducees were among the most educated men
around and probably thought themselves the wisest. Yet here were
two "unschooled, ordinary men" leaving them lost for words. Faced
with the disciples' simple truth, the priests abandoned their supposed
wisdom and resorted to threats.

How did Peter and John come to have such an impact? Well,
codes have their cipher, treasure maps have their X, and every lock
has a key—somewhere. God created the universe and all the wisdom
these learned men hoped to attain. They studied ancient scrolls to gain
knowledge, but Peter and John had stood in the presence of God's
living key. Jesus opened their minds to what was real in the world.

We don't get to stand in His physical presence, but we do get to
invite Him into our lives—and with Him comes the key to understanding. So when you are faced with a worldly dilemma, step back
from conventional wisdom and forget about what others think you
ought to do. Consult with the Lord. The world won't always like it,
but they will take note that you too have been with Jesus.

*Jesus, my Teacher, You counsel me in worldly things and present
them from a righteous perspective. How wonderful that You
are willing and eager to share Your wisdom with me. Amen.*

"He must become greater; I must become less."
JOHN 3:30 NIV

John the Baptist knew exactly who he was and what role he was called to play.

When John's disciples complained that a new preacher, Jesus, was drawing followers from their group, John set his ego aside and said, "Jesus must become greater; I must become less."

John understood his call as the forerunner. His job was to prepare the way for the Messiah. He played second fiddle to the first chair.

Every orchestra needs a second fiddle (or trumpet, or clarinet) for the music to be complete. The lead in a play needs a supporting actor for the story to come across correctly. John prepared the path for Jesus then stepped out of the limelight.

Maybe we're feeling our call to serve Christ isn't good enough. Not everyone can teach or preach—but perhaps we can make coffee on Sunday or hand out bulletins before the service. Physical limitations may prevent us even from getting to church, but we can pray daily for others. Each role serves a purpose in sharing God's story.

John models the right attitude for serving God: we set our own agendas and egos aside. God's light shines through us more brilliantly when we become less.

Lord, put me where You need me most. Whether it be a lofty place or lowly, I am Your servant, ready and enthusiastic to serve. Amen.

What kind of people ought you to be?
2 PETER 3:11 NIV

The first-of-the-year weight-loss ads ask, "Are you the person you want to be?" followed by a commercial pitch about point counting or frozen meals by mail.

That's not the take-it-or-leave-it question asked in this verse from 2 Peter. In no uncertain terms it uses the word *ought*. No choice here. The apostle isn't asking, "What do you want to be when you grow up?" Neither is he giving you a cafeteria menu of options. He is confronting his readers with truth that has little wiggle room.

Today we realize that God's calendar isn't ours. Because Armageddon and our Lord's return have not transpired, does Peter's vision become any less important? Has the human race become any more Christlike? Are homes and families more secure? Have you noticed any slacking of evil? Is there less need for constant spiritual vigilance? Since the answer to all of the above is "no," it is obvious what kind of people we ought to be!

Because the world appears to be on a collision course with God's purposes, His people have to hold to a higher standard. Perhaps the kind of people we ought to be is best expressed by the apostle Paul: "You are God's children whom he loves, so try to be like him" (Ephesians 5:1 NCV).

Father, I am not all that I want to or ought to be.
I want to be better than I am—more faithful, more
in tune with Your will. Show me how. Amen.

(For the director of music. A psalm of David.)
How long, LORD? Will you forget me forever?
How long will you hide your face from me?
PSALM 13:1 NIV

David wrote many psalms, but others were written by Asaph's descendants (1 Chronicles 25:1–2; Ezra 2:41; Nehemiah 7:44) and the descendants of Korah (Psalms 42, 44–49, 84, 85, 87, 88). Most were written during the kingdom period; but some, such as 87 and 137, date to after the Babylonian captivity, in the time of Ezra and Zerubbabel.

Babylonian hymns to Marduk have been discovered that are shockingly similar to Psalms 6, 13, 51, and 69, some of the most beautiful psalms ascribed to David. Textual critics rushed to proclaim this proved that pseudo-Davids stole these from the Babylonians.

A little knowledge of history would have shown better. David wrote these psalms around 1000 BC, about four centuries before the Babylonian captivity. Psalm 137:3 (NIV) records that by the rivers of Babylon, "our captors asked us for songs, our tormentors demanded songs of joy; they said, 'Sing us one of the songs of Zion!'" It seems more likely that the Babylonians knew good music when they heard it!

Dear God, are my expressions of praise music to Your ears?
My words might not be eloquent, but they are sincere.
Hear my song, O Lord! I sing to honor You. Amen.

*I have fought the good fight, I have finished
the race, I have kept the faith.*
2 TIMOTHY 4:7 NIV

It's an ideal we all would aim for—but finishing the race isn't always easy. In 1992, Derek Redmond was determined to win the Olympic 400-meter dash. But less than halfway around the track, his hamstring tore, and Redmond collapsed in agony. Thousands of spectators—and a worldwide television audience—watched the other runners leave Redmond in their dust. But he picked himself up and hobbled after them.

The runner's tears and suffering were too much for his father, who ran out of the stands onto the track to help his son complete the journey.

We'll never know if Derek Redmond could have finished that Olympic race on his own. In his moment of direst need, he didn't have to depend on his own strength.

It's the same in the race for heaven. We might set out with our eyes on the prize, convinced our belief is unshakable. But there are attacks, traps, and diversions along the way. Our faith will take a beating—and might be in tatters as we approach the last lap. We might have to hobble, hop, and crawl just to glimpse the prize in the distance. Let's face it—alone, we might fail.

Leaning on our Father is the guarantee of crossing the finish line.

*Lord, I've done my best. I'm tired. My energy is spent.
There's such a short distance to cross the finish line. Carry
me, please—carry me over to win the prize. Amen.*

*I will utterly consume all things from off the land, saith
the Lord. I will consume man and beast; I will consume
the fowls of the heaven, and the fishes of the sea.*
Zephaniah 1:2–3 kjv

"Doom and gloom" is an apt phrase for the prophet Zephaniah's message. After briefly introducing himself as the son of Cushi, prophesying during the reign of Judah's godly king Josiah (v. 1), Zephaniah launches into a message of looming destruction at the hand of God.

Though Josiah, who became king at age eight, led a revival in Judah, there was still trouble on the horizon. Within a half century, invaders from Babylon would wreck Jerusalem and essentially wipe Judah off the world map.

Zephaniah's message—which may have hinted at that Babylonian invasion, the end of time, or both—is intriguing for its mirror-image deconstruction of creation. The prophet's order of God's "consuming"—man, animals, birds, then fish—is exactly the opposite of His creation of life in Genesis 1.

God can do whatever He pleases—whether creating an orderly universe out of nothing or consuming what He's made in a similarly logical order. But what God really desires is for "everyone to come to repentance" (2 Peter 3:9 niv).

*God, I've asked You "why," expecting some lengthy and
profound answer. But Your response is simple—because You
are God, You have the right to give and to take away. Amen.*

*Eliakim son of Hilkiah, Shebna, and Joah said to the chief
adviser, "Speak to your servants in Aramaic, for we understand
it. Don't speak with us in the Judahite dialect in the hearing of the
people who are on the wall." But the chief adviser said to them,
"My master did not send me to speak these words only to your master
and to you. His message is also for the men who sit on the wall."*
2 KINGS 18:26–27 NET

By the time of the Assyrian invasion, the nobles spoke Aramaic,
while the lower classes still spoke Hebrew. After Alexander the
Great's conquests, commoners spoke Aramaic while everyone who
was educated spoke Greek.

But the scriptures had been written mostly in Hebrew. If they
were not translated, then the people would lose touch with the Law.
The Septuagint was the first translation of the Bible into Greek.

Today there are seven thousand languages. Only 439 languages
have complete Bible translations. A billion people don't have the New
Testament and 250 million do not have a single verse of scripture
in their language. Ask at your church to see how you can make a
difference to someone who has never heard John 3:16!

*Lord, I will be a messenger for You. I will share Your
Word both near and far. Open people's ears to hear
it, Lord. Open their eyes to see You! Amen.*

~ Day 243 ~

"We cannot help speaking about what we have seen and heard."
ACTS 4:20 NIV

Anyone who doubts the Resurrection happened or doubts the power of the Holy Spirit ought to give some thought to this verse from Acts.

One of the men speaking here is Simon Peter. He is addressing the Sanhedrin in the same temple where, a short time before, he had cowered like a whipped dog, protesting he had no idea who this Jesus fellow was. Now he stands there as a miracle worker, having accused the priests of nothing less than the murder of his Lord. He isn't scared, and he isn't backing down. It's the Sanhedrin's turn to be afraid.

Peter's personal courage doesn't come into it, though. He literally can't help but speak because he has seen and heard things that put the powers and policies of the worldly rulers firmly in their place. And that place is an insignificant one!

The Peter who denied Christ never would have spoken like this if he didn't know he had a mighty ally behind, around, and inside him.

If you face it alone, this world can be overwhelming. You might cower, like Peter. But if you believe what he saw and if you claim the Holy Spirit as your constant companion, you can stand up to anyone—in Jesus' name!

I believe it, Jesus! You are the Son of God, the Risen Christ, the one who sent the Helper through whom I have strength to carry out God's will. Amen.

*"Be strong and courageous. Do not be afraid or terrified
because of them, for the L<small>ORD</small> your God goes with
you; he will never leave you nor forsake you."*

<small>DEUTERONOMY 31:6 NIV</small>

We find Deuteronomy 31:6 in a speech that Moses delivered to
the Israelites just before they entered the Promised Land. Moses
told them that he would not be traveling with them into Canaan.
God had chosen to replace Moses with a new leader, Joshua. The
Lord Himself would go on ahead with Joshua to take possession of
the land (Deuteronomy 31:1–7).

The Israelites worried that fighting might occur with the
Canaanites. In Deuteronomy 31:6, Moses encourages them to be
strong and trust that the Lord will be with and protect them. Many
times, Moses reminded the Israelites that they needed to trust in
God. These words are echoed in the New Testament in Hebrews 13:5
(NIV): "God has said, 'Never will I leave you; never will I forsake you.'"

It is interesting to note that conflict still exists in what was once
the Promised Land. As we face troubled times in the world, we can
find comfort in Deuteronomy 31:6.

*O God, You are the one who gives me courage when I
am afraid. Because You go before me, I can be strong
and go forward with confidence. Amen.*

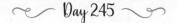

*Then Ananias went to the house and entered it. Placing his hands
on Saul, he said, "Brother Saul, the Lord—Jesus, who appeared
to you on the road as you were coming here—has sent me so
that you may see again and be filled with the Holy Spirit."*
ACTS 9:17 NIV

Ananias was a disciple of the Lord. This kind and faithful man had
heard of Saul of Tarsus and feared to meet him.

Saul (later known as Paul) murdered Christians—that is, until
Jesus visited him. The event left Paul blinded and traumatized. He
hid in the dark of someone's spare room and didn't eat or drink for
three days.

To Ananias, Saul must have seemed a wild and genuinely dangerous man, very different from himself. But because Jesus was
now in this man's heart, the first word Ananias spoke was *Brother.*

Paul must have wept.

It's a problem we still have. How can people so different from us
ever be like us? There are different rituals, languages, and interpretations. And then there are those outside the church but who
still believe. It's confusing and easier just to keep a safe distance
sometimes. No doubt Ananias felt the same. But if Jesus is there
in the hearts of these strangers, He expects us to call them brother
or sister—and mean it! Regardless of those annoying differences.

*Lord, help me to set aside the differences that obstruct my
relationships with other Christians. Anyone who has You
in their heart is my sister or brother in Christ. Amen.*

And so the Lord says, "These people say they are mine. They honor me with their lips, but their hearts are far from me. And their worship of me is nothing but man-made rules learned by rote."
ISAIAH 29:13 NLT

Think of one of the Christian creeds or prayers that you have committed to memory. Perhaps it's the Lord's Prayer; maybe you learned the Apostles' Creed in a catechism class. Now, consider the last time you were invited to recite it. Did you savor each word as it was spoken, reflecting anew on its meaning, or was the experience more of a rote recitation?

From God's perspective, the actions of our hearts speak louder than our words. And if our worship consists of mindlessly repeating words and going with the flow, we are missing out on connecting with a God who fiercely loves us and desires to be in an unscripted relationship with us.

This verse carries a sobering reminder that God looks beyond the words of our mouths and considers the heart that utters them. Creeds and prayers are familiar ways to connect with God and serve as wonderful reminders of His steadfast character. The next time an opportunity arises to recite from memory, consider how to bring the well-known words to life in a new and fresh telling—spoken from the heart.

Father, when I read the Bible I will savor each word and consider its meaning. And when I pray a familiar prayer, I will pray from my heart. Amen.

But God demonstrates his own love for us in this:
While we were still sinners, Christ died for us.
ROMANS 5:8 NIV

"While we were still sinners"! . . .

In other words, God gave His Son to die for a bunch of folks who didn't even deserve it! Did He already know how that would turn out? You would think so, but isn't there a spiritual war going on? Don't people turn from God all the time? What if the disciples had simply run away and hidden?

Maybe God took a huge chance with us.

When someone holds out a begging hand to us, when a relative asks for help, when we spot something we could do for a neighbor, we don't just rush in there. We weigh the options: What will they do with what I give them? Are they worth my time and effort? If I do it now, won't I just have to do it again later? Then we help or walk on by.

God could have answered those questions, "Many will despise what I give them, time and time again they have rejected Me, and they will still be crucifying My Son two thousand years later."

The next time you find yourself deciding whether to help someone, remember, we did not deserve His sacrifice—but He gave it anyway!

Jesus, You generously gave Your life for me—someone undeserving
of Your sacrifice. When someone whom I feel is undeserving
asks for my help, I will remember what You did for me. Amen.

The LORD is slow to anger but great in power; the LORD will not leave the guilty unpunished. His way is in the whirlwind and the storm, and clouds are the dust of his feet.

NAHUM 1:3 NIV

Clouds always point to God's power. He created the clouds. God resides within and beyond the heavens. As this verse tells us, the Lord is so huge, the clouds are merely the dust of His feet.

By watching clouds, we see hints of God's presence. We see God as the Creator when we imagine the different shapes of clouds to resemble animals, funny faces, and flocks of sheep.

Storm clouds remind us that God is also powerful. During the raging winds, crashing thunder, and startling lightning, our fear grows. The devastating violence of a storm can obliterate everything in its path. Is this the same playful God we remember on fair-weather days?

But God is very patient. He waits in His unhurried way for us to acknowledge Him as our King and Savior. He welcomes us back into His arms. He invites us to look up at the clouds in His heaven and understand His many sides—powerful, creative, and loving.

Lord, I look up and see You in the clouds, the sunshine, and the stars. What wonders lie beyond them? Someday I will see You in Your heaven. Amen.

O death, where is thy sting? O grave, where is thy victory?
1 Corinthians 15:55 kjv

This verse personifies both death and the grave. In ancient paintings, death is sometimes depicted as a crowned skeleton with a dart in his hand. Like an ox goad, the dart's sharp point continually irritates and taunts.

The apostle Paul explains that the sting of death is sin, and sin is the parent of death. Yet through the death and resurrection of Christ, we have atonement for our sins. So Christians no longer need to fear death and the grave. Or as Paul said, "But thanks be to God, which giveth us the victory through our Lord Jesus Christ" (v. 57 kjv).

Earlier in this passage, Paul declared that when Jesus returns all believers—alive and dead—will receive new, glorified bodies that are imperishable and immortal (vv. 50–54).

So the question in 1 Corinthians 15:55 is rhetorical. Because of Christ, the deadly darts of sin no longer hold sway over us. Sin has lost its power, death has no sting, and our shackles are loosed! We have nothing to fear and everything to gain.

Thank You, Jesus, for taking away the fear of death.
In death, there is no pain or darkness. Death is only a
glorious portal—the welcome entrance to heaven! Amen.

*I do not understand what I do. For what I want
to do I do not do, but what I hate I do.*
ROMANS 7:15 NIV

Who is this weak-willed, indecisive wimp? Has he no faith, no
moral fiber?

Actually he was the worldwide leader of the early church, and
this verse comes from his letter to Christians in Rome. So what kind
of impression was he giving them?

He was laying out the harsh reality that faith does not make us
perfect. Paul lived, suffered, and died for his adoration of the Lord,
but in day-to-day life he frequently and consistently failed to live
up to his own ideal. That's because his ideal life was Christ's, and
no one could live up to *that* example.

Still he tried, because while his body belonged to sin, his soul
belonged to the Lord—and his mind was the general directing the
battle between the two.

It can be disheartening to fail. Some people fall away from faith
because of failure. But here is the remedy to that situation. In your
struggle, you are no better or worse than Saint Paul. Thankfully,
your ultimate success won't be measured by the number of times
you fall; it will depend entirely on the number of times you reach
for Jesus to help you back up.

*I struggle with perfection, Lord. I try my best and
still I fail. But my best is good enough for You!
Teach me not to be so hard on myself. Amen.*

*The heavens declare the glory of God; the skies
proclaim the work of his hands.*
PSALM 19:1 NIV

The cosmos, the universe, outer space. . .called by any name, it's a place of awe and enchantment, filled with stars, comets, quasars, and our home planet, Earth.

Though the first verse of the Bible clearly states that God created our world, the belief in an infinite, eternal universe held sway with scientists for generations.

But in 1915, Einstein's general theory of relativity challenged that assumption. Over the ensuing decades, scientific observations indicated that our universe did indeed have a beginning, just as the Bible says.

But science goes much deeper than the birth of the universe. It shows an Earth fine-tuned for intelligent life, an amazingly rare possibility even in the vastness of space. The evidence points to a planet designed by a Creator.

With the heavens displaying the Creator's glory, it shouldn't surprise us that scientists have also discovered that the conditions that make life possible on Earth provide a perfect setting to study our universe as well.

Stand outside on a clear night, gazing into the sky. Drink in the glory and majesty of creation. Only a mighty and powerful God could fashion all the wonders we see.

*Father, I marvel at the design of the cosmos created by Your
mighty hands—nothing out of place, the whole in line
with Your perfect will. Oh, the wonder of it all! Amen.*

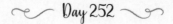

Day 252

*With this in mind, we constantly pray for you, that our
God may make you worthy of his calling, and that by
his power he may bring to fruition your every desire for
goodness and your every deed prompted by faith.*

2 Thessalonians 1:11 niv

God's sovereignty and our free will clash in a glorious kaleidoscope
of grace in the second letter to the Thessalonians.

Here, Paul prayed for the church at Thessalonica, that God would
make them worthy of His calling. God calls; then God makes them
deserving of that calling.

Elsewhere, Paul commanded believers to *live* lives worthy of God
and His calling (Ephesians 4:1). Our effort, our choice.

Here, Paul prays that God will fulfill *our* purposes and actions
prompted by our faith.

But God is the one who calls us "according to his purpose"
(Romans 8:28 niv; 2 Timothy 1:9). In fact, Paul goes so far
as to say that call is "irrevocable" (Romans 11:29 niv).

Let's rest in the fact that all the things we live and plan and
believe, God will fulfill for us.

*By faith I believe that You will fulfill the plans You
have for me. Right now You are working on my behalf,
enlightening me to Your will. I thank You, Father! Amen.*

~ Day 253 ~

For I am convinced that neither death nor life, neither angels nor demons, neither the present nor the future, nor any powers, neither height nor depth, nor anything else in all creation, will be able to separate us from the love of God that is in Christ Jesus our Lord.
ROMANS 8:38–39 NIV

Isn't that a comforting thought?

Of course, the flip side is that lots of things will try to separate us from God—way more things than you can chalk up to mere coincidence! The mockery of loved ones, ill health, loneliness, financial stress, depression, just the sheer scale of an unbelieving world seemingly antagonistic to faith. . .any of these things, or some others specifically targeted to your situation, will try to separate you from the love of God.

Why? Because God's love is a great prize! Otherwise, no one on this earth (or below it) would care. The struggles you experience for your faith are a measure of the reality and importance of what you are going to achieve in the end. It's a real battle, but Paul is telling you that you are on the stronger side. If you'll only hold on to Jesus, He'll wrap His arms—and His love—around you.

Earthquakes, meteor strikes, and superheroes couldn't break that embrace. You'll be home to stay!

Wrap Your strong arms around me, Jesus. Embrace me in love whenever evil tries to separate us. I trust that I will be safe resting in Your arms. Amen.

I have hidden your word in my heart, that I might not sin against you.
PSALM 119:11 NLT

When Jesus was tempted by Satan, He did not yield, because He remembered the Word of God.

It must have been difficult. The Bible says that Jesus had been in the wilderness for a long time. He hadn't eaten for forty days and nights and, being fully human, must have been in a weakened state. It is difficult for anyone to function well after experiencing that kind of hunger.

But Jesus knew the Word of God very well. Each time He was tempted, He was able to ward off trouble by using God's Word as a weapon.

This same weapon is available to us. By reading and meditating on God's Word, we become much stronger in our faith. It becomes easier to battle temptation. The Bible says that we will never be tempted beyond that which we are able to handle (see 1 Corinthians 10:13). And Psalm 119:11 indicates we can find victory by filling our hearts and minds with God's Word.

*Dear God, when I am pushed to my limit, I will
rely on Your Word. I will find comfort, refreshment,
and strength in its everlasting power. Amen.*

∽ Day 255 ∽

*He also broke in pieces the bronze snake that Moses had
made, which was called Nehushtan. Up to that time the
people of Israel had burned incense in its honor.*
2 KINGS 18:4 GNT

One day the Israelites complained bitterly against Moses and God, so
God sent poisonous snakes that bit many of them. When the people
repented, God told Moses to hammer out a bronze snake and hold
it up on a pole, and "anyone who had been bitten would look at the
bronze snake and be healed" (Numbers 21:9 GNT).

You can understand why the Israelites would hang on to such a
symbol of God's power for hundreds of years. It was like a national
heritage. You could even understand why they might think it still
had healing powers many years later. But somewhere during the
centuries, the Israelites began to worship the bronze snake and
burn incense to it.

When King Hezekiah was destroying idols in Judah, he sarcas-
tically named the snake *Nehushtan*. That sounds like the Hebrew
words for "bronze" and "serpent" but means "unclean thing." Then
he smashed it into pieces.

God gives us many helpful, good things, but if we begin to worship those things instead of God Himself—or give them too much
of our attention—then they become idols and must be destroyed.

*Heavenly Father, I'm grateful for the good things You
have given me, but open my eyes if I have turned any of
them into idols. I want to worship only You. Amen.*

～ Day 256 ～

*Now we see only a reflection as in a mirror; then
we shall see face to face. Now I know in part; then I
shall know fully, even as I am fully known.*
1 Corinthians 13:12 niv

"Dark matter," "dark energy," "dark flow"—the scientific model of the universe depends on all of these. The expression *dark* means, "We think something ought to be there, but we can't find it."

Cosmologists face the unenviable task of trying to understand creation while they themselves are a part of it. They envisage a necessarily restricted model and call the bits beyond their comprehension *dark*.

In that, they're not so different from people of faith. Not even the greatest Bible scholars fully understand God's grand plan. His ways have been mysterious since the beginning. And because of that, there are things we don't understand; things we would have difficulty explaining to anyone else; things, if we are honest, that might sometimes cause us to doubt the validity of our faith. But hold on.

Paul addresses those "dark" spots in this verse. He knew those worries. He also knew there was an answer.

The scientific community invests billions in solving its mysteries. Paul advises the rest of us to invest a little faith and a little time. Then we "shall know fully," and there will be no "dark."

*Through faith I have come to know You more fully. Through
faith, I understand some of the dark spots because Your
Word has given them light. Thank You, Father. Amen.*

*The LORD said to Moses, "Speak to the Israelites and say to them:
'These are my appointed festivals, the appointed festivals of
the LORD, which you are to proclaim as sacred assemblies.'"*
LEVITICUS 23:1–2 NIV

Holidays in Israel combined festive celebrations with worship to commemorate God's amazing blessings on the nation.

The weekly Sabbath, although a day for rest and worship, served as a time to "remember that you were slaves in Egypt and that the LORD your God brought you out of there with a mighty hand and an outstretched arm" (Deuteronomy 5:15 NIV).

The Feast of Harvest, or Pentecost, occurred fifty days after the Passover observance. Loaves of bread were presented to the Lord as an offering from the wheat harvest, along with sacrificial animals. Jewish tradition also links this feast to the day God gave Moses the Law on Mount Sinai.

During the Feast of Booths, the Israelites camped out in fragile shelters for seven days as a remembrance of God's care and protection following their escape from Egypt. This joyous feast took place at the end of the harvest season and included a time of thanksgiving to God for the year's crops.

Like the Israelites, let's use all our holidays to celebrate God's goodness, reflecting on the blessings He has given us personally and as a nation.

*Father, the secular world has excluded You from holidays,
especially those set to honor You. As for me, Lord, I will
worship You on holidays and every day. Amen.*

～ Day 258 ～

*The god of this age has blinded the minds of unbelievers,
so that they cannot see the light of the gospel that displays
the glory of Christ, who is the image of God.*
2 Corinthians 4:4 niv

The "god of this age" is undoubtedly Satan. The "unbelievers" are people who think themselves too wise for faith. Their master gave them powerful weapons when he blinded them to their fate and armed them with scorn.

After all, no one likes to be laughed at. A little public humiliation might dampen a strong faith and kill a weak one. So many of us just keep quiet in front of people like that. As a result, they go happily to their fate, and the Lord's heart is twice broken.

How did Jesus deal with the blinded? He got in their faces. His actions might be described as a little scornful. He spat in their eyes, rubbed mud in their eyes, then commanded them to see!

If we can stand a little humiliation for the sake of those who mock us; if we can weather their scorn, knowing they are pawns of Satan but beloved of God; if we can get in their faces, they will have to look. And if we do all that in God's name, then the blind will have no option but to see!

*Heavenly Father, I will stand up for You and wear my
faith proudly. Even where my faith is not welcomed,
I will honor You and lift up Your name. Amen.*

*And because the Israelites forsook the LORD and no
longer served him, he became angry with them.*
JUDGES 10:6–7 NIV

This verse raises an important question: Is anger sin? If so, how can
a loving, sinless God express anger?

To explore these questions, we need to understand the moral
attributes of God. He is good, loving, compassionate, patient, truthful,
faithful, just, and slow to anger. But He does become angry—not
in an imperfect human manner, but with a righteous indignation
against evil.

It was righteous indignation that moved Jesus to drive the
greedy and ungodly out of God's temple. In the same way, after the
Israelites returned to idol worship, they suffered the consequences
of their sin—God allowed neighboring nations to oppress them for
eighteen years (Judges 10:8).

From the beginning of time, God has revealed His wrath against
all forms of wickedness and idolatry. But His disdain toward evil is
also an expression of love for goodness and righteousness.

The apostle Paul taught New Testament believers, "'In your anger
do not sin'. . .do not give the devil a foothold" (Ephesians 4:26–27
NIV). For us as Christians, it's right to express anger against sin and
injustice. It's wrong to let that anger lead us to sin.

Not all anger is sin. But it's an emotion best left to God's control.

*God, help me to control my anger, to express it only when
standing up for goodness and righteousness. Teach me
when and how to be angry so I will not sin. Amen.*

*The apostles left the high council rejoicing that God had counted
them worthy to suffer disgrace for the name of Jesus.*
ACTS 5:41 NLT

The apostles performed "many miraculous signs and wonders among the people" and "more and more people believed and were brought to the Lord" (Acts 5:12, 14 NLT).

Filled with jealousy, the Jewish council arrested the apostles. After much debate, the council released the men, forbidding them to speak about Jesus and punishing each with a flogging.

As the apostles limped away in pain, with sliced and bleeding backs, they rejoiced that God had allowed them to suffer for Him.

How could suffering persecution be cause for celebration?

Years later, the apostle Peter penned, "If you have suffered physically for Christ. . .you won't spend the rest of your lives chasing your own desires, but you will be anxious to do the will of God" (1 Peter 4:1–2 NLT). Persecution keeps us on track with Christ.

It also offers future blessings. "If you suffer for doing what is right, God will reward you for it" (1 Peter 3:14 NLT). However, we are to suffer persecution "in a gentle and respectful way. . .then if people speak against you, they will be ashamed" (1 Peter 3:16 NLT).

Are you experiencing difficulties because of your Christian beliefs? Stand strong. Eternal blessings are yours.

*Dear Jesus, sometimes I am bullied because of my Christian
faith. Surely You understand how that feels. Help me to
stand strong and focus on Your blessings. Amen.*

And he said unto me, My grace is sufficient for thee: for my strength
is made perfect in weakness. Most gladly therefore will I rather glory
in my infirmities, that the power of Christ may rest upon me.
2 Corinthians 12:9 kjv

Eric Liddell, the Scottish missionary to China, once wrote a prayer asking "that no circumstances, however bitter, may cause me to break thy law, the law of love to thee and my neighbor." No matter what, he promised to maintain "a heart full of gratitude."

Liddell didn't mention that he was, at the time, captive in a Japanese internment camp. He didn't know if his family was safe. And he was dying of a brain tumor.

But Eric Liddell's certainty that God loved him—and that Christ had died for him—was enough to prove that his blessings *still* outweighed his problems. He was able to do work that left others in the camp thinking of him as something akin to a saint.

Our down moments need not be hopeless times. When we are at our least, God can fill the space we used to occupy and do marvelous things. When you think you have nothing else going for you, if you have God to lean on, you have more than enough.

Someday you can ask Eric Liddell about that!

Lord, in my weakness You give me strength,
and You are my comfort in the midst of despair.
With You in my heart, I have all that I need. Amen.

~ Day 262 ~

He was sorry that he had made them.
GENESIS 6:6 CEV

Because of the flood, God has often been painted as the bad guy. "I can't trust a God who got angry and wiped everyone out!" people say. Yet this verse tells us God was sorry, not angry.

God did everything possible to avoid the flood. He gave humanity several generations to turn from its wickedness. His long-suffering was so great that He waited until there was only one righteous man left—Noah. And God didn't send the flood without warning. Noah and Enoch were preachers of righteousness. Though they warned the world for a hundred years (the time it took the ark to be built), no one believed them. By the time the rains began, the world reeked of sin. Genesis 4:23–24 indicates there was murder without guilt. A world of killers received the death penalty.

Considering the details of an event, we see a whole new story—and the righteousness of God. Don't be quick to put God down, but carefully research those questions you find disturbing. The Bible has given us every reason to put our whole lives into His hands, today and forever.

You knew that humans would continue to sin, and so You sent Jesus to save us. Your love for us is greater than any other love, O just and forgiving God! Amen.

~ Day 263 ~

Don't be selfish; don't try to impress others. Be humble,
thinking of others as better than yourselves.
PHILIPPIANS 2:3 NLT

Another great verse along these lines is "Your love for one another will prove to the world that you are my disciples" (John 13:35 NLT).

The way we conduct ourselves says volumes about what is most important to us. Isaiah 53:2 tells us that there was nothing beautiful about Jesus' physical appearance that would attract anyone to Him, yet with one look people could see that He was full of love.

Imagine being able to see the love people have just by how they look at you. Perhaps you could know this in the way they speak to you. Maybe it is just in the way they say your name. That is what Jesus had. Those fortunate enough to be in His presence during that short time He was on the earth must have truly been filled with His love.

Today, we are the disciples of Jesus. If we are to fulfill that role, we must conduct ourselves according to Philippians 2:3 and many other verses that were written to guide us. It is now we who need to display this love toward others. With each person we encounter, may we shine with the love of Jesus.

Jesus, let Your love shine through me. Extend Your
love to others through my smile, my words, and
my acts. All for Your glory, Lord. Amen.

*"Call to me and I will answer you and tell you great
and unsearchable things you do not know."*
JEREMIAH 33:3 NIV

In this verse, God is speaking directly to the prophet Jeremiah.

For forty years, Jeremiah had been warning that Judah and Jerusalem would be destroyed for their sins. Now his predictions were coming true: the Babylonian army was poised to attack. King Zedekiah commanded that Jeremiah be thrown into prison for speaking the words of God. While Jeremiah was there, God commanded him to pray. "Call to me," He said, "and I will answer you" (Jeremiah 33:3 NASB).

Jeremiah 33:3 teaches that if we pray to God, He will answer us with wisdom. In the King James Version of the Bible, the word *pray* is listed more than five hundred times. God wants us to pray. When we call on Him in prayer, we know that He hears us (1 John 5:15).

Proverbs 2:6 (NASB) says, "For the LORD gives wisdom; from His mouth come knowledge and understanding." God knows us fully, and He is able to direct us in wisdom and guide us through the works of His Holy Spirit.

Just as God gave Jeremiah wisdom when he prayed, He will do the same for you if you call on Him in faith (James 1:5–6).

*God, I need Your help. I've sought counsel for my
problem, and still I'm not sure what to do. But You know!
Please, God, guide me with Your wisdom. Amen.*

Day 265

*"Woe to you who are rich, for you have
already received your comfort."*
LUKE 6:24 NIV

Some readers may feel that Jesus' teaching is too hard on the wealthy. In Matthew 19:24 He claims the camel will more easily step through a needle's eye than a rich man will make it through the pearly gates.

Jesus' words shouldn't be interpreted as a negative view of wealth. He had wealthy friends who supported His ministry in many ways, including providing a tomb for His burial.

His choice of the Greek word for "comfort" was a message to the wealthy—they had already been paid in full. Their pleasure was momentary, not eternal. "Eat, drink, and have your good times, because there's no tomorrow!"

The regular folks who heard Jesus probably nodded in agreement, while others understood, "He is talking to us too." Riches-lacking person, be content with what you have (Exodus 20:17). Understand that generous financial stewardship has lasting results (Luke 6:38). Nothing is more satisfying than a born-again relationship with Jesus (Hebrews 11:26).

To everyone, Christ sums up His message with "Freely you have received; freely give" (Matthew 10:8 NIV).

We used to sing a hymn titled "Give of Your Best to the Master." One stanza reads:

*Give Him first place in your heart. Give Him
first place in your service; Consecrate every part.*

*Lord Jesus, thank You for Your many blessings. I am grateful
for them all, but nothing compares to my relationship
with You. It is always first in my heart. Amen.*

When Jesus was leaving, he saw a man named Matthew
sitting in the tax collector's booth. Jesus said to him,
"Follow me," and he stood up and followed Jesus.
MATTHEW 9:9 NCV

In New Testament times, the Roman tax structure provided ample opportunity for lucrative kickbacks and payoffs to officials working in the system. These underhanded operations reached down to the lowest level of the tax hierarchy—the publicans or tax collectors.

Utilizing common practices of the day, Matthew's superiors encouraged him to overcharge the general populace, falsely accuse merchants of smuggling in hope of extracting hush money, and impose arbitrary duty taxes on all imports and exports. These and other cunning schemes provided dishonest wealth for tax officials throughout the agency.

Many Jews believed it unlawful to pay tribute in any form to Rome and regarded Jewish tax collectors as traitors. Already despised, a Jewish publican had frequent interaction with pagan Gentiles, rendering him defiled in the eyes of most Jews.

Yet Jesus asked Matthew, a detested publican, to "follow Me," and Matthew immediately complied. He became one of Jesus' twelve disciples and penned the Gospel bearing his name.

Do you have family members, friends, or coworkers living far from God? There is hope. Keep them in your prayers and let Jesus work in their hearts.

Dear Lord, I pray for _____ today. He/she
doesn't know You. Lead him/her to the cross to accept
Your gift of salvation and eternal life. Amen.

Day 267

*When Peter entered, Cornelius met him and fell down
at his feet and worshiped him. But Peter lifted him
up, saying, "Stand up; I too am a man."*
ACTS 10:25–26 RSV

Peter loved Jesus, but he was a flawed human who made terrible mistakes, such as taking his eyes off Jesus, rebuking the Lord, and in a moment of weakness, even denying that he knew Him (Matthew 14:28–31; 16:21–23; 26:69–75). Who would ever imagine that anyone would mistake Peter for a god and worship him?

Yet after Jesus rose from the dead and the disciples were filled with the Holy Spirit, Peter became a powerhouse and a miracle worker. He prayed, and the sick were healed and the dead were raised to life. Even his shadow healed people (Acts 3:1–8; 5:15; 9:32–42)!

So it was when this "holy man" entered the house of the Roman centurion that Cornelius bowed down to worship him. Peter quickly grabbed Cornelius, pulled him to his feet, and set him straight.

When the apostle John nearly worshipped an angel, the angel immediately commanded, "Don't do that!" then added, "Worship God!" (Revelation 19:10 NIV). This is good advice for us when we're tempted to place some leader on a pedestal or succumb to man worship.

*Father, You are my only God, and I worship only You. I will
not bow down to any person or any thing on earth. Amen.*

And he said to me, "Son of man, eat what is before you,
eat this scroll; then go and speak to the people of Israel."
EZEKIEL 3:1 NIV

Why would the Lord instruct Ezekiel to eat a scroll? Simply put, the scroll contained God's words for the defiant Israelites. Its contents were harsh judgment sweetened with blessed redemption. But before Ezekiel could preach the Word of God, he had to ingest it and commit himself to it first.

When Satan tempted Jesus in the wilderness to turn stones into bread, Jesus replied, "Man shall not live on bread alone, but on every word that comes from the mouth of God" (Matthew 4:4 NIV). God's Word nourishes and sustains every believer; it is our meat and potatoes. However, we must digest it and imprint it on our hearts and minds before we can become effective for the kingdom.

The prophet Jeremiah said, "When your words came, I ate them; they were my joy and my heart's delight, for I bear your name" (Jeremiah 15:16 NIV). So it is with every Christian. The scriptures bring joy, life, hope, peace, comfort, encouragement, and all the spiritual nutrients we need to fortify our hearts and minds. They empower us to preach the Good News of Jesus Christ. Have you eaten today?

Nourish me with Your Word, God. Fill me up with Your scriptures.
Lay before me a banquet of Your wisdom, abounding with
love, joy, encouragement, comfort, hope, and peace. Amen.

Day 269

> *"Produce fruit in keeping with repentance. And do not begin to say to yourselves, 'We have Abraham as our father.' For I tell you that out of these stones God can raise up children for Abraham."*
> LUKE 3:8 NIV

Being one of the faithful isn't an inherited position, much as some people might like to think so. We aren't automatically saved because our parents were.

Thinking of themselves as the chosen race had made some of the folk of Jesus' day lazy about their faith. John pointed out that the *choice* was God's—and they shouldn't give Him cause to regret it.

Imagine God as an employer. He's hiring, but He doesn't want people who think they're owed a job. He doesn't "do" nepotism—you won't get the job because your old man worked for the company way back. God has no place for "seat warmers" in His business. He seeks people who want to be there, people who will "produce fruit" from the raw materials He provides.

God, Inc., is a thriving business that's really going somewhere. There are always vacancies for those willing to work. It's a lifelong, recession-proof position with a wonderful retirement package.

It's too good an opportunity to risk losing through complacency. You can bet those stones would jump at the chance—if stones could jump!

Jesus, put me to work. What can I do to spread Your Word? How can I recruit others into Your business of salvation? I am ready, willing, and able, Lord. Amen.

A blacksmith could not be found in all the land of Israel, for the Philistines had said, "This will prevent the Hebrews from making swords and spears." So all Israel had to go down to the Philistines in order to get their plowshares, cutting instruments, axes, and sickles sharpened. They charged two-thirds of a shekel to sharpen plowshares and cutting instruments, and one-third of a shekel to sharpen picks and axes, and to set ox goads. So on the day of the battle no sword or spear was to be found in the hand of anyone in the army that was with Saul and Jonathan. No one but Saul and his son Jonathan had them.
1 SAMUEL 13:19–22 NET

This is a fascinating view of Palestine at the very cusp of the Iron Age. The Philistines, more technologically advanced than the Israelites, guarded all knowledge of iron making as a vital military secret.

Bronze, the metal available to the Israelites, is actually harder than wrought iron, but it cannot be resharpened by a grindstone; it must be completely reforged. By controlling the blacksmiths, the Philistines implemented an effective arms embargo against the Israelites. God used even older technology to end it: five smooth stones and a sling (1 Samuel 17:40, 49–50).

Some humans believe that they are in control. But no, God, You are. You set Your plan in action, and man-made technology can't stop it. How great You are, my Lord! Amen.

*"No one can serve two masters. Either you will hate the one
and love the other, or you will be devoted to the one and
despise the other. You cannot serve both God and money."*
MATTHEW 6:24 NIV

A master rules with complete control and authority. In this verse, money also translates as "mammon," which means all manner of earthly possessions.

Mammon cannot be our master. We can use our possessions and money for God's purpose, but we can't let these things rule our lives. When mammon controls our hearts, we have no time or space for God.

We may try to juggle two masters for a while—and we may even look successful—but Jesus warns us that this is not the way to live. Just as the juggler handles only one ball at a time, we must let go of one to cling to the other.

Today we are easily seduced into thinking we can have it all. But when we try to cling both to our possessions and to God, we eventually have to let go of something.

God is our master. Some things we cling to—our home, job, family—are good things, but we place them out of order in our priorities. What distracts from God is our mammon. He wants to be number one in our hearts.

*In my busy life, God, I am so often distracted, and
my priorities shift away from You. Forgive me,
please. Empower me to do better. Amen.*

Then the LORD gave the donkey the ability to speak. "What have I done to you that deserves your beating me three times?"
NUMBERS 22:28 NLT

The diviner Balaam lived in Pethor, near the ancient city of Mari. Cuneiform tablets discovered at Mari describe a well-established cult of professional diviners who used omens, dreams, and fortune-telling in their trade. For a price, they would utter incantations and offer sacrifices to curse a person or nation.

Fearing an attack from Israel, the Moabite king hired Balaam to come and curse the Israelites.

The diviner set out for Moab, instructed by God not to curse Israel and "do only what I tell you to do" (Numbers 22:20 NLT). However, Balaam intended to get around God's orders and take home his hefty fee, for he "loved to earn money by doing wrong" (2 Peter 2:15 NLT).

Displeased, God sent an angel to slay Balaam, an angel invisible to the diviner but not to his frightened donkey. She bolted. Furious, Balaam struck the animal. God caused the donkey to speak. As a diviner, Balaam wasn't shocked by a talking animal and argued with the beast.

Then God allowed him to see the angel standing with his sword drawn. Balaam fell on his face, confessing his greedy intentions.

Unlike Balaam, let's examine our motives and serve God with a pure heart.

Let me serve You with a pure heart, Lord. Lead me away from temptation and deliver me from evil. Cleanse me of my iniquity, and make me acceptable in Your sight. Amen.

～ Day 273 ～

But to him who does not work, but believes on him who justifies
the ungodly, his faith is reckoned as righteousness.
ROMANS 4:5 DARBY

Have you ever played the Opposite Game? When the leader tells you
to step forward, you step back. When he calls out the color green,
you call out, "Red." It's challenging to the very young because they
have to think before they act.

Well, many people have played the Opposite Game with God.
Today's passage tells us that God will not count us righteous based
on our works. So what do many of us do? We try to please God by
our works! "I've worked hard at being a good person. I hope God
will let me into heaven." "No matter how hard I try to do good, I
still feel that God doesn't accept anything I do."

Abraham is given as a good example. God told Abraham that his
seed would be as numerous as the stars, and Abraham believed God.
God then counted him righteous—and Abraham had not lifted a
finger. What is our approach to the promises of God? Indifference?
Or do we get a sense that God wants to do something in our lives?

Jesus, I understand that the only road to heaven is the
one traveled by believing in You and Your gift of salvation.
Thank You for leading me to eternal life. Amen.

My body and my heart may grow weak.
God, you give strength to my heart.
You are everything I will ever need.
PSALM 73:26 NIrV

You may not have heard of Asaph. He is the man who wrote Psalm 73. Asaph was David's music director and author of twelve of the Psalms.

In Psalm 73 Asaph wonders, if God is good, then why do the righteous suffer and the wicked prosper? He says, "Did I keep my heart pure for nothing? Did I keep myself innocent for no reason? I get nothing but trouble all day long; every morning brings me pain" (vv. 13–14 NLT). Asaph confesses that he sometimes feels like giving up and joining the wicked (vv. 2–3).

In desperation, Asaph seeks God in His sanctuary. There he realizes that while the wicked might prosper for a season, God will defeat them in His own way and in His own time. Asaph ends up praising God, "How good it is to be near You! You are all I will ever need."

When our bodies are tired and sick, when we feel as if we can't go on, Psalm 73:26 reminds us that God is our everything.

Help me to be patient when seeking punishment
for the wicked. In Your time, Lord, and in Your
way, You will deal with them. Amen.

Examine yourselves to see whether you are in the faith;
test yourselves. Do you not realize that Christ Jesus
is in you—unless, of course, you fail the test?
2 CORINTHIANS 13:5 NIV

When we are in church or a Bible group, we know we are among kindred spirits. We can relax a little, knowing we won't be upsetting anyone with our faith and knowing the others will help keep us on track. Christ Jesus will be in us. But much of His work isn't done among the faithful. We need to venture out of our comfort zone, and that's when it gets dangerous.

The world is a trap for the spiritually unwary. There are countless diversions and it's easy to get lost, which is why fellowship with other Christians is so important. But if you don't have that opportunity, if you are a "voice in the desert," it is vitally important that you regularly ask, "Am I doing this for the love of God? Would He approve?" When you can no longer answer "yes" to those questions, then you know you have strayed.

But here's the good news. If you have failed the test, you are far from alone. Simon Peter failed it in spectacular style! But you can revisit that test anytime. Simply open your heart and invite Him back in. He will come.

God, whenever I stray from You, pull me back. My heart is open to You. You are always welcome here. You are my everything. Amen.

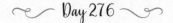

Don't let anyone fool you by using senseless arguments. These
arguments may sound wise, but they are only human teachings.
They come from the powers of this world and not from Christ.
COLOSSIANS 2:8 CEV

"There is no such thing as absolute truth." Ever heard an argument like this? It sounds good on the surface—until you take a step back and start to ponder its meaning. The trouble with this statement is that it declares an absolute truth while maintaining that there is no such thing.

Adam and Eve were deceived in the garden, as the serpent manipulated truth and logic into something that seemingly justified evading God's established guidelines. This legacy of deception continues in our modern world. Positions and viewpoints that appear intellectually solid at first glance break down upon further examination of their components and consequences.

Human logic falls apart in the face of divine wisdom. Worldly philosophy captures and enslaves; the all-knowing, omniscient presence of God radiates both truth and grace. What arguments have you heard lately that have their origins in the roots of this world rather than in the fullness of Christ?

O mighty God, keep me focused on the truth of Your
Word. Remind me to dig deep to the roots of human
logic to determine if You planted its seed. Amen.

"Where then are the gods you made for yourselves?
Let them come if they can save you when you are in trouble!
For you, Judah, have as many gods as you have towns."
JEREMIAH 2:28 NIV

The Lord made His intentions clear at Sinai: He forbade the making and worshipping of idols (Exodus 20:4–5).

In spite of that command, Israel fell into cycles of idolatry, judgment, repentance, and restoration (Judges 2:11–19). Solomon, the king who built God's temple in Jerusalem, formalized idol worship, building altars to the gods of Moab and Ammon for two of his wives. Later, "he did the same for *all* his foreign wives" (1 Kings 11:8 NIV, emphasis added). Since he had three hundred wives and seven hundred concubines, that's the potential for a thousand idols to false gods!

Centuries later, King Manasseh committed a final, awful sacrilege: he brought idol worship into the temple courts (2 Chronicles 33:5–6).

Jeremiah began prophesying during the reign of Manasseh's grandson. Idolatry had so pervaded the land that every town had its own god, and Jeremiah warned, pleaded, wept—to no avail. Jerusalem fell, and her people went into captivity.

What about us? Have we let the false gods of the world—money, things, celebrity worship—take root in our lives? There's only one God—and He demands our attention.

Father, many things distract our attention from You—the internet,
television, books, even the news. Sadly, they have become idols.
Open our eyes to idolatry, God. Turn our hearts toward You! Amen.

"The Sabbath was made for man, not man for the Sabbath."
MARK 2:27 NIV

Remember when Sunday was devoted to multiple church services, good deeds, and dinner in the dining room with an undercurrent of "we don't do that on the Lord's Day"?

In response to what some considered constricting Sunday observance, believers have "updated" fourth-commandment observance. Some say these changes were made to the detriment of the family.

The original intent for keeping the Sabbath holy was for spiritual and physical renewal and worship. When historical Christianity moved God's special day to recognize the Resurrection, the intent remained the same.

In almost one hundred words, compared to murder's four words, the commandment forbids work on the Sabbath (Exodus 20:10). The reason is spelled out succinctly: If the Creator needed a day off for rest after six days of creation work, who are we to ignore His request on our behalf?

Today our typical day of rest seems to favor football, barbecues, and maybe a honey-do chore list. And Sunday-morning church chores for active members can be exhausting.

So how can the Lord's Day be honored? As a family, decide how to make Sunday special. Plan what you could do for others. Decide on activities you won't participate in. Discuss how to handle kids' Sunday sports. Above all, make the day memorable.

Lord, in our family, Sunday will be a day of rest and remembrance of You. Show us ways that we, as a family, can honor this day and spend it with You. Amen.

*In the morning, LORD, you hear my voice; in the morning
I lay my requests before you and wait expectantly.*
PSALM 5:3 NIV

"Lay my requests" originates from the Hebrew word *arak*, which means to arrange or set up as in a legal contract.

We act as lawyers preparing our case. We plead our claims before the Lord: *Lord, here is what I want/need/deeply desire. I know You love me and have promised to hear me.*

But as in any legal contract, both parties have duties or responsibilities. God listens. We wait in expectation.

Often we forget our side of the legal contract. God fulfills His side of the bargain to hear our prayers. We take off on our merry way, trying to solve our dilemma without Him.

We leave His presence without lingering with the Lord to listen and to worship Him in the silence of our heart. Then the next morning we return with more demands and "gimmes."

God knows our human hearts and understands. He gently waits to hear from us—and He delights when we keep our end of the bargain and linger in His light with hearts full of anticipation and hope.

*Dear God, my hope is in You. Thank You for listening to my
prayers and knowing exactly what I need. I wait patiently,
expectantly, knowing that You will answer me. Amen.*

∽ Day 280 ∽

Am I now trying to win the approval of human beings, or of
God? Or am I trying to please people? If I were still trying
to please people, I would not be a servant of Christ.
GALATIANS 1:10 NIV

"Why does she stay with him?" Or "Oh, he could do so much better
than her." Who hasn't seen someone stay in a one-sided relationship,
trying desperately to please a self-centered partner?

It's often a tragic waste of love. And to what end? To win the
affections of a flawed individual?

Everyone who puts their faith in this world ends up trying to
please a flawed individual or system. It might be a partner, relative,
or boss. We give them credit for being somehow better than us, but
they are, after all, only human. Even our best attempts to fulfill their
noblest desires could never be better than imperfect.

There is someone out there who can take our love and make it
all it should be. Through Him, the romantic ideal of "happily ever
after" becomes a reality. He has already died for us, and what greater
sacrifice could a lover make?

No earthly partner or authority figure could give more or do
more with what we have to offer.

So why focus on humans when we could do so much better?

Jesus, You must really love me to have suffered and given
Your life for me. You loved me before any human did,
and Your love for me lasts forever. I love You too. Amen.

Jesus Christ is the same yesterday and today and forever.
HEBREWS 13:8 NIV

Although the writer of Hebrews is disputed, clearly the letter is written for Jewish converts who were tempted to revert to Judaism. The writer encourages them to hold fast and persevere based on the surety of Jesus' death on the cross for eternal life.

To understand the context of verse 8, however, look at 13:7 (NIV): "Remember your leaders, who spoke the word of God to you. Consider the outcome of their way of life and imitate their faith."

Two thousand years later, we're reminded to remember those who walked the earth with Jesus Christ, obediently taking the first steps toward making disciples of all nations (Matthew 28:19). They were the ones whose eyes were fixed on the changeless Christ, and their faith reflected it. They're the ones who passed the faith to us.

So as we remember our Christian role models of the past, the disciples, a Sunday-school teacher, a parent who led us to Christ, we too are asked to imitate their faith, which was built on Jesus Christ, our only absolute that was, is, and forever will be.

Precious Jesus, thank You for all the disciples, past and present, who led me to You and helped me to grow in my faith. Lord, bless them all. Amen.

*Godly sorrow brings repentance that leads to salvation
and leaves no regret, but worldly sorrow brings death.*
2 CORINTHIANS 7:10 NIV

Here the apostle Paul identifies two types of sorrow with totally different results. One is from God, the other from the world; one brings life, the other death.

Paul's previous letter of admonishment to the Corinthian church caused the new believers grief. The apostle explained that although he hated to hurt them, he didn't regret writing those words, adding, "For you became sorrowful as God intended" (v. 9 NIV).

Before accepting Christ, each individual experiences varying degrees of conviction—an intense sense of shame and reproof. The guilt associated with realizing our sins and our need for repentance is uncomfortable and troubling temporarily. Yet it is that sorrow that produces humility, a contrite heart, and a change of mind that leads to liberating salvation! Paul wrote, "See what this godly sorrow has produced in you: what earnestness, what eagerness to clear yourselves. . .what readiness to see justice done" (v. 11 NIV).

On the other hand, worldly sorrow destroys and creates inner turmoil. Deep sorrow for lost possessions, jobs, or relatives often produces illness or leads people to pursue desperate means of coping.

The Lord wills for us to experience godly sorrow and—as we trust Him—He helps us overcome all worldly sorrows through His grace and mercy.

*Loving Lord, Your grace, mercy, and love fill me up. You turn my
worldly sorrow into heavenly joy! I praise You, Father. Amen.*

Day 283

Great is our Lord and mighty in power;
his understanding has no limit.
PSALM 147:5 NIV

God has phenomenally *great* power. Genesis 1:16 tells us that He created all the billions upon billions of stars; and in Psalm 147:4, David tells us that God knows the exact number of stars in the entire universe. What's more, He calls *every one* of them by name—as if they were His pets! Remember this astonishing fact the next time you need an answer to prayer and wonder if God is big enough to take care of it.

But there's more: the second half of this verse says God's "understanding has no limit." When you're praying for wisdom in a complex or desperate situation, fix this thought firmly in your mind. You may have no clue as to the right answer, but God certainly does! His understanding is without end.

At times, we don't understand why God allows us to go through troubled times, but He certainly knows—and He cares deeply for each one of us. He not only knows every star by name; He knows *your* name too.

Psalm 147:5 is one of the most powerful scriptures in the Bible. When we meditate deeply on its words, they can fill our minds with peace and assurance.

God, who am I among all the stars in the universe? But You
know their names, and You know mine too! You know me,
You understand me, and that brings me peace. Amen.

*What does "he ascended" mean except that he also
descended to the lower, earthly regions?*
EPHESIANS 4:9 NIV

Paratroopers who led the Normandy invasion jumped, in the dark
of night, into enemy territory. They took every weapon and as much
ammunition as they could carry. Then they loaded kit bags with more
weapons and equipment, tied them onto their ankles, and threw
them out of the plane before they jumped. They were knowingly
cutting their already-slim chances of survival.

Now imagine yourself making the same jump. Your greatest enemy
controls the region below. But over the drop zone, the jumpmaster
unties your kit bag, taking away all your weapons. He says there are
some good folks below who *might* help—though they don't have many
resources themselves. Oh, and there won't be a pickup point, because
you will definitely *die* down there.

Would you make the descent?

Jesus' crucifixion and ascension get glory and attention, appro-
priately. But a key part of any venture is the beginning. He had to
descend to earth—"enemy territory"—before He could complete
God's plan of salvation.

God isn't asking anything nearly as scary of us. The next time
you think it would be good to help somebody, *but*. . .remember that
without taking that first step in faith, people continue in need. Jesus
weighed risks against love. Love won—and down He came!

*Love came down. I will remember that, Father. Love
came down to save me. Give me courage to set aside
my fears and to help save others in need. Amen.*

Then they got up early the next morning and went to the top of the range of hills. "Let's go," they said. "We realize that we have sinned, but now we are ready to enter the land the LORD has promised us."
NUMBERS 14:40 NLT

Before entering the land God promised to Israel, Moses sent out twelve scouts to explore the region.

After forty days, the men returned and reported, "It is indeed a bountiful country. . .but the people living there are powerful" (Numbers 13:27–28 NLT).

Two scouts, Caleb and Joshua, urged the people to go at once and take possession of the land. But the other ten spread fear, saying, "We can't go up against them! They're stronger than we are!" (Numbers 13:31 NLT). Hearing this, the Israelites revolted against Moses and wanted to stone Caleb and Joshua.

During the riot, God's presence appeared above the tabernacle.

For their unbelief, God sentenced the Israelites to wander forty years in the desert. Those twenty years and older would never live to enter the Promised Land, except Caleb and Joshua.

The riot dissolved into sorrow.

Ignoring God's verdict, the men prepared for battle and went up to take the land, but the inhabitants attacked and soundly defeated the Israelites.

Rebuffed opportunities often disappear, never to return. Let's tune in to God's gentle prodding and act on His instructions.

Father, sometimes Your voice whispers to my heart, but I don't listen. Forgive me. Help me always to tune in to Your words and act on Your instructions. Amen.

Run in such a way as to get the prize.
1 Corinthians 9:24 niv

Athletic games were well known in the Hellenistic world. As pagan customs they were abhorrent to Orthodox Jews, yet the metaphor of racing and boxing is often used by Paul. No doubt, in other days, he had been a spectator.

The apostle understood the parallel between life in Christ and the intense striving of a runner. Elsewhere, the writer of Hebrews compares the cheering crowd in a stadium to the encouragement of fellow Christians on the course of life (Hebrews 12:1–2).

For believers in Corinth, Paul underscores the necessity of living life with eternal goals in view. To all runners, from spiritual sprinters to experienced marathoners, the apostle's advice conjures memories of hearing the cracking starter gun, pushing away from the blocks, being aware of others on the course who may cause a trip-up, keeping one's eyes on the goal, and being mindful of the commitment that helps a runner put one foot in front of the other, regardless of anything.

Runners in the Spirit heed the directive to "[fix] our eyes on Jesus" (Hebrews 12:2 niv). He is the originator and the perfecter of your faith. He is the secret of success; He is the motivation that ensures the prize—eternal life.

*O Jesus, the world sometimes tries to block my way in
this race called "life." Help me to overcome the obstacles
and keep my eyes fixed on You and heaven. Amen.*

Keep falsehood and lies far from me; give me neither
poverty nor riches, but give me only my daily bread.
PROVERBS 30:8 NIV

Agur, a personal name meaning "hired hand," wrote the thirtieth chapter of Proverbs. Unlike the majority of Proverbs, written by King Solomon, the wisdom offered here came from a common man, a day laborer. He admitted his lack of credentials in verses 2–3, but he clung to the Word of God as his shield (vv. 5–6).

In verse 7 he offered his "wish list" to God. "Two things I ask of you. . .before I die": Keep falsehood and lies from me; and make me neither rich nor poor, but give me only enough for each day. He continued building on that theme by saying the rich man was likely to take credit for his own success; but a poor man faced the temptation to steal (v. 9). Solomon said much the same thing in chapter 10. Poverty "ruined" the poor, but the wealth of the wicked brought punishment (10:15–16).

Agur's wish list concerned overcoming temptations to sin. What areas of our lives do we want God to clean up before we die? Are we satisfied with only daily bread? Or do we seek more? Like Agur, let us construct our wish lists around the quality of our character and not around experiences.

Dear God, guide me in the things I wish for. Lead me to ask only for
those things that will strengthen my relationship with You. Amen.

And he shall make a strong covenant with many for one week,
and for half of the week he shall put an end to sacrifice and offering.
DANIEL 9:27 ESV

In this prophecy, the angel Gabriel (yes, *that* Gabriel) tells Daniel what will happen in the future. After the Messiah dies and shortly before His return, a man will make a seven year peace treaty with Israel. Sacrifices and offerings will be allowed in Israel, and then in the middle of the treaty he will stop them.

Now, who could have known more than two thousand years ago that Israel would still be around? Most ancient civilizations have been buried under the sands. Furthermore, how could anyone have known that Israel would be in need of a treaty? If you pay attention to the news at all, you'll find trouble between Israel and the Middle East mentioned repeatedly. The last few United States presidents have all tried unsuccessfully to broker peace in the region.

God is pretty amazing to tell us in minute detail what will happen thousands of years in the future. It's even more amazing to find this important messianic prophecy on the brink of fulfillment in *our* lifetime!

Come, Lord Jesus. Fulfill Gabriel's prophecy. Lead me not to
fear worldly turmoil, but instead to anticipate that wonderful
day when You return to redeem Your people. Amen.

When he had seen the vision, immediately we
sought to go into Macedonia, concluding that God
had called us to preach the gospel to them.
ACTS 16:10 NASB

With the blessing of the Antioch brethren, Paul teamed up with Silas and embarked on a second missionary journey. Leaving Antioch, they traveled northward through Syria and into the southern provinces of Asia Minor.

Forbidden by God to speak the word in Asia, Paul and Silas traveled through Phrygia and Galatia to Mysia. At Mysia, "they were trying to go into Bithynia, and the Spirit of Jesus did not permit them" (Acts 16:7–8 NASB).

A bit perplexed, they proceeded to the seaport town of Troas. There, in a nighttime vision, a Macedonian man appeared to Paul saying, "Come over to Macedonia and help us" (Acts 16:9 NASB). Without delay, Paul and Silas sailed from Troas to the region of Macedonia.

Although Paul and Silas set specific goals for the mission trip, they continued to seek God's direction and changed their itinerary as necessary. These changes gave the men a fruitful European ministry.

Are you listening for Christ's direction in all areas of your life or simply pushing ahead with your own agenda? Seek Christ's guidance and make adjustments to stay on track with Him. Don't miss out on God's best for you.

God, so often I go my own way and miss out on Your
best for me. Set my heart more in tune with Your
guidance. Help me to stay on course. Amen.

Greet Mary, who has worked very hard for you.
ROMANS 16:6 NET

Mary is the New Testament equivalent of Miriam, the name of Moses' sister. There are at least five different women named Mary and possibly as many as seven. We read of Mary, the mother of Jesus; Mary Magdalene; the sister of Martha and Lazarus (perhaps the same woman as Mary Magdalene); the mother of James and John; the wife of Clopas; the mother of John Mark; and the unidentified Mary of Romans 16:6.

One strong indication that the Bible is a record of true-life events is how many people carry the same name: five to seven are called Mary, three or four James, three John, and two Judas—wouldn't that be an awful name to be stuck with! There are even three people named Jesus.

When was the last time you read a novel with two characters with the same name? No one writing fiction would create people with the same name. It's far too confusing!

One proof of the Bible's extraordinary character is its internal structure. Read it and judge for yourself: Does this read like a novel or a biography?

*Father, I believe the Bible is truth. Some people say
that some or all of it is fiction. But I know better.
The Bible is the Word of God. The Bible is You! Amen.*

"Those who are wise will shine like the brightness of the heavens, and those who lead many to righteousness, like the stars for ever and ever."
DANIEL 12:3 NIV

In the verses immediately preceding this one, God told Daniel about the resurrection of the dead, when the righteous would be raised back to life to discover that they were now immortal (Daniel 12:2). Not only that, but if they had led others to live righteous lives as well, both by word and by example, they would shine like stars forever.

In the Bible, stars symbolize angels (Job 38:7), and Daniel had already seen an angel whose face blazed like lightning and whose supernatural body gleamed with light (Daniel 10:5–6). He had a good idea how beautiful and powerful our resurrected bodies would be.

Several hundred years later, the apostle Paul described our resurrected bodies in greater detail. Though our bodies are now perishable, dishonorable, and weak, they will be raised imperishable, glorious, and powerful (1 Corinthians 15:42–43). Not everyone will shine with the same level of brilliance and glory, since "star differs from star in splendor" (1 Corinthians 15:41 NIV).

Shine brightly for Christ now, and He'll see to it that you shine brightly for all eternity.

Mighty God, I will be a light for You. I will lead others to Christ, and together we will light the way to You and Your heaven. Amen.

～ Day 292 ～

If anyone is in Christ, he is a new creature; the old things
passed away; behold, new things have come.
2 Corinthians 5:17 nasb

It's safe to say that the science pages of the *Corinth Daily* never carried a story about the discovery of any "new creature" that the apostle Paul described. It didn't report any paleontologist's find of new-creature bones.

Of course not—Paul's new creature was a creative description of what happens to any person who enters into a relationship with God's Son, Jesus the Christ. It's his answer to those who snipe, "How can you call him a Christian? Why, I remember when he. . ."

As in any large metropolis, the Corinthian population had more than its share of disreputables. The church of that city was busy with outreach evangelism. As men and women accepted Christ, it was necessary to make assurance that the new believer was a new creature in Christ. His old ways were ancient history. He was encouraged to make amends and share how everything about him was new.

There is more than one message in this fascinating verse: (1) Accept a new child of God with open arms. (2) Don't let Satan beat you down for your past life. (3) Newness is how God sees you; your job is to make amends and share the new life.

Savior, You've made me brand-new! I've exchanged my
worldly garments for a heavenly robe. My life will never
be the same, and I thank You, Lord Jesus! Amen.

"Though it is the smallest of all seeds, yet when it grows,
it is the largest of garden plants and becomes a tree,
so that the birds come and perch in its branches."
MATTHEW 13:32 NIV

Insignificant beginnings can lead to magnificent finishes. Jesus picked up the tiniest of all seeds—a mustard seed—to show the disciples. This seed is about the size of the point of a sharpened pencil tip.

Once planted, the seed grows slowly in a gradual process. The seedling takes days or even weeks before it gives any sign of breaking through the ground. Why does growth drag on so slowly?

The mustard seed requires deep roots. The plant grows its roots three times faster than the stalk in order to be well grounded. Mustard trees grow up to twenty-one feet tall with the roots reaching down to sixty-three feet in the ground.

God planted mustard-seed-sized faith within each of us. Our faith may seem inadequate and so small we no longer think it exists. But often during these times, we are not aware of the deep transformation occurring within our souls.

God is pushing our roots deeper. We can help nourish this growth through prayer and the study of His Word.

Miraculous growth from a very small seed is possible only through the work of the Master Gardener.

Your greatest work in me, Father, comes when I'm
completely unaware. In my darkest hours when I feel
separated from You, You nourish and strengthen the
roots of my faith. Thank You, Father. Amen.

Eye for eye, tooth for tooth, hand for hand, foot for foot.
Exodus 21:24 asv

The movie thug straightened up, wiping his mouth with the back of his hand. Seeing blood, he started forward with menace. "I'll get you for that. An eye for an eye, buddy."

How often have we heard the phrase "eye for an eye," taking it to mean retaliation and revenge? The words have their origin in the second book of the Bible, where, in context, they're not about revenge but fairness in judgment! God told the people of Israel that when two fighters came before the court, a judge was to render a punishment that fit the crime. If the victim lost an eye, for example, the judge was not to take the life of the other man. In modern terms, there was to be no "cruel and unusual punishment."

How do we deal with wrongs against us? God holds us to a higher standard than the rest of the world. Jesus was severely treated on the cross, yet He prayed, "Father, forgive them." That is God's standard for us: forgiveness, not revenge. And we attain it not through the Law, but by grace.

God, give me grace to forgive my enemies. I have been hurt and betrayed, but so was Jesus, and He readily forgave! Help me to be more like Him. Amen.

They are darkened in their understanding and separated
from the life of God because of the ignorance that is
in them due to the hardening of their hearts.
EPHESIANS 4:18 NIV

Stubbornness is a terrible thing. How many of us haven't let stubbornness harden our hearts against something we would really rather be doing? Perhaps we feel awkward, afraid, or unwanted, so we stand back and pretend we never wanted to take part in the first place. Wild horses couldn't make us admit we care.

But this isn't a high school dance or a club or a wedding reception. Hardening your heart against God's Word isn't something that's going to spoil your weekend then quickly pass. The consequences are too awful to think about, so the hard hearts *don't* think about them. The question is, should we think about it for them?

Most of the hard hearts we meet will be normal people—just stubborn about the wrong things. Does that mean we should leave them behind, saying it serves them right? God doesn't want that. The hard hearts have no idea what they are walking stubbornly toward. The Christian does. Do we allow their fears to separate them from the Lord forever, or do we make sure they know they are wanted?

Hard hearts are a challenge to the man and woman of faith. Let's soften some!

Lord, I reach out to You in prayer asking that You soften
the hearts of those too stubborn to come to You themselves.
Open their hearts to receive You, Lord. Amen.

He makes winds his messengers, flames of fire his servants.
PSALM 104:4 NIV

Psalm 104 is a beautiful psalm about God the Creator. It is sometimes called "the creation psalm." It begins and ends with praises to God and outlines His mighty works.

We can better understand this verse by reading Hebrews 1:7. There Paul quotes Psalm 104:4 and explains what the first part means. Paul says, "In speaking of the angels he [God] says, 'He makes his angels spirits, and his servants flames of fire'" (NIV). Paul continues in Hebrews 1:14 (NIV), "Are not all angels ministering spirits sent to serve those who will inherit salvation?"

The second part of Psalm 104:4 can be explained through one of many references to fire in the Bible: God's manifestation as a pillar of fire that led the Israelites out of Egypt (Exodus 13:21–22). God was in the fire, commanding it to go on ahead and light the way for the Israelites when they traveled by night.

Psalm 104:4 reminds us that God sends His angels to engage with us. It provides reassurance to all believers that God is in control.

Angels are among us, Lord, proof that You love us and desire to protect us. Thank You, Father, for sending Your angels. Thank You for Your love. Amen.

～ Day 297 ～

Whatever you do, work at it with all your heart,
as working for the Lord, not for human masters.
COLOSSIANS 3:23 NIV

There are moments, as when we're watching a beautiful sunset or when a loved one strokes an arm in passing, that we don't hesitate to think of as gifts from God. Then there are the times we choose to see as tedious, like when work is unappreciated or when we are stuck in the company of someone we might think is boring. Those times are no less gifts from God. He is beside us always. The only difference is in how we behave, in how grateful we are.

Brother Lawrence, a seventeenth-century lay brother in a Carmelite monastery, practiced "the presence of God." Believing God was always with him, Lawrence turned the washing of the dishes and the repairing of sandals into acts of worship—simple things he would give his best to as a thank-you to the Lord.

It's easy to think you are working for the Lord when you are on some great quest. It's much more difficult to find a purpose in menial chores or to find a child of God in a self-centered bore.

But believe in the presence of God, and there is nothing you can do that can't also be an opportunity to raise a smile on high.

Jesus, everything You did, You did for God and for me.
You never complained or refused difficult tasks. I want to be
like You—content and willing to do God's work. Amen.

For as he thinketh in his heart, so is he.
PROVERBS 23:7 KJV

Some Christians become so desperate for financial success and relief from economic uncertainty that they subscribe to the magical thinking sweeping society today. The "secret" to prosperity is said to be simple: think about the things that you want God (or the Universe) to give you, focus on them, repeat to yourself, "They're already mine," and they will be yours.

A verse often quoted by such teachers is "For as he thinketh in his heart, so is he"—as if you only need to think about something to bring it into existence. However, this verse is *actually* talking about dining with a stingy man who says, "Eat and drink. . ." but "his heart is not with you" (NIV). He pretends to be generous, but he's actually cringing as you eat up his food. In his heart, he's stingy, and as he thinks in his heart, so *is* he.

Certainly God has promised to answer our prayers, and Jesus said, "Everything is possible for one who believes" (Mark 9:23 NIV), so yes, we should have more faith, but faith alone is not enough. God's promises are conditional on His will for us, our obedience, etc. (1 John 5:14–15; Isaiah 59:1–2). After all, God is God, not our servant.

God, thank You for Your gracious gifts. Teach me not only to have faith in Your generosity, but also to be worthy and accepting of whatever You choose to give me. Amen.

"Heaven and earth will disappear,
but my words will never disappear."
MARK 13:31 NLT

If there is anything we can be sure of in this world, it is that what God says is true. Jesus said that even the earth will eventually be no more, but His words will continue to be as true as they always have been.

As humans, we often change our minds as we navigate through our lives. As we mature in our thought processes, our point of view changes. Sometimes we reach an age where our reasoning has evolved to include different ways of seeing any particular issue. Perhaps it is that we learn more information than before and can make more informed choices with how we feel about things. This is not how it works with God.

Our Lord has been consistent since before there were people on the earth. And because of His infinite wisdom, His Word will never change. Perhaps it would be wise for us not to trust in other people, who may well have an entirely new set of ideas later. Instead, let us invest all of our faith in the one whose Word will never change.

We can be assured, as Mark 13:31 shows us, that what God says will still be true tomorrow, next week, next year, and forever.

True God, I can always count on Your Word. What You have
said is the truth and the same today as it will be forever.
I trust in You, Father. Your wisdom never fails. Amen.

> *"The prophets prophesy lies, the priests rule by their own authority, and my people love it this way. But what will you do in the end?"*
> JEREMIAH 5:31 NIV

"You get the government you deserve." Charles Wheelan, PhD, author of *The Naked Economist*, could have been speaking about the priests and prophets of Jeremiah's day. The prophets prophesied lies instead of God's truth. Priests ordained by God instead ruled by their own authority. And the people lapped it up.

Centuries earlier, the prophet Micah saw much the same problem. He said, "If a liar and deceiver comes and says, 'I will prophesy for you plenty of wine and beer,' that would be just the prophet for this people!" (Micah 2:11 NIV).

Unfortunately, the people of Judah would reap what they had sowed: siege, destruction, death, exile. . .

The apostle John described another time when people loved sin. Even after the seven trumpets sounded, "the rest of mankind who were not killed by these plagues still did not repent of the work of their hands" (Revelation 9:20 NIV). When they appeared before the great white throne, their end was pronounced: "Each person was judged according to what they had done" (Revelation 20:13 NIV).

As for the Jews of Jeremiah's day, our choices today will determine our end. Let's be careful what we wish for.

Father, help me to choose wisely and be obedient to Your teaching. I want my actions to have pleased You on that day when I approach Your throne. Amen.

Anyone who listens to the word but does not do what it says is like someone who looks at his face in a mirror and, after looking at himself, goes away and immediately forgets what he looks like.
JAMES 1:23–24 NIV

Imagine there was a magic mirror that showed your true nature. Would you look? Would you expect to like what you saw there?

James tells his readers there is such a mirror: the Word of God as he had it then, the Bible we have now.

Some folks have a love/hate relationship with mirrors. They don't look too closely because they are scared of what they might see, but from a distance they think they look fine. Some Christians have a similar attitude to the Bible. They can quote it at length and know where all the books are, but they pretend not to see what it asks of them.

A closer inspection of the Bible does more than show our faults; it shows the beings God created us to be. It's up to us to remember that image when we are away from the "mirror." And how better to remember than by actually living the Word every day?

Being a faithful servant of the Most High isn't easy. But it's who you were meant to be. And don't you forget that!

Dear God, when I look in the mirror, I want to see Jesus. Help me to be a reflection of the life He lived and the things He taught. Amen.

See, I set before you today life and prosperity, death and destruction.
DEUTERONOMY 30:15 NIV

When God created humanity, He gave us the power, responsibility, and privilege of free choice. Every person is accountable for his or her individual actions.

Moses told the Israelites, "I command you today to love the LORD your God, to walk in obedience to him, and to keep his commands, decrees and laws; then you will live and increase, and the LORD your God will bless you in the land you are entering to possess" (Deuteronomy 30:16 NIV). In previous chapters, Moses had underscored the blessings of obedience and the horrible curses of disobedience. In Deuteronomy 30:15, he urges the Israelites to choose.

The choice was, and still is, clear: life and prosperity or death and destruction. Without question, we reap the benefits or consequences of whatever choices we make. Obedience leads to present and future blessings, while disobedience leads to present and future miseries. To obey God's Word brings great rewards, but to turn away from God to worship the gods of this world ultimately brings ruin.

The choice is ours to make. As Moses taught, choose wisely.

Lord, bless me with the wisdom to choose the right way. Set me on a righteous path that leads away from worldly gods and, ultimately, to You. Amen.

For God's gifts and his call are irrevocable.
ROMANS 11:29 NIV

We are surrounded by a culture that is obsessed with gift giving.

Each month we are bombarded by advertisements that proclaim the next holiday and the appropriate gift to go with it: January—New Year's Day; February—Valentine's Day; March—Saint Patrick's Day; April—Easter; May—Mother's Day; June—Father's Day; July—Independence Day; August—Back-to-School; September—Labor Day; October—Halloween; November—Thanksgiving; December—Christmas.

When you add in individual celebrations for birthdays, anniversaries, adoptions, and job promotions, we're facing a full social calendar, complete with gift-giving obligations!

In contrast, God gives gifts to us freely—and for no occasion at all except for the simple fact that He loves us. And when He gives a present, there are no returns. The gift has been chosen so perfectly that there is no need to stand in a returns line at the department store to exchange it for something else. God's giftings are permanent, and they fit us, individually, to a tee.

The same is true of God's calling. When God calls to us, beckoning us to share in His ministry, He never rescinds His word. He never thinks, *Gee, I wish I hadn't given you that.* He shares Himself, His giftings, and His callings with us to reach a hurting world. And He never takes them back.

Father, thank You for all those "just because" gifts—priceless one-of-a-kind gifts just because You love me. Help me to take good care of them and use them to please You. Amen.

"I will appoint rulers to take care of them. My people
will no longer be afraid or terrified, and I will not
punish them again. I, the LORD, have spoken."
JEREMIAH 23:4 GNT

Quite a few people see disaster and trouble around the world and wonder why God doesn't stop it. This verse gives us insight into how God works in the world. He works through people. Repeatedly in the Old and New Testaments, we find God using people to reach out to a hurting world. He has used shepherds and kings, men and women, angels, and even a donkey to move in the affairs of this life.

In the book of Acts we see men and women of the church moved by the Spirit to minister to vast numbers of people. God is not silent. He is not far off. He is still moving in the churches, hospitals, soup kitchens, disaster-relief workers, and people of ordinary occupations to touch the lives of others. To those who say that God does nothing, we may tell them that God has always moved through people. Let's stop saying that God isn't working and instead volunteer to serve. Then we'll find God moving through us!

God, every day I see You working through good people
in the world. Acts of love and mercy surround me.
Enlist me as a volunteer! Work through me too. Amen.

～ Day 305 ～

But you, man of God, flee from all this,
and pursue righteousness, godliness, faith,
love, endurance and gentleness.
1 TIMOTHY 6:11 NIV

Paul loved Timothy as a son, calling him his "true son in the faith" (1 Timothy 1:2 NIV). The apostle had a vested interest in helping the younger man succeed in life and ministry and wrote him two letters full of advice.

In the sixth chapter of 1 Timothy, Paul discussed the danger of the love of money (1 Timothy 6:10). The word *but* at the start of verse 11 changes focus. Unlike people who had wandered from the faith, Timothy was a true man of God. Paul advised him to run away from the love of money and to run toward the right things. He repeats his command in 2 Timothy 2:22.

Two of those good things, godliness and righteousness, are closely connected. Godliness is vertical—our reverence toward God; righteousness is horizontal—how our right relationship with God impacts our relationships with others. Put together with faith, love, endurance, and gentleness, it's a powerful mix.

Flee the bad. Pursue the good. That was Paul's recipe for a godly life.

Dear Father, I worship and praise You for leading me toward
righteousness. Staying close to You and living right in faith, love,
endurance, and gentleness makes me a better person. Amen.

Thus says the LORD to his anointed, to Cyrus, whose right
hand I have grasped, to subdue nations before him.
ISAIAH 45:1 ESV

Who will be the next president? What will be the name of a child who will be born to one of your neighbors in ten years? Why don't you know?

What's so fascinating about this verse is that God tells us in advance the name of the person who will liberate Israel from Babylonian oppression—150 years before his birth! Much of Bible prophecy is literal, where God gives names (such as Cyrus the Great), times (such as seventy years before Israel is released from captivity), and places (such as Bethlehem, where the Christ child was to be born).

So when we read Matthew 24 and other places where end-times prophecies are recorded, we can be sure of their literal fulfillment. For instance, we do not look for a Christ to come out of a nation, but out of the sky when the sun has turned dark (Revelation 6:12–14). Prophecy confirms the presence of God and keeps us from being deceived.

Dear God, I am wary of false prophets—there are so
many these days—but I know I can always rely on the
truthfulness of the prophecies in Your Word. Amen.

There is only one Lawgiver and Judge, the one who is able to save and destroy. But you—who are you to judge your neighbor?
JAMES 4:12 NIV

Have you ever "gotten even" with someone over something? Have you ever reacted unkindly to someone else's unkindness?

We've all done it. It's our way of passing judgment on others. This is what we think they deserve, so we give it to them.

Does that kind of judgment make us better people? No, never.

So what's the alternative? Oh yeah, soppy old love! And we dismiss it as the soft option, the option that gets us taken advantage of, the way that makes us look foolish to others.

But how foolish do we look when we lower all our personal standards to get even, when we make ourselves as bad as our enemies because *they* deserve it? That's just a win-win situation for the enemy.

Jesus wasn't vague when He told us to love God and one another. It's the answer to every problem, and anyone who dismisses it as the soft option obviously hasn't tried it.

Judging others usually only makes us deserving of a harsh judgment in return. Don't judge—love. Then, when it comes our time to face the Lawgiver, His judgment on us will be a love we didn't deserve either.

*Jesus, I am no better than anyone else, so who am I
to judge my neighbors? Help me, Jesus. Help me not
to judge them but to love them instead. Amen.*

Seven times a day I praise you for your righteous laws.
PSALM 119:164 NIV

In the Bible, the number seven symbolizes completeness. God created the world in seven days. Seven days complete a week. Major festivals, such as the Passover and Feast of Tabernacles, and wedding feasts lasted seven days. In Pharaoh's dream, the seven good years followed by seven years of famine represented a complete cycle. In the New Testament, seven churches are mentioned in Revelation.

The psalmist prayed seven times a day. He lifted up praises to God throughout the entire day. He filled the minutes of his life with gratitude and attention to God.

The Bible tells us to pray without ceasing. A fixed-hour prayer ritual is called "praying the hours" or the "daily office." Hearts and minds turn toward God at set times. We make an effort to create space in our busy lives to praise God and express our gratitude throughout the day.

We can create any kind of prayer schedule. Each stoplight we pass, the ring of the alarm on our watches, or a pause during television commercials can serve as a simple reminder to pray. We can be alert during the day for ways God protects and guides us.

Seven moments a day—to thank the Lord for all the moments of our lives.

Sometimes I forget to pray; busyness gets in the way. But I can change that! I will set aside specific times throughout my day to pray and praise You, Lord. Amen.

Confess your trespasses to one another, and pray for
one another, that you may be healed. The effective,
fervent prayer of a righteous man avails much.
JAMES 5:16 NKJV

The exact authorship of the book of James is uncertain. While this book of the New Testament is often attributed to James the half brother of Jesus, the author identifies himself only as "James, a servant of God and of the Lord Jesus Christ" (James 1:1 NIV).

This less-than-well-identified James encourages us to admit our faults to other trusted Christians. Why? So that we can support and pray for one another that we might be healed. The healing mentioned in this verse isn't limited to physical healing. More often, it means healing the heart of its sinfulness. James adds that the earnest prayers offered by Christians bring results. The results might not be what we expect, but we can be assured that they are God's results—His will for our lives.

Are you carrying the burden of your faults all by yourself? Why not have a heart-to-heart talk with a Christian friend?

Heavenly Father, there are things that I am keeping to myself
that weigh heavy on my heart. Help me to share my burden
with the right Christian friend. Lead me, Lord. Amen.

"Now therefore, put away the foreign gods which are in your midst, and incline your hearts to the Lord, the God of Israel."
Joshua 24:23 nasb

Although Abraham, Isaac, and Jacob worshipped the true God, this didn't always hold true with their wives. Jacob's wife Rachel "stole her father's household idols and took them with her" (Genesis 31:19 nlt). Worship of these idols passed on to future generations.

While slaves, the Israelites added Egyptian gods to their other pagan deities and brought them along when fleeing out of Egypt.

The Israelites knew God performed miraculous feats like dividing the Red Sea, providing manna in the wilderness, and destroying Jericho's walls. Nevertheless, many worshipped pagan deities as they prepared to receive their inheritance in the Promised Land.

In an electrifying speech, Joshua challenged the Israelites to "choose for yourselves today whom you will serve," and the people answered, "Far be it from us that we should forsake the Lord to serve other gods" (Joshua 24:15–16 nasb).

Joshua ordered them to demonstrate their allegiance to God by destroying their idols. That generation of Israelites abandoned the false deities and followed God to the end of their lives.

Is anything hindering your relationship with God? Perhaps there are things you need to stay away from in a renewed commitment to Him. Choose today whom you will serve.

Dear God, make clear to me the things in this world that have become my idols. You are my God, and I choose to serve only You. Amen.

~ Day 311 ~

*Jesus said to the people who believed in him, "You are truly
my disciples if you remain faithful to my teachings."*
JOHN 8:31 NLT

Jesus taught us how to live in two ways. He spoke words of wisdom, making very clear what God expects of us. But even more importantly, He taught by example. It seems that people say, "Jesus did this," or "Jesus did that," more often than "Jesus told us to do this." We remember things best by being shown.

We can *say* anything we want. We can tell everyone we are followers of Jesus, and we can put on quite a show for those around us. All of us have probably known people who attend church and pretend to be Christians on Sunday, but seem to be anything but Christians during the rest of the week.

Jesus said, though, that we are truly His followers if we are faithful. That means we continue to be Christians outside of the church. We live the Word of God every day; and although we may have failures, we strive to live as closely to Jesus' teachings as we can. As it is so well said in John 8:31, we must remain faithful. The Lord is certainly faithful to us!

*Jesus, Your faithfulness to me is so great. You've set the
perfect example for living, and You are so patient with me
while I try to be like You. Thank You, Jesus. Amen.*

Discipline me, LORD, but only in due measure—
not in your anger, or you will reduce me to nothing.
JEREMIAH 10:24 NIV

Jeremiah struggled with his constant messages of gloom and doom to the people of Israel. The ending verses of chapter 10 record his personal plea for compassion in the midst of discipline: correct me with justice, not anger. His prayer echoes that of the psalmist, who twice asked God, "Do not rebuke me in your anger" (Psalm 6:1; 38:1 NIV).

Since the Bible teaches that there is none righteous, a cry for justice and not anger seems pointless. Wouldn't justice demand punishment? The ultimate punishment for sin is death (Romans 6:23).

Isaiah tells us that justice is the "measuring line" (28:17 NIV). The American justice system metes punishment to lawbreakers; but the civil courts seek to restore what is lost to those who have been wronged.

If human judges offer justice to the oppressed, how much more so will God! Isaiah said, "The LORD longs to be gracious to you; therefore he will rise up to show you compassion. For the LORD is a God of justice" (30:18 NIV).

God's anger may diminish us (the literal translation of Jeremiah 10:24), but His just discipline produces "a harvest of righteousness and peace" (Hebrews 12:11 NIV).

Lord, rain down Your justice upon us. We need Your righteousness and peace.

Lord, I pray for my nation. Rain down Your justice
upon it, and with mercy lead it to repentance,
Your righteousness, and peace. Amen.

Jesus told him, "Because you have seen me, you have believed;
blessed are those who have not seen and yet have believed."
JOHN 20:29 NIV

Before His ascension into heaven, Jesus appeared to several people, including some of the disciples. One of them, Thomas, had not been part of the initial sightings of Jesus. When others told him, he refused to believe—saying he needed direct proof to be convinced of the Lord's resurrection.

One week later, Thomas got his proof when Jesus walked through the locked doors of a room where the disciples were staying. The Lord invited Thomas to feel His hands and touch His side. In their exchange, Jesus mildly scolded Thomas for his skepticism, saying, "Stop doubting and believe" (20:27 NIV).

If we let them, these words Jesus spoke to Thomas can hit us right between the eyes. Aren't we all like "Doubting Thomas" at times? Don't we often want everything in black and white—or for God to appear in a burning bush (Exodus 3), a miraculous cloud (Exodus 13:21–22), or through the words of a talking donkey (Numbers 22:28–33)?

But the fact is that God *does* appear to us—through His Word, His Son, and His Spirit. Jesus says to all of us, "Blessed are those who have not seen and yet believe. Stop your doubting."

Dear God, Your presence is all around me. I see You in the sun,
the moon, the stars, and countless other ways. Still, there are
moments when I doubt You. Forgive me, Father. Amen.

He who sits in the heavens shall laugh.
PSALM 2:4 NKJV

Ever wonder whether God has a sense of humor? It shouldn't surprise us to find that we who were made in His image laugh as He does. But it's important to read this verse carefully to find out what gives God the chuckles.

Psalm 2 provides a telescope to focus on details in the future. We can see what will happen after Jesus returns to earth: He will set up His kingdom and dole out territories for His faithful servants to rule the world with Him. After a while, though, some people will refuse His rule and plot against Him. Therein lies the humor.

God laughs at the ludicrous. The people secretly plot against a God who reads their very thoughts. They send their strongest to fight the one who holds the universe together single-handedly. They think they can outwit the Creator, whose wisdom and power generated the miles of blood vessels and billions of cells that make up their arrogant beings. It is funny, when you think about it.

No one can outsmart God or outwit His plans for our lives. There's comfort in that thought—and that's no joke.

Mighty God, I am grateful that You are my Creator,
the one who laughs at vain human attempts to outwit You.
How foolish men are! Always, You will prevail. Amen.

*We are hard pressed on every side, but not crushed;
perplexed, but not in despair; persecuted, but not
abandoned; struck down, but not destroyed.*
2 CORINTHIANS 4:8–9 NIV

Throughout his epistles, the apostle Paul alluded to the Grecian games of biblical times—this verse is one such instance. Just as Jesus used contemporary parables to drive His messages home, Paul used familiar references to encourage and help the early Christians.

Interestingly, three expressions of 2 Corinthians 4:8–9 refer to the customs of wrestling, the fourth to running in a race. To the wrestler, "hard pressed" meant having no way of resistance. Puzzled by his antagonist's skill, a wrestler could be "perplexed," not knowing what move to attempt. The grappler who "struck down" his opponent first was deemed the conqueror. "Persecuted," meanwhile, refers to one being pursued in a footrace. In each of the four clauses, the first part refers to the outward experience of our earthly experience, the latter the excellence of the power we have in Christ.

Paul and the disciples were no strangers to hardships, persecution, and trials. So he penned these words encouraging the early Christians that absolutely no problem, tragedy, or sickness could defeat the believer.

That still holds true today. When the outward man suffers and our human resources are exhausted, the Christian spirit soars!

*Lord, when my resources are all used up, You bless me
with encouragement and strength to carry on. Nothing
can defeat me as long as I have You. Amen.*

Why, you do not even know what will happen tomorrow. What is your
life? You are a mist that appears for a little while and then vanishes.
JAMES 4:14 NIV

For thirty-five years, Arthur Stace wrote "Eternity" in chalk across
Sydney, Australia. His graffito was written in lights across the Sydney
Harbor Bridge during the 2000 Olympics.

Stace had been a drunk and a criminal before finding faith. His
one-man campaign was an attempt to start people thinking about
where they were going after the "mist" of this life blows away.

James points out that this life shouldn't be about material possessions and earthly things. Those, he says, are already God-given.
We are here to do His work. The question is, will we or won't we?

The "work" He asks from us is that we love each other. That's a
big ask sometimes, and that's why we get a lifetime to practice. This
life is where we learn to love Him before we meet Him.

The apostle James and Arthur Stace remind us we have a decision to make. Are we content not to think about it, are we pinning
our hopes on the things of this world, or will we do His work as
preparation for heaven?

In the words of the minister who inspired Stace, "You've got to
meet it. Where will you spend eternity?"

God, I feel joyful knowing that I will spend eternity with
You. Help me to do Your work here on Earth—to love others
and lead them into forever love with You. Amen.

David son of Jesse reigned over all Israel. He reigned over Israel forty years; he reigned in Hebron seven years and in Jerusalem thirty-three years. He died at a good old age, having enjoyed long life, wealth, and honor. His son Solomon succeeded him. King David's accomplishments, from start to finish, are recorded in the Annals of Samuel the prophet, the Annals of Nathan the prophet, and the Annals of Gad the prophet. Recorded there are all the facts about his reign and accomplishments, and an account of the events that involved him, Israel, and all the neighboring kingdoms.
1 Chronicles 29:26–30 net

Kingdom history really isn't that hard. King David's place in Bible history is easy to remember. He became king of united Israel around 1000 BC.

The kingdom split into northern Israel and southern Judah after the death of his son Solomon. Israel was pretty much always bad, while Judah alternated between bad and good kings, tending more and more toward bad ones. The Tel Dan Stele provides archaeological confirmation that both kingdoms were politically separate and that the Davidic lineage ruled southern Judah. In 722 BC the Assyrians destroyed northern Israel, and in 586 BC the Babylonians destroyed Jerusalem.

When I study the history of Your kingdom in the Bible, Father, I see that You never change. Your goodness, power, and justice last forever. Amen.

When we came to Macedonia, our bodies had no rest, but we were troubled on every side. Outside were conflicts, inside were fears.
2 Corinthians 7:5 nkjv

When friends are going through prolonged difficult times, it's easy to give them pat answers: stay focused on God and continue praising the Lord, no matter what happens; and if you do this, you'll have peace in the midst of life's storms; the storm will soon pass, and all will be well again (Isaiah 26:3; 1 Thessalonians 5:16–18). That's good advice as far as it goes, but it's not the full picture.

When Paul and his companions were going through extremely hard times in Macedonia, suffering sleep deprivation, surrounded by conflicts, and nearly overwhelmed by problems, Paul frankly confessed that he felt fear. Fear may not have wholly debilitated him, but certainly anxious thoughts constantly tried to fill his mind.

God sent him comfort and peace, and Paul said: "God, who comforts the downcast, comforted us by the coming of Titus." It not only uplifted Paul to see his good friend, but what caused him to rejoice "even more" was that Titus brought good news (2 Corinthians 7:6–7 nkjv).

Let's bring comfort and good cheer to the downcast, not just good advice (Proverbs 12:25; Isaiah 61:1–2).

Father, sometimes I don't know what to say to those feeling downcast. Teach me, please, how I might comfort them and bring them good cheer. Amen.

*Therefore, since we are surrounded by such a great cloud
of witnesses, let us throw off everything that hinders
and the sin that so easily entangles. And let us run
with perseverance the race marked out for us.*
HEBREWS 12:1 NIV

The first Olympic competition, in 776 BC, was a running race. When this letter to the Hebrews was sent to Jewish Christians, the ancient Olympics were still being conducted. The recipients were familiar with the race.

Runners often ran naked, not wanting their clothing to interfere with their running. They knew the route of the race, as it was marked out for them well in advance.

As they completed the race in an amphitheater, the crowds cheered them on to the finish line. The arena was full of spectators, many of them veteran athletes who had run the race in the past and knew how hard it was to finish well.

The Christian life is like a marathon, a race in which God is our aim. As we run, a huge crowd cheers us on. They encourage us to throw off anything that hinders our pace and may keep us from finishing. This great cloud of witnesses urges us onward, living the Christian life by faith as they did.

Don't give up—keep running toward the finish line of heaven.

*This race through life is hard, but I will stay strong and give
it my best effort. If I fall, Lord, lift me up. If I become weak,
carry me. We'll cross the finish line together. Amen.*

"Do not be afraid of them or their words. Do not be afraid, though briers and thorns are all around you and you live among scorpions."
 EZEKIEL 2:6 NIV

Ezekiel's call was a difficult one. He was to preach judgment to the rebellious, obstinate, and stubborn Israelites (vv. 3–4). Whether they would receive the message was questionable, but for certain they would seek to kill the messenger. Yet God's summons to the prophet was delivered with words of encouragement: "Do not be afraid."

Have you ever sensed God prompting you to speak when you preferred to remain silent? As Christians we are called to exhort, encourage, and occasionally rebuke in the spirit of God's love.

Living for Christ is far from a popularity contest. In fact, we are often misunderstood or ridiculed for our spiritual convictions, until we feel as if we are embedded in a field of briers and thorns while venomous scorpions surround every side. But God's mandate is the same as it was in Ezekiel's day, namely, communicate the truth of God's Word with love and without fear.

Just like the prophet of old, we are called to simply speak and leave the rest to God.

Dear Lord, when I hesitate to speak about the truth of Your Word, prod me to do so. Remove my fear so that I can boldly speak out in love. Amen.

Be on your guard; stand firm in the faith; be courageous; be strong.
1 CORINTHIANS 16:13 NIV

You have probably heard this verse before.

Paul's letters often included commands to fellow believers, instructions for living the Christian life. When he wrote, Paul chose his words wisely.

"Be on your guard; stand firm." These words invoke the image of an army facing its enemy. Instead of running, it stands and fights against its oppressor. Its soldiers are strong and courageous. This is the image that Paul wanted to impress on the Christians at Corinth. They should be vigilant, stand instead of run, and be courageous and strong. When they were persecuted for their Christian beliefs, they were to react as soldiers in the army of God.

Standing firm in our faith is not something that comes easily. We are tempted by evil every day. We forget that we must always be vigilant. When someone treats us unfairly or when we face obstacles that seem insurmountable, we can remember Paul's words in 1 Corinthians 16:13. Face evil with courage and strength. Stand firm as a soldier in the body of Christ.

Dear God, bless me with courage and a tough armor of faith so that I can stand firm as a soldier in the body of Christ. Amen.

"I am as strong now as I was when Moses sent me on that journey, and I can still travel and fight as well as I could then."
JOSHUA 14:11 NLT

Caleb was descended from the Kenizzites, a people residing in Canaan during Abraham's time. At some point before the Exodus, members of the Kenizzites turned to God and joined the Israelite tribe of Judah.

Unlike many Israelites, who simply mimicked the religion of their birth, the Kenizzites possessed a deep trust and faith in God.

Caleb demonstrated these convictions when Moses sent him and eleven other men to scout out the Promised Land. Only he and Joshua returned with a favorable report.

For his faithfulness, God promised, "I will bring him into the land he explored. His descendants will possess their full share of that land" (Numbers 14:24 NLT).

When the time came to distribute the land, Caleb requested Hebron, a city that had terrified ten of the scouts years before. At eighty-five years of age, Caleb prepared to battle the Anakites still living in Hebron and take the town as his inheritance.

Caleb's life reflected his trust in God. Along with an allotment of the Promised Land, he left the priceless legacy of faith to his family.

Like Caleb, let's endeavor to leave a heritage of faith in God to those we love.

Heavenly Father, I want my family to be with You forever. Lead me to be a faithful example for them. Lead me to show them the path to You through Jesus Christ. Amen.

Day 323

*Speaking to one another with psalms, hymns, and songs from
the Spirit. Sing and make music from your heart to the Lord.*
EPHESIANS 5:19 NIV

We are surrounded by music. Our radio alarm clocks awaken us
each morning, TV musically underscores the dramatic moments
in our favorite shows, and commercial writers come up with catchy
jingles to sell their latest, greatest whatchamacallit. Our computers
reprimand error keystrokes with familiar beeps, and apps streaming
music keep us company during our exercise sessions. We live in a
symphony (or a cacophony) of sound.

Now, rewind your thoughts to a different era two thousand
years ago. Electricity was limited to lightning in the night sky, and
amplification depended on the acoustics of the amphitheater. In
this relatively quiet environment, Paul suggests that making music
together is, in fact, a good way to connect with God.

Picture a solitary soul receiving encouragement from the community of believers worshipping together in song. In a time when
music had to be participatory in order to be experienced, imagine
the hearts of each worshipper storing up precious phrases of song
as treasured memories.

Biblical generations broke the silence of their world by singing
praise to God. In the loudness of our modern world, we must create
our own times of silence. And in the stillness, our hearts sing their
own song of praise. Be still—and listen.

*Thank You, Lord, for stillness. Thank You for quieting
my heart so that I can hear Your precious voice.
Speak to me, Father. I'm listening. Amen.*

∽ Day 324 ∽

*And the sun stood still, and the moon stayed, until the
people had avenged themselves upon their enemies.*
JOSHUA 10:13 KJV

Ever have one of those days when you never seem to have enough
time to do what you need to do? Well, in our passage, the full armed
forces of five kings had come against the city of Gibeah, which
Joshua had agreed to protect. As Joshua prepared his men to fight,
God promised him that He had already delivered the enemy into
Israel's hand and that none of them would stand before the Israelites
(v. 8). After they had smashed the overwhelming foe in battle
and watched God drop bombs of hailstones on them, Joshua asked
God to stop the clock. The sun and moon paused, and Joshua's men
had another day of light to erase the menace.

The longest day in history was also a day for believing in the
Lord for victory. Joshua went against the combined armies of five
kings because he believed the Lord's promise, and he saw God
fight for him. In that spirit, he prayed a great prayer. May we be
emboldened to pray great prayers when we see the Lord following
through in our lives!

*God, fight for me! I believe in victory over my troubles and
my enemies. Their words and deeds pierce me like arrows,
but with Your great love, You protect me. Amen.*

Each of you should use whatever gift you have received to serve others, as faithful stewards of God's grace in its various forms.
1 PETER 4:10 NIV

There are no useless lives. But there are lives taken out of service. God doesn't do that, and His enemy isn't responsible either. Those lives are put "on the bench" by the people living them.

You might think people incapacitated by illness are taken out of the game by God—but they have a role in bringing out the best in others. People who are swamped by the evil around them might feel unable to do any real good—but their courage is a great example.

This message is for the ones who through fear of failure or worry about their inadequacy deliberately sideline themselves. There are no useless lives. There is a point to your being on this earth. If the least you can offer is a smile, if you can only sit and listen, then smile and listen. The most seemingly insignificant act on your part might be what makes the difference to another struggling soul.

Think you have nothing to offer? You're wrong. Get back in the game and make your play, however feeble it might seem to you. God will take it and do great things with it. He just needs you to be in the game.

Lord, when I am physically or emotionally unable to give my all, remind me of my gifts, especially those I'm unaware of, and teach me to share them with others. Amen.

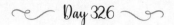

Abimelech moved on to Thebez; he besieged and captured it. There was a fortified tower in the center of the city, so all the men and women, as well as the city's leaders, ran into it and locked the entrance. Then they went up to the roof of the tower. Abimelech came and attacked the tower. When he approached the entrance of the tower to set it on fire, a woman threw an upper millstone down on his head and shattered his skull. He quickly called to the young man who carried his weapons, "Draw your sword and kill me, so they will not say, 'A woman killed him.'" So the young man stabbed him and he died. When the Israelites saw that Abimelech was dead, they went home. God repaid Abimelech for the evil he did to his father by murdering his seventy half-brothers.

JUDGES 9:50–56 NET

Abimelech may be the first person in history seriously injured by a large kitchen appliance! The millstone cracked his skull, but he was still able to talk, so perhaps the wound wasn't mortal. One has to wonder if, in his male-chauvinist pride, Abimelech acted a little prematurely in asking to be killed.

Pride is an evil thing, Father. It creeps up and hardens a heart with stubbornness. Keep me humble, please. There's no room for pride in my heart. Amen.

*Correct your son, and he will give you comfort;
he will also delight your soul.*
PROVERBS 29:17 NASB

Solidarity within the family is a primary request on everyone's wish list. Solomon, the great creator and collector of wise sayings, well knew the danger of uncorrected children. As a son of King David, he keenly remembered the pain he and his brother Absalom brought to the family. Both siblings were desperately in need of a strong corrective hand.

Another translation reads, "Discipline your children, and they will give you rest" (NRSV). Is there a parent who hasn't lain awake waiting to hear the front door open and a son or daughter's footsteps on the stairs?

As Solomon's father learned, a permissive mom or dad isn't just damaging a child, but herself or himself too.

Poet Henry Wadsworth Longfellow, who had no sons, wrote that one's greatest foe begins within: "None but one [can harm you]—none but yourself, who are your greatest foe." The poet lived by this thought. He taught its truth to his children, "grave Alice, and laughing Allegra, and Edith with golden hair."

We cannot, as Longfellow suggested, keep our children "in the dungeon in the round tower of my heart." But we can prepare them to live disciplined lives in a corrupt society.

*Lord, help me to be firm and just when disciplining my
children. Give me wisdom to correct them steadfastly yet gently
and to lead them toward living their lives for You. Amen.*

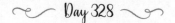

In the same way, you who are younger, submit yourselves to your elders. All of you, clothe yourselves with humility toward one another, because, "God opposes the proud but shows favor to the humble."
1 PETER 5:5 NIV

Do you suppose teenagers enjoy hearing this verse? If it were only for teens, they might have a right to feel put upon. But it isn't. We can *all* find someone older and wiser if we have the eyes to look.

So the question is this: Do we have the humility to learn from those older people? If we do, our submission becomes a positive thing. Through it we move onward and upward. If we don't, we set ourselves up as the authority, as people who know it all. That's exactly the kind of person the next generation likes to rebel against and try to topple. So the generations are separated because of pride.

It's tougher to rebel against humility. If our children see the benefits of positive submission, the peace and wisdom it brings, they might follow the example and learn from us. In turn, they become the teachers. It's a process that never ends. We will always be younger than someone, so we'll always have more to learn. And even when we're "as old as the hills," we won't be as old as God.

Father, open my heart to wisdom offered by those older than me. Set their wise words inside my heart so I might learn from them and pass them on to younger generations. Amen.

*A person can do nothing better than to eat and drink and find
satisfaction in their own toil. This too, I see, is from the hand of God.*
ECCLESIASTES 2:24 NIV

Ecclesiastes has earned a reputation for pessimism in the Old
Testament canon. After all, the teacher (presumed to be Solomon)
repeats the word *meaningless* thirty-five times in twelve chapters.

In the second chapter, he examines the worth of pursuing pleasure
and the worth of work. He concludes, "This too is meaningless"
(2:23 NIV).

In spite of his seeming pessimism, the teacher finds nuggets
of meaning. Sometimes he compares two items, such as by saying
"wisdom is *better than* folly" (2:13 NIV, italics added). Four times he
uses the formula found in 2:24: "nothing better than." To borrow a
movie title, this is "as good as it gets" in this life.

What are those rock-bottom sources of satisfaction?

- your work (2:24; 3:22)
- eating, drinking, and all of life (2:24; 8:15)
- being happy (3:12)
- doing good while you can (3:12)

Live each day to the fullest and find joy in the simple things. If we
follow the teacher's advice, we will find the meaning that escaped him.

*Dear God, open my eyes to the simple things in life.
So often, these are the things that bring the most
joy. Help me to enjoy life more fully. Amen.*

"Come now, let us reason together, says the LORD: though your sins are like scarlet, they shall be as white as snow; though they are red like crimson, they shall become like wool."
ISAIAH 1:18 RSV

The sins described as being "like scarlet. . .red like crimson" refer to God telling a murderess, "Your hands are full of blood" (v. 15 RSV). This murderess was "the daughter of Zion" (v. 8 RSV), the people of Judah. God stated that unless they stopped sinning, He would not pay attention to their offerings and faithful keeping of feast days. He would turn away His face when they prayed.

God wanted to hear prayers of repentance, and He wanted that repentance to be followed by action. He commanded: "Cease to do evil, learn to do good" (vv. 16–17 RSV).

They were in the habit of living selfishly and trampling on others, but God promised that if they repented, though their sins were like scarlet, every stain would be washed away. The word *scarlet* means "double-dyed" and refers to dipping white garments in scarlet dye twice to make certain that it would not wash out. Yet God said He *would* wash every stain away.

This message is still true for us today: God can forgive the deepest sins and wash us clean, "as white as snow."

I will confess my sins to You, God. I praise You for Your forgiveness. How wonderful You are to forgive even my worst sins and reward me with a clean heart. Amen.

*But Ruth replied, "Don't ask me to leave you and turn back.
Wherever you go, I will go; wherever you live, I will live. Your
people will be my people, and your God will be my God."*
RUTH 1:16 NLT

During a famine in Israel, a man named Elimelech moved with his
wife, Naomi, and their two sons into the land of Moab. Life became
easier, and each son married.

Sadness descended on the family when Elimelech died. Then
each son passed away, leaving behind their widows, Ruth and Orpah,
and their mother, Naomi.

By now the famine in Israel had ended, and Naomi decided to
return home to Israel, with Orpah and Ruth accompanying her.
Along the way, Naomi urged her daughters-in-law to "go back to
your mothers' homes" instead of coming with her (Ruth 1:8 NLT).

Orpah returned, but not Ruth. She refused, determined to stay
with her mother-in-law and take Naomi's God as her own.

What attracted Ruth to this heartbroken woman?

During the years in Moab, Naomi must have radiated an authentic
faith in God. No doubt this faith peeked out even as Naomi worked
through the pain and anger of the grieving process.

Life was hard then; it's hard now. But God is greater. Does your
faith shine during difficult times? Trust God to get you through,
and others will notice.

*Heavenly Father, I am inspired by women like Ruth who
face difficult times with stalwart faith that radiates toward
others. Help me to be that kind of woman. Amen.*

For the love of money is a root of all kinds of evil.
Some people, eager for money, have wandered from the
faith and pierced themselves with many griefs.
1 Timothy 6:10 niv

Even if you haven't been an avid Bible reader, you probably have heard this verse.

Two of the most popular topics covered in the Bible are love and money. In fact, out of Jesus' approximately forty parables, nearly half refer to money. Ironically in this verse, the words *love* and *money* are written side by side, forming a simple equation of sorts: Love of money = evil. Ouch, that stings! Doesn't everybody love money?

In Paul's words to Timothy, it's not money that's evil, rather the extent to which our hearts are involved. What applied to people almost two thousand years ago applies one hundred percent to us today. Our hearts need constant examining when it comes to money. How much commitment and priority do we give to obtaining money? And once we've got it, how passionate are we in getting, spending, or saving more? Paul cautions that some of us who are eager for money have wandered from the faith. Wandering from faith separates us from God, and separation from God equals grief. Paul's words earlier in this chapter are a timeless reminder that we bring nothing into this world, and we take nothing out.

Dear Lord, sometimes I pray asking You for money. Teach
me to have the right motive in those prayers and pray for the
sake of needing money and not for the love of it. Amen.

*They dress the wound of my people as though it were not
serious. "Peace, peace," they say, when there is no peace.*
JEREMIAH 6:14 NIV

Jeremiah wrote in the final days of the nation of Israel. The people
had sinned and worshipped idols for too long; judgment was certain
and would no longer be delayed.

God's anger burned fiercely against the leaders of Israel, religious men who should have fought beside Jeremiah. Instead, they
"all practice[d] deceit" without shame (v. 13 NIV). So much without
shame, they didn't even know how to blush (v. 15). They spoke the
message the people wanted to hear, much like Neville Chamberlain,
who proclaimed, "Peace in our time," when faced with the Nazi threat.

God often emphasizes His message by repeating it. That happened with this indictment. Word for word, God repeats the judgment
of 6:13–15 in verses 10–12 of chapter 8. The prophet Ezekiel also
spoke against leaders claiming a false peace (Ezekiel 13:10). The
persistence of false prophets in promising peace was enough to make
Jeremiah question his own message (Jeremiah 14:13).

May God grant us courage to speak His message in the face
of opposition.

*God, I see great leaders of great lands proclaiming
falsehoods to their citizens. Give me courage to speak
out and declare the truth of Your Word. Amen.*

Dear friend, you are faithful in what you are doing for the brothers and sisters, even though they are strangers to you.
3 JOHN 1:5 NIV

Don't you sometimes wish you were a missionary, devoting yourself completely to God and the Word? All you would do is leave behind everything you've known to risk the ridicule of strangers, the ill-treatment of antagonistic powers, and perhaps an ignominious death.

No? Don't fancy that? Really?

Those called by God (the "brothers and sisters" in this verse) get a sense of mission—a willingness to sacrifice and the strength to do the Lord's work. Most of us are never asked to do anything so terribly dramatic.

Before you heave a sigh of relief, though, don't think you have nothing to do. There are "brothers and sisters" risking all for God right now. Some of them will cross our paths; others we'll never meet. Most will be strangers, like the men John thanked Gaius for helping. They are our frontline troops in the battle for souls—and if we aren't fighting alongside them, we can at least support them.

Do what you can to help those called to give their all. Never think of them as strangers. Instead, remember this: someone who loves us loves them too.

Lord, I pray for Your missionaries serving in the darkest and most dangerous parts of the world. Protect them. Bless them with the tools they need and show me how I can help them. Amen.

"As long as the earth endures, seedtime and harvest, cold and heat, summer and winter, day and night will never cease."
GENESIS 8:22 NIV

As disagreements about global warming continue, there are some God-given, "Mother Nature" absolutes that will never change.

Today's fascinating verse appears at the end of the Noah narrative—when the great flood has done its damage, the water has receded, and God invites the ark family to come out, telling the patriarch to build an altar and make a sacrifice.

Noah's faithfulness and the sweet-smelling sacrifice he kindles give God new hope in what's left of His creation. He determines never again to destroy His creatures in such a violent manner. And as a pledge of His great faithfulness, the Creator promises to keep His young world spinning on its axis, ensuring the natural cycles and beauty of nature.

In Eden, God instructed Adam to care for that corner of creation—its flora and fauna, all gifts to man from the creative hand of God (Genesis 1).

Consider this: If today God returned to our Eden, would He still say, "It is very good"? (See Genesis 1:31.)

Heavenly Father, every day I marvel at the beauty of Your creation. The mountains, oceans, woodlands, and valleys—all so lovingly made by Your hands. Thank You for the earth! Amen.

But everything exposed by the light becomes visible.
EPHESIANS 5:13 NIV

Isn't it incredible how quickly light dispels the darkness?

In his letter to the Ephesians, Paul wasn't speaking of a literal light but rather of a spiritual light. When our lives are in Christ and we're displaying goodness and righteousness and living in the truth, Paul writes, we're shining in the Lord.

Paul reminds his readers that before they received the light that comes from the Lord, they lived in darkness, a darkness that caused them to live a fruitless life. Paul preached that everything done in darkness eventually becomes exposed by light.

David believed no one would know about his sin with Bathsheba (2 Samuel 12:7–9); Haman thought his plot against the Jews wouldn't be exposed (Esther 7:1–10); and Achan believed his thievery would go unnoticed (Joshua 7:19–20). Yet in each of these people's lives, the deeds they had done in darkness were exposed by the light of God's truth.

This exposure came through confrontation. As Paul writes, it's not enough to stay away from the darkness, but we must be willing to expose it. For only by being brought into the light is sinful behavior evident.

Does our light burn bright enough to drive away the darkness and bring God glory, or have we let our light diminish until it barely dispels anything?

Jesus, You said, "I am the light of the world. He who follows Me shall not walk in darkness, but have the light of life" (John 8:12 NKJV). I will follow You, Lord, and reflect Your bright light. Amen.

Hear, O Israel: The LORD our God is one LORD.
DEUTERONOMY 6:4 KJV

Deuteronomy 6:4, known as the "Shema," is perhaps the best-known statement of Jewish faith and doctrine, recited in synagogues across the world. Jesus affirmed its importance in Mark 12:29–30.

"Hear," from the Hebrew word *sh'ma*, implies more than can be clearly understood from the English translation. The word *sh'ma* appears more than one thousand times in the Hebrew Old Testament and is translated by more than thirteen different words in the King James Version. Of those translations, the third most common is "obey." The implication is clear: if one hears God, one will also obey God.

When Joshua challenged Israel to stay true to the Lord after his death, the people responded, "His voice we will [*sh'ma*]" (Joshua 24:24 ESV). Centuries later, when Samuel confronted King Saul, he said "Why then did you not [*sh'ma*] the voice of the LORD?" (1 Samuel 15:19 ESV).

James spoke to the duality of hearing without obeying in his epistle. He exhorted believers: "Be doers of the word, and not hearers only" (James 1:22 ESV).

Let's not deceive ourselves. If we hear the Word of God but fail to obey, we haven't truly heard it at all.

*Father, please don't allow Your Word to slip past me
unattended. Open my ears to hear it. Let it resound
in my heart, and I will obey You. Amen.*

*He has shown you, O mortal, what is good. And what
does the LORD require of you? To act justly and to love
mercy and to walk humbly with your God.*
MICAH 6:8 NIV

Has mankind ever lived up to these lines? Well. . .no.

The mythological golden age of King Arthur's Camelot—with its
Round Table and knights doing good deeds across the land—should
have epitomized all those virtues. But it didn't.

King Arthur was an impressive man. But he was still just a man
and, as such, flawed. In legend, Arthur had a son by an enchantress,
who would bring his kingdom to an end. He devoted too much time
to being king, not enough to being a good husband. So Guinevere's
attentions wandered to the handsome Sir Lancelot.

When the king is flawed, the rest of us have an excuse not to live
up to his ideals. But there is a land where it's possible to act justly,
love mercy, and walk humbly. Its ruler is perfect. Unflawed. You can
aspire to be your best with Him, knowing that no one will ever bring
His kingdom down. That kingdom is all around you.

Would you like to be a lady of nobility and virtue? Then choose
your king wisely!

*God, my King—how great You are! You lead perfectly,
rule justly, and teach wisely. I am so blessed to be Your
daughter and to dwell in Your kingdom forever. Amen.*

"I do believe; help me overcome my unbelief!"
MARK 9:24 NIV

Healing was a significant part of Jesus' ministry. Throughout the four Gospels we read about Jesus healing lepers, the blind, and those possessed by evil spirits.

The verses prior to Mark 9:24 tell of a father who brings his son to the disciples, asking them to cast out an evil spirit. After a failed attempt, an argument occurs. Jesus arrives to witness the chaos. The father explains his plight and informs Jesus that His disciples' healing skills aren't up to par. He then tells Jesus, "If you can do anything . . .help us." Jesus corrects him by saying, "*If* you can? Everything is possible for one who believes" (vv. 22–23 NIV, italics added).

Interestingly, Jesus didn't always choose to heal upon request (Matthew 13:58). So why did He heal this man's son, despite his doubt? Mark 9:24 may give us the answer. In one breath, the man confidently states his belief, and in the next he honestly confesses his doubt, asking Jesus for help.

The father's contradictory response speaks for us all. Like him, we confidently profess our faith until we are tested, then find ourselves slipping into doubt. In times like these, we must be honest about our faith, praying for God to strengthen it. Only then can God truly begin the healing process.

Dear Lord, there are days when my faith is strong and others when I slip into doubt. Strengthen my faith! Destroy those seeds of doubt. Prevent them from growing within me. Amen.

"In that day," declares the LORD, "you will call me 'my husband'; you will no longer call me 'my master.'"
HOSEA 2:16 NIV

This Old Testament book tells the story of the faithful and forgiving Hosea, married to the prostitute Gomer. Hosea represents God's deep love and commitment to His people. Gomer, in her sinful and wandering ways, symbolizes Israel.

God based this illustration on the marriage relationship. God is the loving husband, fully devoted to his wife, even considering her infidelity. He never gives up and continually searches for her, protecting her, restoring her to His side. God's forgiveness and love redeem that relationship.

God also wants *our* hearts. He desires a relationship with us based on love and forgiveness. He enters into a covenant with us, like the marriage between Hosea and Gomer.

God is the loving, faithful husband, constantly pursuing us no matter what we do or where we roam. Though it is difficult to grasp how much He loves us, we find hope in His promise. God will keep His commitment to us. His love song to us is forgiveness, and His wedding vow is unconditional love.

Thank You for loving me so fully and unconditionally, God. I find comfort in knowing that as much as any person on earth could love me, You love me more. Amen.

Day 341

*"Nor will people say, 'Here it is,' or 'There it is,'
because the kingdom of God is in your midst."*
LUKE 17:21 NIV

For centuries, the Jewish people had waited for their "glory day." Through ancient prophecies came mental pictures of the kingdom of God—a physical kingdom with a real king who would deliver them from Roman rule.

In Luke 17 the Pharisees demanded that Jesus tell them when the kingdom of God would arrive. Jesus' answer, that the kingdom of God already existed, surely confused them. Probably more puzzling to them was where it existed!

As Christians, we too find ourselves waiting. We wait for good to win over evil and for Christ's second coming. We long to experience the glory of God's kingdom. Jesus' answer applies to us too. God's kingdom is already here!

But where? Some Christians confuse "church" with the kingdom. But the church and the kingdom are not the same. If we've discovered the kingdom, it means God (our King) has delivered us from the darkness of sin through His Prince, Jesus. God sits on a throne, in our very own hearts, governing our souls and consciences. How glorious! Church is simply a place for those who submit to the rule of the King to come together, proclaim God's reign, and invite others to find it. Wait no longer—every day is glory day!

*Dear Father, Your kingdom is within me—a place of peace,
contentment, and love. I look forward to that day when I
will live with You forever in Your heavenly home. Amen.*

*This made Saul very angry. "What's this?" he said.
"They credit David with ten thousands and me with only
thousands. Next they'll be making him their king!"
So from that time on Saul kept a jealous eye on David.*
1 Samuel 18:8–9 nlt

King Saul proved himself to be a valiant and successful warrior. We're told "he fought against his enemies in every direction. . .and wherever he turned, he was victorious" (1 Samuel 14:47 nlt).

Then Saul grew prideful and no longer followed God's commands. As a result, God rejected him as king of Israel (1 Samuel 15:26). Saul realized his son would never inherit the throne.

When young David returned victorious from the battlefield and received higher praise than Saul, the king's jealousy flared and quickly turned to anger. Instead of celebrating, Saul became a raving madman, fearful of losing his throne to the valiant warrior.

Although David proved himself loyal to the king, Saul's suspicion and jealousy blinded him to the talents and accomplishments of his faithful subject. David's success on the battlefield made everyday life in Israel more secure, but Saul couldn't see or appreciate these gains.

Jealousy and suspicion make terrible taskmasters. Let's cheer when others succeed, especially in areas of our own expertise.

*God, jealousy slips into my heart. When others succeed,
I sometimes fake my happiness for them. Help me to overcome
jealousy and to treat others as Jesus would. Amen.*

Do not quench the Spirit.
1 THESSALONIANS 5:19 NIV

Fire is a destructive force, showing no mercy toward what it consumes. However, fire also gives off warmth and light, enabling us to do many things.

Paul was instructing the readers of his letter not to put out the fire of the Spirit. Continual prayer, a thankful attitude in the midst of their circumstances, whether good or bad, and belief in God's will for their lives were the qualities they were to be displaying.

In addition, they were to speak out against the idle, come alongside the timid, and examine the things they were being taught. They needed to hang on to what was good and stay away from evil. By living in this manner, they wouldn't be quenching the Holy Spirit.

Jesus spoke of the importance of the Spirit, especially in the book of John. He preached that the Spirit not only teaches us about God but also brings back to mind the lessons we have already learned (John 14:25–26).

We know that when a fire is neglected, it soon begins to go out. With proper attention, though, a fire will continue burning, giving off warmth and light to those around it.

Are we doing the necessary things to keep the fire lit, or are we allowing it to burn out?

*Lord, help me to keep my heart open to the Holy
Spirit's fiery intervention—the teaching and lessons
that come from You and Your Word. Amen.*

*But if I say, "I will not mention his word or speak anymore in his
name," his word is in my heart like a fire, a fire shut up in my bones.*
JEREMIAH 20:9 NIV

The prophet Jeremiah faced a challenge. He'd been called to minister the Word of God to Judah during that nation's final years of decline. With passion and fervor, the prophet preached that unless God's people repented, judgment and calamity would soon follow.

The people resented and ridiculed Jeremiah, treating him with contempt for those unwanted proclamations. Frustrated, the man called "the weeping prophet" lamented, "The word of the LORD has brought me insult and reproach all day long" (Jeremiah 20:8 NIV). So he sought to silence his spiritual stirrings.

No matter how hard Jeremiah tried, though, he couldn't suppress the divine message God placed on his heart. Despite the personal cost, Jeremiah continued to proclaim the Word.

In a world that rejects the Gospel, God is seeking Christians who are eager and willing to share the truth of His Word—no matter the consequences. The apostle Paul declared, "I am not ashamed of the Gospel of Christ: for it is the power of God unto salvation" (Romans 1:16 KJV).

When our love of God exceeds our fear of rejection and reproach, we can't help but proclaim the Good News with unabashed boldness.

*I love to share the Good News, Lord—Your amazing gift
of salvation, offered freely to anyone who asks. Open
ears to hear it! Open hearts to receive it! Amen.*

～ Day 345 ～

His feet were like burnished bronze, refined in a furnace,
and his voice was like the roar of many waters.
REVELATION 1:15 ESV

The first chapter of Revelation records John's attempt to capture his vision of "the Living One" in mere words. He includes a description of God's voice—like "the roar of many waters."

Although translated in the New International Version as "rushing" waters, the Greek word is *polys*—a common English prefix indicating "many." The same word is used in Revelation 14:2 and 19:6 to refer to God's voice, adding the detail that it also sounds like loud thunder pealing across heaven. When Ezekiel saw the vision of the return of God's glory to the temple, he also described God's voice "like the sound of many waters" (Ezekiel 43:2 ESV).

Revelation tells us the blood of the Lamb has purchased men "from every tribe and *language* and people and nation" (Revelation 5:9 ESV, italics added). When Daniel saw his vision of "one who looked like a man" (Daniel 10:16 NIV), His voice sounded "like the sound of a multitude" (Daniel 10:6 NIV).

Is it too much to imagine that we, His children, are His voice in the world? Together, our individual voices become a roar.

We are Christians—hear us roar.

Heavenly Father, what an awesome responsibility to be
Your voice in the world! I lift up my voice and join the
world's Christians in singing Your song. Amen.

*Here are more of Solomon's proverbs, copied by scribes
at the court of King Hezekiah of Judah.*
PROVERBS 25:1 GNT

The royal chronicler informs us that King Solomon "spoke three thousand proverbs and his songs numbered a thousand and five" (1 Kings 4:32 NIV). Somebody was obviously counting. Only *one* of Solomon's songs comes down to us in the Bible, and it is named the Song of Songs.

Slightly more of Solomon's proverbs survived until the present day—about nine hundred. But at first only about seven hundred of his proverbs were preserved. Then in King Hezekiah's day, over two centuries after Solomon, someone discovered an amazing treasure: very likely a worn, old scroll containing about two hundred "more of Solomon's proverbs." Scribes copied them out, enriching the already-existing collection. We don't know where the other 2,100 proverbs went to, but we can be very thankful for what we do have.

One hundred years later, another scroll of the scriptures was misplaced and lost—the *entire* Law of Moses. Then, during King Josiah's day, Hilkiah the priest happened to find it (2 Chronicles 34:14–15).

We owe a huge debt of gratitude to little-known heroes like Hilkiah and the completely unknown person in King Josiah's court for rescuing the Word of God from oblivion.

*Dear God, Your Word will live on forever. Nothing can
obliterate it. The scriptures echo Your voice speaking to
Your children from generation to generation. Amen.*

And I saw that all toil and all achievement spring from one person's envy of another. This too is meaningless, a chasing after the wind.
ECCLESIASTES 4:4 NIV

Labor isn't meaningless. Achievement isn't meaningless either. Man's envy of his neighbor is the spoiler. What we do to be like others, what we want because other people have it, those are the meaningless things.

"Keeping up with the Joneses" is all very well in this life, but the Joneses (whoever they might be for you) are mortal, and their example is finite. When they go the way of all mortal things, their works, achievements, and everything we emulated—or wished we were or wished we had because they had it—all that goes with them, like dust blowing in a good stiff breeze.

For a life's work to be meaningful, its effects should be independent of the life that made it. Great men and women get that for a while—until history forgets them. Humble, faith-filled souls find real meaning not in trying to get what their neighbors have, but in reaching out to those neighbors and others in God's name, making their labor the Lord's work.

If you must chase after the wind, make it the Holy Spirit, otherwise known as the Wind of Heaven. Then your achievements will mean something forever.

Lord, remind me that that my labor and all that I achieve should bring You glory. Allow my work to leave Your footprint on earth even after I am gone. Amen.

This is my body, which [is] for you:
this do in remembrance of me.
1 CORINTHIANS 11:24 DARBY

For the most part, when people remember heroes, they celebrate their accomplishments. But with the Lord's Supper, Jesus commands us to remember His death. How fascinating!

Why not let a cup of wine remind us of the time He turned the water into wine? Or have the bread remind us of when He multiplied the loaves to feed five thousand? Instead, He calls us to the circumstances of His death.

At the Passover, a lamb was sacrificed. But Jesus was the Lamb of God who came to take away the sins of the world. That is why we remember His death. Only by His dying on the cross then rising again could we be saved from our punishment of hell and the slavery of sin.

Some things lose their fascination with familiarity. It's normal for a familiar passage of scripture to lose its force over time. Chances are, if we have taken Christ's death for granted, we have accommodated sin too. Let us stir up our hearts over the death, burial, and resurrection of Christ, for they are the bedrock of our faith and will lead us to triumph over all sin.

Jesus, fill my mind and heart with thoughts of Your
death, burial, and resurrection. I am so grateful for Your
sacrifice. I don't ever want to take it for granted. Amen.

"What is this that God has done to us?"
GENESIS 42:28 NIV

It was Jacob's bewildered boys who asked this question. The answer blew their minds and brought them face-to-face with forgiveness.

You remember Joseph with the beautiful coat, whose brothers sold him into slavery? They thought they had seen the last of their fair sibling, until a famine drove them to Egypt for a "care package." But lo and behold, who was providing the lifesaving handout? Their brother Joseph.

The irony of this historical incident cannot be misunderstood. Before recognizing Joseph, the brothers were overwhelmed by finding their silver payments returned in the sacks of grain. Rightfully, they gave God credit for such generosity. Of course, it was God working in the heart of Joseph that began the process leading to recognition, renewal, and the reward of reconciliation. No coincidence here.

Perhaps no other biography is as convincing that God is always at work for our good. In many ways, Joseph foreshadows what was to come from another Father. Read Joseph's full story (Genesis 37–50). Open your heart to God's lifesaving provision.

Of the four hundred–plus verses comprising Joseph's story, none are more thrilling than Genesis 50:19–20 (NIV): "Joseph said to [his brothers], '. . .You intended to harm me, but God intended it for good.'" That's just like Him!

God, I believe that You are always at work for my good.
Scripture says that You weave things together for good
to those who love You—and I love You! Amen.

"But if you remain in me and my words remain in you,
you may ask for anything you want, and it will be granted!"
JOHN 15:7 NLT

Wow! Really? Is that true? Is God some magical genie who will grant us unlimited wishes?

As silly as this may sound, there are some who pray this way. They assume that they have license to treat God as a concierge of some kind, who is standing by to rush to fulfill our every request.

When we think about our children, we remember that our love for them is so great that we would give them anything they want. In the midst of thinking this, however, our intelligence kicks in, and we realize what might happen if we did, in fact, give our kids everything they want. The result would probably be some pretty rotten kids!

As we present our requests to God, we need to realize that He knows what is best for us and that we should never demand "our way." We must not forget the first part of John 15:7, which says, "If you remain in me and my words remain in you." This should clearly tell us that our first desire needs to be that God's will is done.

Since God only wants to give us the very best, and He knows how to make that happen, why would we pray for anything else?

Father, I say, "Thy will be done!" You know best. I want what
You want for me, even if it's not what I ask for. Amen.

But the Lord *replied, "Is it right for you to be angry?"*
Jonah 4:4 niv

Jonah is one of the most familiar characters in the Bible.

His adventure began when God told Jonah to go and spread the word in the wicked town of Nineveh that God would soon be passing judgment on them. Jonah refused to go and ran away. He ended up on a boat that he eventually got tossed off of in the midst of a raging storm. Jonah didn't drown though; instead God was merciful and spared Jonah by sending a big fish to swallow him.

Once Jonah repented, God delivered him out of the fish. Jonah then traveled to Nineveh and preached. The people listened and repented. Jonah should have been happy with the results, but that wasn't his reaction.

After seeing God's compassion for people he despised, Jonah got mad. He was so angry that he wanted God to take his life. Instead God taught Jonah about compassion. It was a lesson Jonah refused to submit to.

Jonah had forgotten his role as the clay and God's position as the potter. When we reverse our role with God's, we're going to find ourselves angry and frustrated. We are blessed with many rights, but questioning God isn't one of them.

*I'm guilty of questioning You, God. I wonder why You do
what You do, and in anger and frustration I sometimes
go against Your will. Forgive me, please. Amen.*

With great power, the apostles gave their testimony of the resurrection of the Lord Jesus. Great grace was on them all.
ACTS 4:33 WEB

It isn't coincidental that a description of these first-century believers includes the words *power* and *grace*. You remember that the martyr Stephen was described in the same way (Acts 6:8). No doubt, he was a part of this congregation.

Here in Luke's history of Christian beginnings, this description of Christ's followers appears two chapters after Luke's report on the day of Pentecost (Acts 2). A reading of that event reveals the unity of those believers. His description of believers in chapter 4 underscores their continued unity and the power of their Resurrection testimonies.

In New Testament use, the word *grace* is linked with the graciousness of God. It's His blessings bestowed on His faithful children, the result of His gracious sharing; so these Spirit-filled believers shared with one another.

The mark of the grace-filled Christian is his or her spirit of unity and genuine love for others.

It is told that when Emperor Hadrian sent out a man to investigate "these Christians," the spy returned with a mixed report, but paramount was his observation, "Behold how they love one another."

That love sprang from their unity in God's great grace.

Heavenly Father, Your power and grace are the sparks that light the fire of Love. Teach me to set the world on fire for You. Help me to love others as You love me. Amen.

All these died in faith, not having received the promises,
but having seen them from afar off and embraced [them],
and confessed that they were strangers and sojourners on the earth.
HEBREWS 11:13 DARBY

When we are in trouble, we often look to God and His promises. The expectation, of course, is that He will deliver us sooner rather than later. What's so amazing about this verse is that the Bible lifts up Abraham as a man demonstrating great faith—by believing God would fulfill His promise after Abraham's death!

Abraham had rejoiced in God's promise of a son years before he received him. Then he rejoiced in receiving a land of his own, even when he came to realize that it wouldn't be in his lifetime. The fulfillment of the first promise—given miraculously—probably helped Abraham to believe God for the other promise.

God calls us to experience the same faith as Abraham, to believe in a better world to come when every righteous promise will be fulfilled. May each promise you believe be a stepping-stone to greater faith.

Father God, I stand on Your promises. By faith,
I believe that each one of them will be fulfilled in
Your own way and in Your own time. Amen.

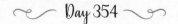

"And I bought the field at An'athoth from Han'amel my cousin,
and weighed out the money to him, seventeen shekels of silver."
Jeremiah 32:9 rsv

It was a very dark hour for Jerusalem and for Jeremiah personally. Jeremiah had warned the Jews for decades that if they didn't repent, God would send the Babylonians to conquer them. Sure enough, a vast Babylonian army was now camped around Jerusalem, and the siege ramps were in place. The Jews were trapped inside, couldn't get out to their fields, and were low on food. Jeremiah was worst-off of all. The rulers of Jerusalem had thrown him in prison because of his unpopular message.

In Jeremiah's lowest moment, his cousin Hanamel showed up. Hanamel needed money for food and wanted to sell his field. The only problem was, it was in the village of Anathoth, some distance outside the walls of Jerusalem where it couldn't do Jeremiah any good. Yet following God's instructions, Jeremiah bought the field. Why? Because as hopeless as things were at the moment, God said things would soon get much better (Jeremiah 32:36–44), and Jeremiah believed God. And it happened!

If you're trapped in a corner like Jeremiah was, remember what God asked him: "I am the LORD, the God of all flesh: is there any thing too hard for me?" (Jeremiah 32:27 kjv).

When I face problems with no ready solutions,
I know that You have the answers. Show me the way,
Lord. Nothing is impossible for You. Amen.

Stand firm then, with the belt of truth buckled around your
waist, with the breastplate of righteousness in place.
EPHESIANS 6:14 NIV

The first piece of God's armor seems simplistic: a belt. However, for a Roman soldier, the belt held all the other pieces of equipment. When Isaiah described the branch from the rod of Jesse, he said, "Righteousness will be his belt" (Isaiah 11:5 NIV). In the armor God has provided us, the belt consists of His truth, while His righteousness covers our vulnerable breasts.

When the Israelites ate the Passover, they were to be travel ready, with sandals on, staffs in hand, and cloaks tucked into their belts (Exodus 12:11).

In one memorable object lesson, God commanded Jeremiah to buy a belt and then leave it to rot. Israel was like that rotten belt: bound to God for His "renown and praise and honor" (Jeremiah 13:11 NIV), they had instead become completely useless.

Just as God commanded the Israelites preparing to leave Egypt, God commands those who wait for His return to "be dressed ready for service" (Luke 12:35 NIV).

Starting with our belts.

Lord, get me ready for Your return. I don't know when You
will come, but prepare me with a clean heart, arm me with
Your Word, and give me the will to serve others. Amen.

Then Belshazzar gave orders, and they clothed Daniel
with purple and put a necklace of gold around his neck,
and issued a proclamation concerning him that he now
had authority as the third ruler in the kingdom.
DANIEL 5:29 NASB

When a supernatural hand appeared during Belshazzar's blasphe-mous feast and scrawled a coded message on the wall, no one could interpret its meaning except Daniel. For this accomplishment, Belshazzar crowned Daniel as third ruler of the kingdom. Not that it mattered, for the same night an invading army conquered the kingdom and executed Belshazzar.

For many years Bible critics scoffed at this narrative. History recorded Nabonidus as the last king of Babylon, not Belshazzar. But in recent times, Babylonian cuneiforms found at a ziggurat in Ur have confirmed Daniel's account. King Nabonidus made his son Belshazzar second ruler before departing for years of adventure in the west. This also explains why Belshazzar made Daniel third ruler rather than second.

Nonetheless, the critics now had new objections. In Daniel 5, Nebuchadnezzar, not Nabonidus, is called Belshazzar's father. However, the Semitic word used for father can also imply grand-father. Ancient documents indicate that Nabonidus married Nebuchadnezzar's daughter, Nitocris. This made their son, Belshazzar, Nebuchadnezzar's grandson.

We can always trust the Bible to be true, even when current data hasn't caught up with the specifics found in God's Word.

Thank You, God, for bringing hidden truths to light. Amen.

~ Day 357 ~

While Jesus was still speaking, some people came from the
house of Jairus, the synagogue ruler. "Your daughter is
dead," they said. "Why bother the teacher anymore?"
MARK 5:35 NIV

What hopelessness. Jairus, a synagogue ruler, pleaded with Jesus to heal his sick child. Jesus was en route to the man's home when they got the news that the child had died. Why trouble the Galilean teacher further? It was kind of Him to come, but there's nothing He can do now, the naysayers thought. Yet Jesus' response was one of encouragement and hope: "Don't be afraid; just believe" (Mark 5:36 NIV).

When Jesus entered Jairus' home, he heard the crying. "Why all this commotion and wailing? The child is not dead but asleep," He said. But they laughed. After removing the doubters, Jesus took the child by her hand and said, "Little girl, I say to you, get up!" and the child was brought back to life (vv. 39–42 NIV).

When the odds are stacked against us and circumstances riddle us with hopelessness, our tendency is to manage our burdens as well as we can and stop praying. Doubtful, we wonder: Can God restore an unhappy marriage? Can He heal cancer? Can He deliver me from financial ruin? *Will* He?

Jesus knows the way out. Only believe; have faith in Him and never lose hope.

Jesus, my hope is in You. Even when it appears that all hope is
lost, I will hold on to the hope that You will deliver me. Amen.

For we are His workmanship, created in Christ Jesus for good works,
which God prepared beforehand that we should walk in them.
EPHESIANS 2:10 NKJV

Paul says we are created in Christ Jesus and designed to do God's work. God has a plan for each of us.

Because we are "created in Christ Jesus," Christ is the example of what Christians should be. "Therefore, if anyone is in Christ, he is a new creation; old things have passed away; behold, all things have become new" (2 Corinthians 5:17 NKJV). We are saved through Christ to do the good works that God has planned for us.

How can you know God's plans for your life? First, you should meet with Him in prayer each day and seek His will. Studying the Bible is also important. Often God speaks to us directly through His Word (Psalm 119:105). Finally, you must have faith that God *will* work out His plan for your life and that His plan is good. Jeremiah 29:11 (NIV) says, "'For I know the plans I have for you,' declares the LORD, 'plans to prosper you and not to harm you, plans to give you hope and a future.'"

Are you living in Christ's example and seeking God's plan for your life?

Father, what is Your plan for me? I know that it is good. Reveal it
to me, Lord. Speak to me through prayer and Your Word. Amen.

But when the kindness and love of God our Savior appeared. . .
TITUS 3:4 NIV

Eleven words. Their message is a simple one: when love and kindness from God appear, changes occur.

In Paul's letter to Titus, he addressed the conduct that those who know Christ should have. They should submit to authority, not speak ill of anyone, strive for peace, and have a humble attitude.

Paul also gave a reminder about the approach that they should be taking with those who didn't yet know Christ. Instead of being prideful, they would do well to remember that once upon a time they engaged in jealousy, lying, hatred, disobedience, and foolish living. It was only when Jesus came into their lives that those behaviors changed.

Paul would know full well what he was writing about. For he once lived in a state of hatred toward others and approved of the mistreatment of those who believed in Christ. Paul wasn't about peace at all. But then Jesus appeared (Acts 9:1–19). Suddenly Paul was putting off his bad conduct in exchange for the behavior that showed God was in his heart.

God's love and kindness are powerful attributes that continuously transform hearts. How has His love changed your heart?

God, Your love has lifted me up from a life of sin.
You have transformed my heart and made me Your
beloved child! How wonderful You are! Amen.

Day 360

*"You are the light of the world. A town built
on a hill cannot be hidden."*

MATTHEW 5:14 NIV

The painter William Holman Hunt portrayed Christ as *The Light
of the World.* Despite the fact that Jesus is holding a lamp in the
painting, there is no doubt that Hunt meant the Lord—not the
lamp—was the light referred to.

The title is from a description Jesus used for Himself. He said
that whoever followed Him would not walk in darkness. Then Jesus
qualified that by saying He would be the light of the world while
He was in the world!

Then, in anticipation of His death, Jesus passed the duty of
illumination to the disciples and, through them, to us.

In the painting Jesus stands before a door that has no handle on
the outside. The implication is that He has to be invited in. But once
Jesus is inside you, don't keep Him to yourself—not while others
still walk in darkness. As a follower of the Lord, you stand on the
"hill" of God's love and shine a guiding light for others.

Bringing people heavenward isn't just a job for pastors and
theologians. It's a job for all of us who claim Him—as He said, *you
are the light of the world!*

*Dear Jesus, when Christians work together, they form a
powerful beacon that lights the way to heaven. I give my
light, Lord, to make Your light shine even brighter. Amen.*

*For which cause we faint not; but though our outward man
perish, yet the inward man is renewed day by day. For our
light affliction, which is but for a moment, worketh for
us a far more exceeding and eternal weight of glory.*
2 Corinthians 4:16–17 kjv

Paul had a heavenly mindset. In a tone befitting a poet, he encouraged the early church as he compared this earthly life against the ecstasy of the eternal for every Christian.

Our bodies—the "temporal temples" of the Holy Spirit—are just that. . .temporary. In 1 Corinthians 15:31 (kjv), the apostle wrote, "I die daily." His statement was both figurative and actual. Physically, our bodies deteriorate with age—and spiritually, we seek to "die" to our self-serving, carnal natures. This presents an interesting dichotomy—namely, the death of self leads to life. As the body grows old, the spirit grows young and is invigorated in Christ daily.

With the voice of wisdom, Paul declares that however heavy our sufferings seem to us, they cannot compare to the far more exceeding and eternal weight of glory we will experience with God throughout eternity.

Paul beautifully contrasted things present to things future—a moment to an eternity, lightness to weight, affliction to glory. This is the mindset God wants all believers to attain.

*Heavenly Father, sometimes my body suffers and my feelings
are hurt. But then I think of You and remember—my human
self is only temporary; my life with You is eternal. Amen.*

But Paul kept insisting that they should not take him along who had deserted them in Pamphylia and had not gone with them to the work.
ACTS 15:38 NASB

A young man, Mark, accompanied Barnabas and Paul as they set out on the first missionary journey, but he returned to Jerusalem before completing the trip.

When planning the second missionary journey, Barnabas wanted to include Mark again, but Paul adamantly disagreed. The young man had deserted them the first time, dumping his share of the work onto the other team members. Paul had no desire for a repeat performance.

However, Barnabas insisted Mark come along. Unable to agree on the issue, Paul teamed up with Silas and headed north, while Barnabas took Mark and sailed west to Cyprus.

Barnabas provided Mark with the encouragement and training he needed to reach his full potential. Mark went on to pen the Gospel of Mark, effectively minister in the early church, and even become an appreciated coworker with Paul.

Has someone failed you? Before completely writing the person off, look for signs of a teachable spirit and growing maturity. Direction and encouragement may be exactly what someone needs to succeed at a task. Perhaps there is a Mark in your life, and Christ is calling you to be a Barnabas.

Father, give me patience with those who are young and not yet mature enough to understand. Help me to lend wisdom gently and when the time is right. Amen.

He [will come] to be glorified in his holy people and to
be marveled at among all those who have believed. This
includes you, because you believed our testimony to you.
2 THESSALONIANS 1:10 NIV

In the opening chapter of his letter to the Thessalonians, Paul contrasts the everlasting destruction awaiting those who don't know the gospel with the glory awaiting those who have believed.

Several things will happen on the day "when the Lord Jesus is revealed from heaven in blazing fire with his powerful angels" (2 Thessalonians 1:7 NIV). Among them: God will be glorified in His holy people—in *us* (v. 10). In Paul's letter to the Ephesians, he mentioned that we believed "for the praise of his glory" (Ephesians 1:12 NIV). The more we are transformed into the likeness of the Lord, the more we reflect His glory (2 Corinthians 3:18).

This verse tells us we will also "marvel" at the Lord. A few translations (KJV, NKJV, HCSB) use *admire* instead of *marvel*. Both words have similar implications, but *marvel* suggests a stronger degree of the same feeling. We will do more than look at the Lord with approval and respect. When we come face-to-face with the Lord in all His glory, we will be amazed—surprised and even bewildered.

Let's begin to seek that amazing, surprising, bewildering God in our lives here and now.

You amaze me, God. Often I am surprised by the ways You
work things out. I can only imagine the surprise and wonder
that I'll feel when I meet You face-to-face. Amen.

～ Day 364 ～

These are evil times, so make every minute count.
EPHESIANS 5:16 CEV

Just think: Paul wrote these words to the church at Ephesus almost two thousand years ago. If the times were evil then, what would Paul say about the state of affairs in the twenty-first century? When was the last time you turned on the news and failed to hear about the evil humanity visits upon itself?

And speaking of the world, it has its own system for time management and making every minute count. The bookstore on the corner has titles galore giving advice on how to best utilize every second of every day in order to become the most productive, best worker/parent/child/human being you can dream of becoming.

But God's plan for time management serves a different goal than self-actualization. And while it may seem tempting to crawl back into bed and hide beneath the covers of denial instead of facing the harsh reality of the world, God has a different idea.

Every minute counts because we, as believers, carry an eternal hope that the world needs to hear. Bad things do happen to good people, but ever-present in the trials of this world is a loving God who cares deeply for His children. Who will you share this Good News with today?

Dear God, how should I share the Good News with those who have suffered at the hand of evil? Show me ways to encourage them that You love and care for them. Amen.

For Demas, having loved this present world, has deserted me and gone to Thessalonica; Crescens has gone to Galatia, Titus to Dalmatia.
2 TIMOTHY 4:10 NASB

Imprisoned in Rome and aware of his impending execution, Paul wrote one last letter to encourage and embolden Timothy, his son in the faith.

He counseled Timothy to "suffer hardship with me, as a good soldier of Christ Jesus" (2 Timothy 2:3 NASB), and wrote out the characteristics of an effective worker for Christ.

Paul also included a brief update of mutual coworkers. All were faithfully serving Christ in various regions, except for one man, Demas. He had deserted Paul and abandoned the ministry altogether.

Why? Demas let his love for the comforts and delights of the present world extinguish his love of Christ.

Perhaps Paul had Demas in mind when he wrote, "No soldier in active service entangles himself in the affairs of everyday life, so that he may please the one who enlisted him as a soldier" (2 Timothy 2:4 NASB).

Demas threw away eternal rewards for temporary pleasures. In contrast, Paul endured hardship for his beloved Savior.

Near the end of his life Paul wrote, "I have fought the good fight, I have finished the course, I have kept the faith" (2 Timothy 4:7 NASB).

May Paul's epitaph also be ours.

God, when my days on earth are through, I pray that, like Paul, I can say, "I have done my best for You, and I have kept the faith." Amen.

Contributors

Dana Christensen is a freelance writer and musician living in Colorado. Her husband, two sets of identical twins, precious daughter, and yellow Lab bring much joy and laughter to her life.
17, 35, 54, 58, 68, 70, 92, 102, 112, 151, 162, 167, 184, 208, 220, 226, 246, 276, 303, 323, 364

Stephen Fierbaugh is the author of *Surviving Celibacy* and a speaker on Christian singles' topics. He is also a contributing author to *The Great Adventure*. He is a missionary with Pioneer Bible Translators, where he serves as Director of Information Technology at the International Service Center in Dallas, Texas. Stephen is a graduate of Johnson Bible College.
10, 18, 46, 57, 73, 84, 93, 106, 120, 145, 155, 172, 187, 200, 215, 239, 242, 270, 290, 317, 326

Jean Fischer has been writing for nearly three decades and has served as an editor with Golden Books. She has cowritten with Thomas Kinkade and John MacArthur and is one of the authors of Barbour's Camp Club Girls series. Other books include *The Kids' Bible Dictionary* and *199 Bible People, Places, and Things*, also for Barbour.
7, 22, 39, 85, 96, 104, 115, 126, 139, 177, 197, 204, 221, 244, 264, 274, 296, 309, 321, 358

Darlene Franklin has written devotionals for several previous Barbour collections. She also has six books and novellas in print (with six more on the way), all with Barbour Publishing. Check out her blog at www.darlenefranklinwrites.blogspot.com.
5, 23, 25, 36, 50, 60, 83, 95, 111, 119, 137, 144, 165, 175, 192, 210, 228, 252, 277, 287, 300, 305, 312, 329, 333, 337, 345, 355, 363

Steve Husting is a mild webmaster by day and fearless writer by night. He loves chocolate, hiking, and making the Bible's message clear to his readers. He and his wife, Shirley, live in Southern California with their son.

12, 49, 81, 100, 109, 163, 173, 186, 224, 262, 273, 288, 294, 304, 306, 314, 324, 348, 353

Tina Krause is a freelance writer, editor, and award-winning newspaper columnist. She has nine hundred published writing credits and is author of the book *Laughter Therapy*. Tina and her husband, Jim, live in Valparaiso, Indiana, where they enjoy spoiling their five grandchildren.

3, 13, 19, 28, 40, 56, 74, 90, 103, 121, 132, 148, 158, 170, 181, 189, 196, 206, 222, 232, 249, 259, 268, 282, 302, 315, 320, 344, 357, 361

David McLaughlan used to write whatever turned a buck; now he writes about faith and God. It doesn't pay as well, but it docs make his heart sing! He lives in bonny Scotland with his wife, Julie, and a whole clan of children.

16, 21, 27, 38, 42, 45, 48, 55, 75, 80, 88, 98, 105, 129, 134, 136, 146, 152, 156, 160, 168, 180, 185, 191, 194, 199, 203, 205, 212, 216, 219, 225, 227, 230, 233, 236, 240, 243, 245, 247, 250, 253, 256, 258, 261, 269, 275, 280, 284, 295, 297, 301, 307, 316, 325, 328, 334, 338, 347, 360

Paul M. Miller is a freelance writer in Oak Harbor, Whidbey Island, Washington. He is an active drama ministry director and Sunday school teacher and a retired publishing company editor and playwright. Paul is the father of two adult children.

8, 24, 31, 51, 71, 87, 97, 116, 128, 131, 141, 153, 157, 161, 178, 188, 201, 238, 265, 278, 286, 292, 327, 335, 349, 352

Kathie Mitchell is a grandmother who has enjoyed writing since childhood. She has written for her church, placed in several writing contests, and has several pieces in Barbour's *365 Fun Bible Facts*. She and her husband, Mike, live in Milton, Pennsylvania. They have two married children and four grandsons.

9, 26, 37, 47, 59, 69, 89, 94, 114, 140, 149, 171, 179, 202, 214, 229, 251, 257, 260, 266, 272, 285, 289, 310, 322, 331, 342, 356, 362, 365

Paul Muckley is a long-time editor who has also written several books. He and his family live in Ohio.

1, 65, 77, 124, 182, 241

Todd Aaron Smith has fourteen books published, some of which have appeared on the CBA bestseller lists. Todd also works with a ministry for native Mayan children living in Guatemala and southern Mexico. He and his family live near Kansas City.

2, 11, 20, 32, 33, 44, 61, 79, 108, 117, 138, 159, 207, 223, 254, 263, 299, 311, 350

Ed Strauss was a freelance writer in British Columbia who passed into heaven in 2018. He authored or coauthored more than 50 books for children, tweens, and adults.

4, 6, 29, 43, 53, 64, 82, 99, 101, 107, 118, 122, 130, 143, 154, 166, 176, 198, 211, 218, 235, 255, 267, 283, 291, 298, 318, 330, 346, 354

Lisa Toner is a freelance writer whose work has been published in Christian and secular publications and websites including *Family Fun*, *Primary Treasure*, *Pack-O-Fun*, and Focus on the Family's *Clubhouse* and *Clubhouse Jr.* Lisa graduated from the University of Nebraska with a bachelor's degree in journalism and has an extensive background in sales, advertising, and public relations.

She volunteers as a teacher for middle school students at her church.

Martha Willey is a wife and the mother of three teenage boys. She works in an elementary school as an aide to students with special needs. Her writing has been published in *DevoZine*, *Encounter*, *Grit*, *Simple Joy*, and *Cross and Quill*, as well as the Barbour books *Whispers of Wisdom for Caregivers* and *The Book Lover's Devotional*. A member of Northwest Ohio Christian Writers, her interests also include reading and cross-stitching.

Jean Wise is a freelance journalist/writer and Christian speaker at retreats, gatherings, and seminars. She has published articles in publications such as *The Lutheran*, *Spirit-Led Writer*, *Christian Communicator*, *Sacred Journey*, and *God Answers Prayers—Military Edition*. She has contributed devotions to two Barbour books, *Daily Comfort for Caregivers* and *The Book Lover's Devotional*. She lives in northwest Ohio where she is a reporter at a daily newspaper, writing feature articles. Find out more at her website, www.jeanwise.org, or her blog, www.healthyspirituality.org.

Scripture Index

Permissions